MICROSOFT ACCESS 7.0 FOR FOR WINDOWS 95

EDWARD G. MARTIN
CHARLES S. PARKER
TERRY DUKE

Acquisitions Editor Robert Linsky
Developmental Editor Elizabeth Hayes
Project Editor Michele Tomiak
Art Director Scott Baker
Production Manager Ann Coburn
Manager of Electronic Publishing Michael Beaupré
Electronic Publishing Coordinator Ellie Moore
Product Manager Scott Timian
Vice-President, Director of Editorial, Design, and Production Diane Southworth

Text Type 10/12 Times Roman

Address for Editorial Correspondence
The Dryden Press, 301 Commerce Street, Suite 3700, Fort Worth, TX 76102

Address for Orders
The Dryden Press, 6277 Sea Harbor Drive, Orlando, FL 32887-6777
1-800-782-4479, or 1-800-433-0001 (in Florida)

ISBN 0-15-505064-8

Printed in the United States of America

5 6 7 8 9 0 1 2 3 4 059 9 8 7 6 5 4 3 2 1

The Dryden Press
Harcourt Brace College Publishers

HOW TO USE THIS MANUAL

This manual contains numerous features that help you master the material quickly and reinforce your learning:

- *A Table of Contents.* A list of the manual's contents appears on the first page of the manual. Each chapter starts with an *outline,* a list of learning *objectives,* and an *overview* that summarizes the skills you will learn.
- *Bold Key Terms.* Important terms appear in bold type as they are introduced. They are also conveniently listed at the end of each chapter, with page references for further review.
- *Color as a Learning Tool.* In this manual, color has been used to help you work through each chapter. Each step is numbered in green for easy identification. Within each step, text or commands that you should type appear in orange. Single keys to be pressed are shown in yellow boxes. For example,

  1 Type WIN and press ↵

- *Step-by-Step Mouse Approach.* This manual stresses the mouse approach. Each action is numbered consecutively in green to make it easy to locate and follow. Where appropriate, a mouse shortcut (toolbar icon) is shown in the left margin; a keyboard shortcut may be shown in brackets at the right, as follows:

As your skills increase, the "click this item" approach slowly gives way to a less-detailed list of goals and operations so that you do not mindlessly follow steps, but truly master software skills.

- *Screen Figures.* Full-color annotated screens provide overviews of operations that let you monitor your work as you progress through the tutorial.
- *Tips.* Each chapter contains numerous short tips in bold type at strategic points to provide hints, warnings, or insights. Read these carefully.
- *Checkpoints.* At the end of each major section is a list of checkpoints, highlighted in red, which you can use to test your mastery of the material. Do not proceed further unless you can perform the checkpoint tasks.
- *Summary and Quiz.* At the end of each chapter is a bulleted summary of the chapter's content and a 30-question quiz with true/false, multiple-choice, and matching questions.
- *Exercises.* Each chapter ends with two sets of written exercises (Operations and Commands) and six guided hands-on computer applications that measure and reinforce mastery of the chapter's concepts and skills. Each pair of applications present problems relating to school, personal, and business use.

- *Mastery Cases.* The final page of each chapter presents three unguided cases that allow you to demonstrate your personal mastery of the chapter material.
- *A Note about the Manual's Organization.* The topics in this manual are arranged in order of increasing difficulty. Chapters 1 and 2 present beginning and intermediate techniques and should be completed in sequence, for each skill builds upon the previous one. However, Chapter 3 includes several *independent* modules that present advanced skills. These modules may be followed in any order or omitted, as time and interest allow.
- *End-of-Manual Material.* The manual also provides a comprehensive reference *appendix* that summarizes commands and provides alphabetical listings of critical operations, a *glossary* that defines all key terms (with page references), and an *index* to all important topics.

WHAT'S NEW IN MICROSOFT ACCESS 7.0 FOR WINDOWS 95

1. *New ways to filter data:* The ability to filter data (limit the set of records to be used for display, reports, calculations, etc.) has been dramatically improved. Among the user's new options in filtering are the following:
   - Filter by Selection—Simply highlight the filter value directly in the table, click a button, and the records are limited to those containing that value in that field. Records can be futher limited by repeating the process.
   - Filter by Form—View the datasheet or form with blank fields and type the filter values in as many fields as you want (or pick them from a list of existing values).
   - Filter value can now be saved with tables, queries, or forms. Sort orders associated with a set of filter values can also be saved.
2. *Improved process for query creation and use:*
   - Select queries can now automatically generate simple summary statistics.
   - Sort order can be changed in datasheet view without having to switch to design view.
   - The toolbar associated with the query design process contains many new features.
3. *Redesigned toolbars and buttons:* New-style buttons include drop-down list boxes and portable palettes.
4. *More easily formatted reports and forms:* Changing the way Access displays data in a report or form can be achieved much more easily than in earlier versions. Instead of changing the properties of a field, the formatting toolbar gives the user palettes that can be dragged anywhere on the window. These palettes can be used to change the format, style, size, color, and so on, of data displayed in any field. Also, a spell-check feature has been included.
5. *New look for Access's desktop:* In addition to the new features, Access has a new appearance that makes it easier for the user to find and use Access's features. New looks have been given to the desktop, the database window, and the design screens for tables, queries, forms, and reports.

MICROSOFT ACCESS 7.0 FOR WINDOWS 95

1

DATABASE MANAGEMENT

OUTLINE

OBJECTIVES

After completing this chapter, you will be able to

1. Explain the general capabilities of a database management program.
2. Describe the procedures to launch and exit Microsoft Access.
3. Explain the various components of the Microsoft Access screen.
4. Create a table and enter data into records.
5. Review data using appropriate menu commands, toolbar buttons, and keyboard actions.
6. Add and delete records from the table.

DB

OVERVIEW

This chapter presents the basic techniques for using Microsoft Access, Version 7.0 (called Access in this module), a well-known database management program. First, you will learn to launch Access, to interpret its screen, to use its menu structure, and to understand what process the buttons on the screen represent. You will then learn how to create a table to contain data. Exiting and launching is presented next. The chapter then examines entering data into records and basic editing, followed by viewing records and creating printed lists. The chapter ends by examining how to delete records.

DATABASE MANAGEMENT

A database management system (DBMS) is a program that allows you to organize data so that they can be easily stored, accessed, modified, and maintained. As shown in Figure DB1-1a, data can be categorized by a hierarchy composed of a *database, table, record,* and *field.* An Access **database** is a single table or a collection of related

FIGURE DB1-1 ■ UNDERSTANDING THE DATA HIERARCHY

(a) The hierarchy categorizes data into levels of *database, table (file), record,* and *field.* (b) A table presents data in rows (records) and columns (fields).

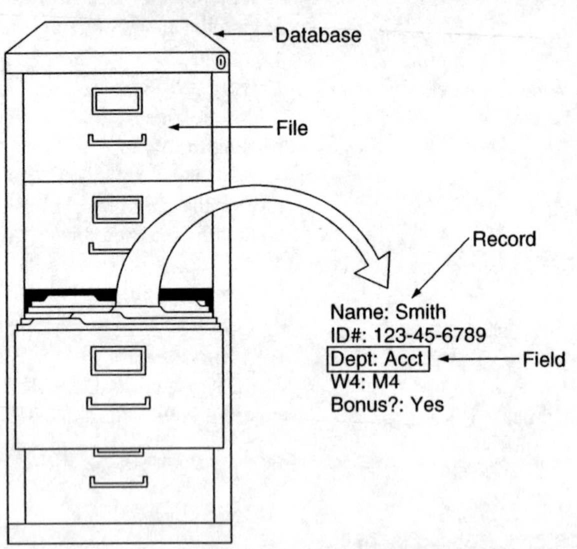

(a)

Table 1 : Table

	Field 1	Field 2	Field 3	Field 4
▶	Data	Data	Data	Data
	Data	Data	Data	Data
	Data	Data	Data	Data
	Data	Data	Data	Data
	Data	Data	Data	Data
*				

Record: 1 of 5

(b)

tables and other objects contained in a file. As shown in Figure DB1-1b, a **table** is a two-dimensional representation of data. Each horizontal row in a table represents one record. A **record** contains information about an individual entity—a person, place, or thing. Each vertical column in a table contains one **field**—an individual element of data that contains one or more typewritten characters or an image (Access can store a graphic image as well as text or numbers in a field). The data contained in a given field are known as field values. For example, "Smith" could be the value stored in the LAST NAME field.

Using a database management system is a process of creating and working within each of these structures. Chapters 1 and 2 of this manual discuss the use of Access as a file management system—working with one table at a time. Chapter 3 explores the use of multiple tables in a true relational database application.

Microsoft Access is a Windows 95 application, so it is based on a **graphical user interface (GUI),** which uses symbols and menus instead of typewritten commands to help you communicate with the computer. It is like using a picture of a cigarette with a slash through it in place of a written No Smoking sign. Communication with the computer using a GUI becomes more universal. Many of the symbols and operations have become standard throughout the industry. The GUI environment that Access operates in is called Windows 95. GUI symbols are called *icons* or *buttons*, depending on the context. Typically, a symbol is called an **icon** when it represents a program, a file, or a folder. It is called a **button** when it represents an option that a user may exercise within a program like Access.

GETTING STARTED

Before you begin, be certain you have all the necessary tools: a hard disk or network that contains Windows 95 and Microsoft Access, and a formatted disk on which you will store the files you create. This text assumes that you will be using Access on a hard-disk drive, although directions for networks are included.

STARTING WINDOWS 95

Before launching any Windows 95 programs, you must first start Windows 95. In the Windows 95 environment, you work in rectangular boxes called **windows.** A window may contain an application or a document. A window may also request or provide information (in which case, the window is called a **dialog box**).

USING A HARD-DISK DRIVE. This text assumes that the Windows 95 and Access programs are on your hard disk, which is identified as Drive C. To start Windows 95,

STEPS

1 Turn on your computer to boot the operating system

Windows 95 should start automatically. A "Starting Windows 95" message may appear. If your system boots to a menu, go to Step 3 in the next section, "Using a network." If a C:\> prompt appears on your screen,

2 Type WIN and press ↵ (This key may also be labeled "Enter" or "Return")

If a *Welcome to Windows 95* dialog box appears,

3 Click the *Close* button or press Esc

You should now be at the Windows 95 desktop as in Figure DB1-2. (The actual contents of your window may differ.) This is the screen that first appears when you start Windows 95.

4 Insert your data disk into Drive A (or B)

USING A NETWORK. Access may be available to you through a local area network. In this case, Access is kept on the hard-disk drive of another computer that is shared by many users. To use Access, you must run the program from your own microcomputer. So many network configurations are in use today that it is difficult to predict

FIGURE DB1-2 ■ THE WINDOWS 95 DESKTOP

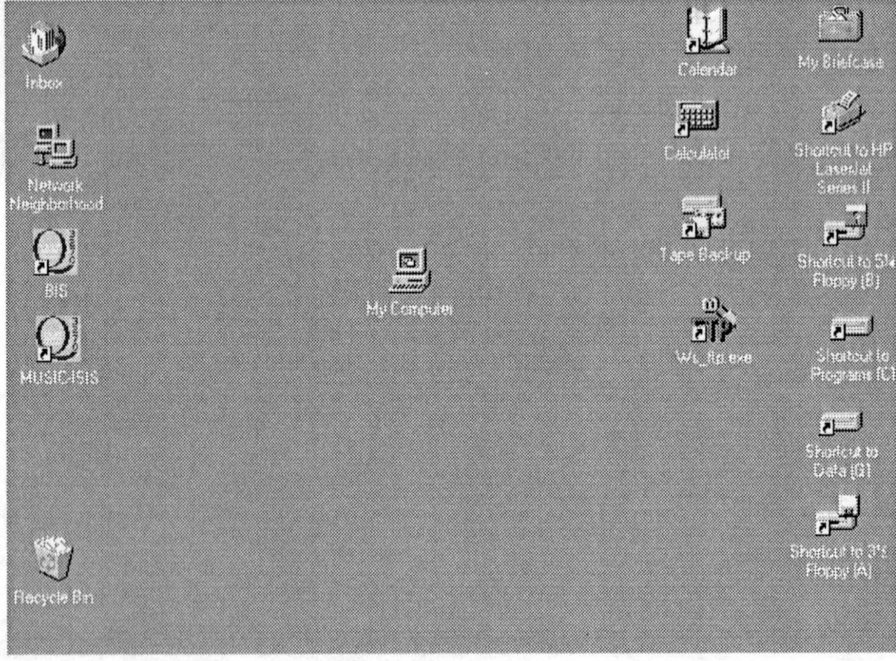

which one you will use. Check with your instructor for exact directions. In general, however, to launch Access,

STEPS

1 **Boot the network operating system (perhaps with your own disk)**

2 **Type any command needed to get the network menu**

In many networks, this is done by typing LAN and pressing ↵.

3 **Make sure your data disk is in Drive A**

4 **Select (or type) the appropriate command on your screen to access Windows 95**

MOUSE AND KEYBOARD OPERATIONS

Skip this section if you are already familiar with using a mouse and keyboard.

USING A MOUSE. A **mouse** is an input device that allows you to control a **mouse pointer** (graphical image) on your screen and select program features. Currently, it appears as a small arrow. As you move your mouse on a flat surface, the mouse pointer moves on your screen in a similar fashion. In Access, the mouse pointer may appear in the forms displayed in Figure DB1- 3a. **Pointing** means moving the mouse. To *point* your mouse,

STEPS

1 **Slowly move your mouse on a flat surface or mouse pad (a small rubber pad) and notice the direction that the mouse pointer moves on your screen. If you run out of space, simply lift your mouse and replace it.**

2 **Point to the *Start* icon (it is in the lower left corner of the screen)**

3 **Point to the *My Computer* icon (it could be anywhere on your screen)**

Clicking involves quickly pressing and releasing the left mouse button. This action will normally select the item at which the mouse pointer is positioned. Try this:

4 **Click *Start* to see its menu**

5 **Click anywhere in the desktop to close the menu for now**

Another basic mouse action is called **double-clicking**. Double-clicking involves quickly pressing and releasing the left mouse button twice. Try this:

FIGURE DB1-3 ■ MOUSE POINTERS AND ACTIONS

(a) Common mouse pointers.
(b) Common mouse actions.

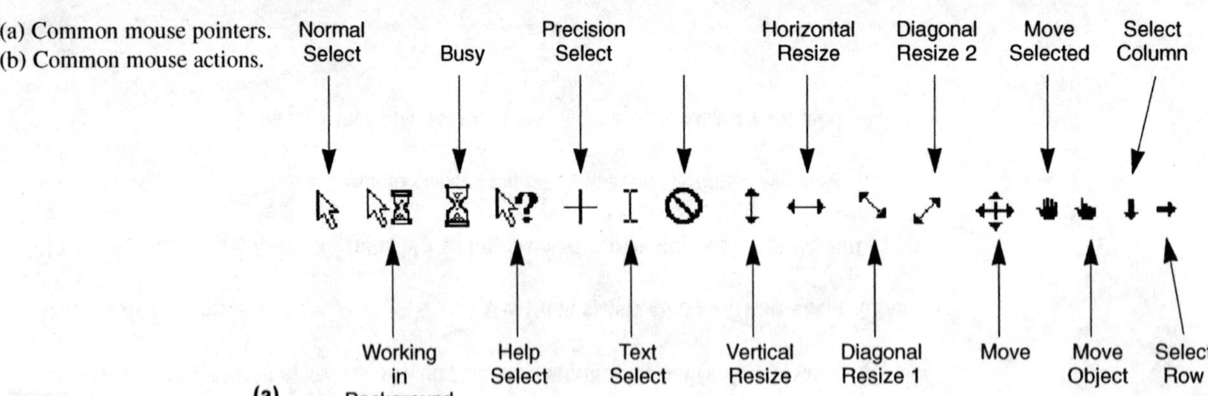

Mouse Action	Description
Pointing	Moving mouse, and thus mouse pointer, to desired item.
Clicking	Pressing and quickly releasing the left (normally) or right mouse button.
Dragging	Pressing and holding left mouse button, while moving mouse to desired location with object pointed to.
Dropping	Releasing mouse and thus object pointed to after dragging.
Double-Clicking	Rapidly pressing and releasing the left mouse button twice.

(b)

6 Point to the *My Computer* icon again and double-click

Note: If a window does not appear, you may not be clicking quickly enough. Double-click the icon again. Or, click the icon to select it, then press Enter.

Now:

7 Click the "X" *(Close)* button at the upper right corner of this window

Many Windows 95 programs also support a feature called *drag-and-drop.* This feature allows you to use a mouse to move a selection (text or object) from one place to another. This feature will be illustrated later. The common mouse actions are summarized in Figure DB1-3b.

Tip: It is possible to reverse the actions of the mouse buttons for the convenience of left-handed people. They can be performed from the Windows 95 Control Panel. Instructions can be found in the Windows 95 documentation and Help screens.

USING A KEYBOARD. At times, Windows 95 features may also be accessed by keyboard. Keystrokes required to operate the Access menu system are discussed under the section "The Menu Bar" (later in this chapter).

Most programs also provide special keystrokes called **shortcut keys.** Shortcut keys provide quick access to certain commands. Shortcut keys involve pressing a function key, either alone or in combination with the Ctrl, Alt, or Shift keys. For example, to close Windows using its shortcut key,

STEPS

1 **Press Alt + F4 (Hold the Alt key while pressing the F4 key and then release both keys)**

2 **Press N to cancel the command**

This manual presents its tutorials using the mouse approach. Where appropriate, keyboard shortcuts will be shown in brackets at the right of the step.

LAUNCHING ACCESS

The procedure to start Access is the same as that used to start any Windows program. The *Access* icon is usually found in the Microsoft Office program group.

STEPS

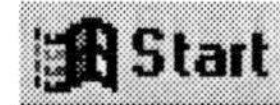

1 **Click the *Start* button to bring up its menu**

2 **Point to *Programs* at the top of the list**

Note: The letter "P" is underlined. This indicates that you can press P if you want to select it.

3 **Point to the *Microsoft Access* item** [→]

4 **Click the *Microsoft Access* item to launch it** [↵]

(If Microsoft Office appears on the Program Menu, point to it for its submenu and then click Microsoft Access.)

DB

Note: To use the Microsoft Office Shortcut toolbar to start Access, click the *Start a New Document* button, *Blank Presentation*, and then *OK*.

An Access copyright screen may appear briefly but will be replaced by the Access window.

5 If needed, press Esc to remove the *Microsoft Access* dialog box

THE ACCESS WINDOW

The main display screen presented by Access should look like Figure DB1-4a. (If the *Microsoft Access* dialog box is occupying the center of your screen, close it by clicking the *Close* button now.)

This screen is divided into five areas. From top to bottom, they are

- The title bar
- The menu bar
- The toolbar
- The work area
- The status bar

The **title bar** on the Access window is the same as it is in all other windows. It contains, from left to right, the title of the application that is running (in this case, Microsoft Access), two size buttons (two of these three: *Maximize, Minimize,* or *Restore*), and the *Close* button.

THE MENU BAR

The **menu bar** now displays the names of three pull-down menus: *File, Tools*, and *Help*. You can access these menus three different ways.

- *Click* the menu name (point to it and press the left mouse button once)

This is the *mouse approach*.

- Hold down the Alt key and then press the *underlined letter* of the menu name. For example, Alt + F would access the *File* menu.

This is the *keyboard approach.*

- Also, you can press Alt, then use the arrow keys to move the highlight to whichever of the menus you want to access. Then, press Enter to access or pull down the highlighted menu.

In this text, instructions will usually be given for using the mouse approach to execute various commands, but you may substitute one of the other methods if it is more convenient. Now, try the following exercises:

STEPS

1 Click *File*

You will see that a secondary menu is pulled down—or displayed—below the menu name. Once the menu is activated, the highlighted area will follow your mouse pointer

FIGURE DB1-4 ■ THE ACCESS WINDOW

(a) This is the blank desktop presented by Access to the user when the program is first started.
(b) The symbols next to the menu items give important clues to the action performed by the item.

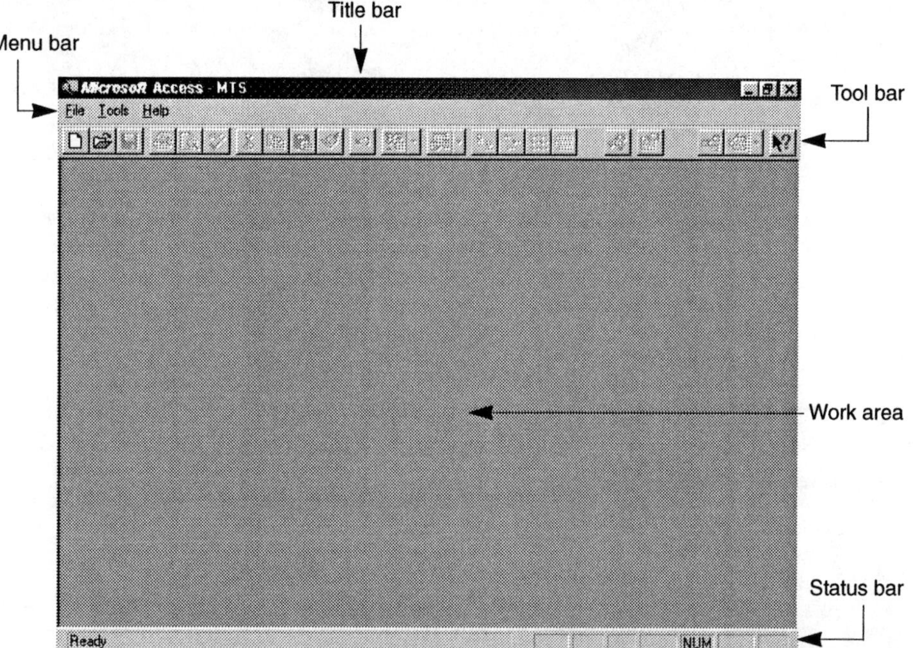

(a)

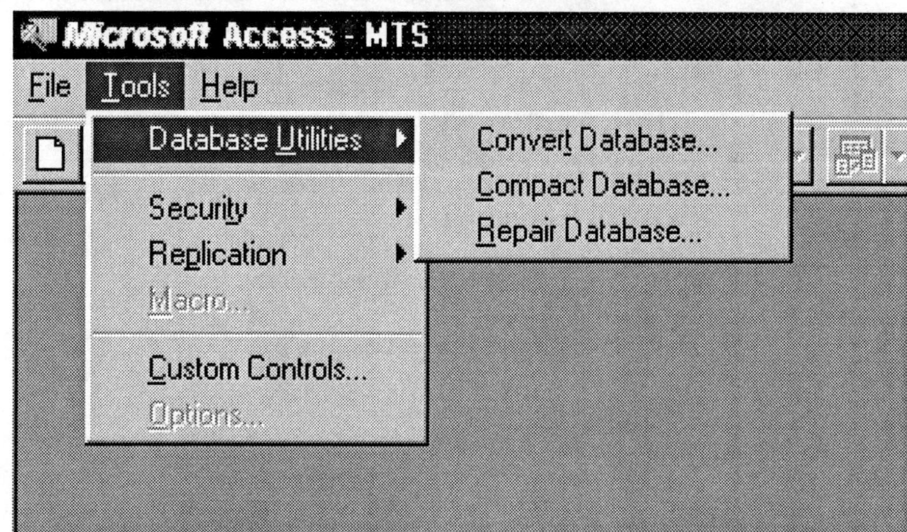

(b)

as you move it vertically from item to item on the secondary menu. If you move the mouse pointer horizontally along the menu bar, Access displays secondary menus associated with the other main menu choices.

2 Move the mouse pointer horizontally and vertically while observing that the highlight follows the pointer

Tip: Do not click any of the choices on the pull-down menus that appear or you may find yourself on an unplanned private adventure. If you selected a choice by mistake, press Esc or click the *Cancel* button on any dialog boxes.

Notice that some of the commands on the pull-down menus have an ellipsis (...) to their right, like *New Database...* and *Toolbars...* under the *File* menu. The ellipsis symbol indicates that whenever this command is executed, Access will open a dialog box that will ask you for any information necessary to execute the command.

Other menu choices are followed by a little triangle pointing to the right. Pointing to one of these items will immediately open another level of menu choices. The Access menus are arranged in a top-down "tree" manner with some menu commands branching to submenus of additional choices. You simply follow the menu tree with your mouse pointer until you have arrived at the specific choice you want. Then execute the command by clicking the left mouse button. To see an example of this,

3 Point to *Tools*

4 Point to *Database Utilities*

Note that a lower level menu opens automatically when you point to a menu choice followed by the triangle symbol, as is seen in Figure DB1-4b. To close the menus,

5 Point to any blank area in the Access window and click the left mouse button

Next, use the arrow keys instead of the mouse to move around in Access's menus.

6 Press Alt

This highlights *File* (or, in other Windows 95 applications, whatever the *left*-most menu choice might be).

7 Press → twice to highlight *Help*

8 Press ↓ to pull down the *Help* submenu

When a menu choice has been highlighted, you can execute that choice by clicking it with the mouse or by pressing Enter. There is yet another way to execute a menu command.

Examine the *Help* menu. Notice that each command on this menu has one underlined letter—a mnemonic code. If you press *that* letter on the keyboard, Access executes that command just as if you had clicked it with the mouse. The underlined letter is usually—but not always—the initial letter of the word. To demonstrate that pressing the underlined letter will execute the command,

9 Press A to execute the *About Microsoft Access* command

You will see a box that contains copyright and version information. When you have inspected the contents of this box,

10 Click the *OK* button

The box disappears.

As you have seen, menu choices can be made by using the mouse, by pressing Alt followed by arrow keys, pressing Enter when your choice is highlighted, or by using Alt in combination with mnemonic letter keys. Use whichever method you prefer. *However, Access, like other Windows 95 applications, are designed to be controlled by the mouse, so it is probably best to become accustomed to using the mouse.*

THE TOOLBAR

The **toolbar** is a row of buttons beneath the menu bar that provides a quick way for you to initiate many important Access features or processes. The number and type of buttons that appear on the toolbar will change as you perform different tasks. It is also possible to customize toolbars to suit your own preferences and work habits. Each set of buttons is appropriate to the task that you are performing. The toolbar has 22 buttons when the desktop is blank, but 19 of them are dimmed (meaning that the processes they represent are not available). Most of the dimmed buttons represent commands used in processing and manipulating data, and because no files are open and no data has been entered, using these buttons would have no point.

Tip: If you are unsure of a button's function, place the mouse pointer over the button and wait for a moment. A description of the button's function will be displayed at the left-most portion of the status bar and the button's name will be displayed under the mouse pointer.

The three active buttons include the two left-most buttons—the *New Database* buttons, used to create a new database file, and the *Open Database* buttons, used to open an existing database file—and the right-most button—the *Help* button, which is used to get information about a screen feature.

Between the toolbar and the status bar is a large blank area (called the Work Area), which will later be filled with dialog boxes, data tables, and other objects that you will use.

THE STATUS BAR

The lower portion of the Access Window is the **status bar**. Useful messages and other information are displayed from time to time on the status bar. For example, a description of the button's function is displayed there, as you have seen. If your mouse is not pointing at a button, the status bar says "Ready," meaning that Access is ready for your instructions.

CHECKPOINT

- ✓ Display the Access opening desktop screen.
- ✓ Identify the title bar, menu bar, toolbar, work area, and status bar.
- ✓ Display each menu and submenu.
- ✓ Identify the menu choices that will lead to another menu.
- ✓ Identify the menu choices that will lead to a dialog box.

ACTIVATING AND USING THE HELP FEATURE

To make it easier for you to use Access, the program contains a variety of Help features—on-line documentation that you can read on the screen. Help provided by Access is **context sensitive**. That is, the Help screens that Access displays are pertinent to the task you are trying to perform.

Tip: If you are an experienced Windows 95 user, the Access Help screens will look familiar. Use the same techniques that you have used in the Help feature of other Windows 95 applications.

ACTIVATING HELP

Several methods are available for asking Access for help or advice in performing a task. They include the following:

Method	Action	Comment
Help	Click *Help* on the menu bar.	This provides a more generic level of help. You will be shown the Help Contents screen. In Windows 95 applications, Help will always be the right-most choice on the menu bar.
F1	Press F1.	You will be shown a help screen relevant to the task at hand.
The Help Button	Click the *Help* button.	The mouse pointer will change shape to an arrow superimposed over a question mark. Then, point to the object on the screen (button, menu choice, etc.) that you want help with and click.

USING THE HELP FEATURES

Do not be reluctant to explore the Access Help screens. You cannot do any damage to your data or perform some action you will later regret. You can only learn more about Access.

USING THE *HELP* MENU. To search for help on a specific topic,

STEPS

1. **If needed, launch Access and then press Esc**

2 Click *Help* (menu bar), *Microsoft Access Help Topics,* and then the *Contents* tab

Like many dialog boxes you will be seeing, this screen displays labeled tabs at the top. You can click the appropriate tab with the mouse to display the set of choices you desire. The screen you see should resemble Figure DB1-5a; however, the contents of your list box may differ.

Notice that there are several content areas represented with the *book* icon.

3 Click a book icon representing a content area of your choice, then click *Open*

Depending on what you have selected, you may have to open additional books to reach the documentation. Eventually, you will see one or more document icons displayed as question marks superimposed over a page. These represent on-line Help documents that you can read by clicking one and then clicking *Display.*

4 Click a topic document, then click *Display*

Access will display the document to you. If you find the answers to your questions in this document, you can click the *Close* button to leave the Help window. After reading about a topic, explore another method of searching for topic-specific help. First, return to the Help Contents page:

5 Click *Help Topics*

USING THE HELP INDEX. Instead of reading through Help's table of contents, you can use the Index feature to search for an index entry on a specific topic. Like any other index, it is arranged alphabetically rather than by topic title. Suppose you need to make a backup copy of an Access database file. To locate a Help document on this procedure (use Figure DB1-5b as a guide),

STEPS

1 Click the *Index* tab

2 Type Backing up databases

As soon as you begin typing, Access begins searching. In fact, as soon as you have typed "Backing," Access has already found the topic.

3 Click *Display*

4 If a *Topic Found* dialog box appears, click *Backup a Database* and then *Display*

FIGURE WP1-5 ■ USING ACCESS HELP

(a) Table of Contents for Access Help.
(b) Searching for help on a particular topic.

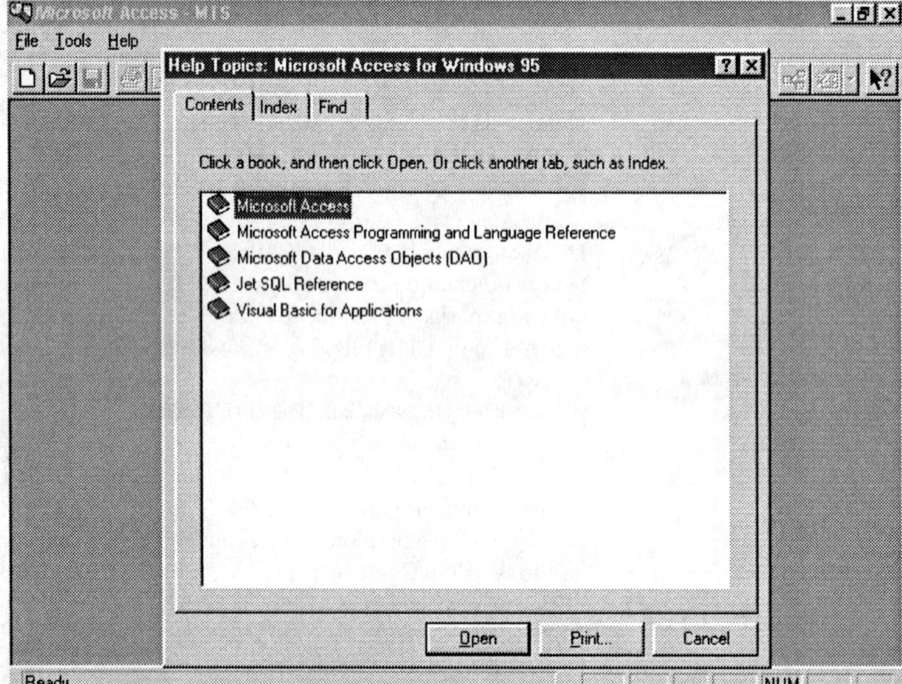

(a)

Microsoft Access - MTS
File Tools Help
Help Topics: Microsoft Access for Windows 95
Contents Index Find
1 Type the first few letters of the word you're looking for.
backing
2 Click the index entry you want, and then click Display.
background processing
backing up databases
backslash (\)
BackStyle
backup
backward compatibility
bands, -see sections
base of natural logarithms
base table
Base
base-16
base-8
base-n logarithms
Beep
Beep
BeginTrans
Between
Display
Print...
Cancel
Ready
NUM

(b)

(continued)

FIGURE DB1-5 ■ *(continued)*

(c) Help explains how to back up a database.

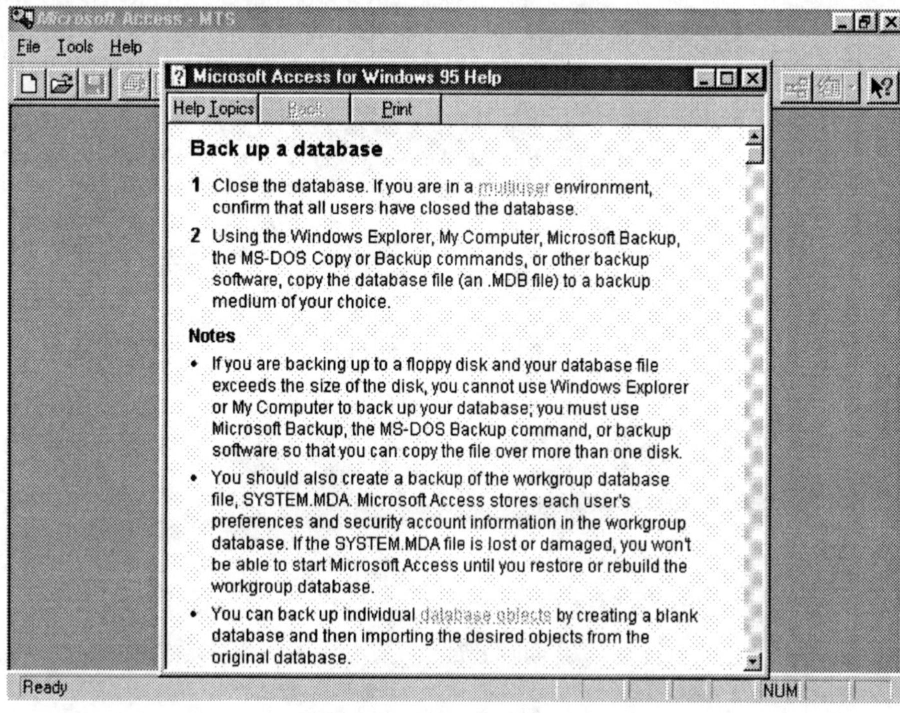

(c)

Tip: If many topics related to the search criteria had been found, you could have scrolled through them, selected the one you wanted, and then clicked the *Display* button.

The Access Help window shows you a screen of information about the topic you selected. You should see a screen like the one shown in Figure DB1-5c. Interspersed throughout many Help screens and at the bottom of many Help screens, you will see underlined words or phrases. If you click a word or phrase that is underscored with a dashed line, Access will show you the definition of the word or phrase. Click the box containing the definition and it disappears.

For example, near the bottom of this Help screen, is the phrase "database objects."

5 **Click *database objects* (if needed, use the scroll bar to locate)**

Access will show you the definition of that topic. It is a topic that you will be learning about in the next few sections. To make the definition disappear after you have read it,

6 **Click any part of the screen**

Take the time now to read about backing up databases. It is a very important topic. Note also that a *Print* button appears near the top of the window containing the Help topic. By clicking this button, you can generate a hard copy of the help text.

In some Help screens, you will see a word or phrase that is underscored with a solid line. If you click on this, you will be taken to another Help screen which explains the process represented by that word or phrase, or you will be shown a list of topics to choose from.

> **Tip: When reading Help screens, click the *Maximize* button. Help will expand to fill your screen and you will be able to see more Help feature text at one time.**

To exit Help:

7 Click the *Close* button [Alt + F4]

USING F1. Remember that pressing F1 will take you to context-sensitive Help screens. Using F1 is very useful when you need help filling out a dialog box. For example,

STEPS

1 Click *File*

The file menu should appear.

2 Click *New Database...*

The *New* dialog box should appear, similar to the one in Figure DB1-6a. If you attempt to get help by clicking the Help choice on the menu bar, you will discover that it is not available. Access will only beep at you. Because the *New* dialog box is the focus, no action outside the boundaries of that box is accepted. But,

3 Press F1

and you will see a Help screen like Figure DB1-6b that directly relates to this particular dialog box.

4 Press Esc to remove the Help caption

5 Click *Cancel*

USING THE *HELP* BUTTON. At times you will want to perform an operation but will not remember which toolbar button is used to activate that feature. At other times you will be presented with a screen that has unfamiliar features. Access offers many tools for creating files, reports, and forms; entering and editing data; customizing

FIGURE DB1-6 ■ OTHER WAYS OF GETTING HELP FROM ACCESS

(a) This dialog box will create a database file named CUSTOMER when the user clicks the *OK* command button.
(b) Access provides help on how to fill in the *New Database* dialog box.

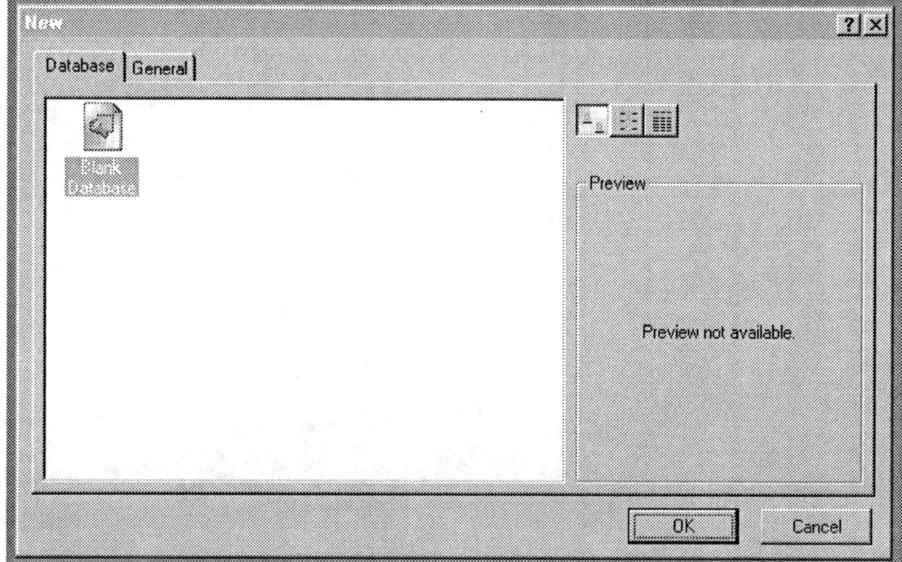

(a)

(b)

(continued)

features, and so on. Even experienced users my be unsure of the function of a particular button, dialog box, or other feature. However, Access will identify most of the components of any screen if you use the *Help* button. The *Help* button (if available) is at the right-most button on the Access toolbar. When you click this button, the mouse pointer changes to an arrow accompanied by a question mark, just like the symbol on the *Help* button itself. Perform the following exercise to see how the *Help* button works:

FIGURE DB1-6 ■ *(continued)*

(c) The *Help* button provides information on specific screen features.

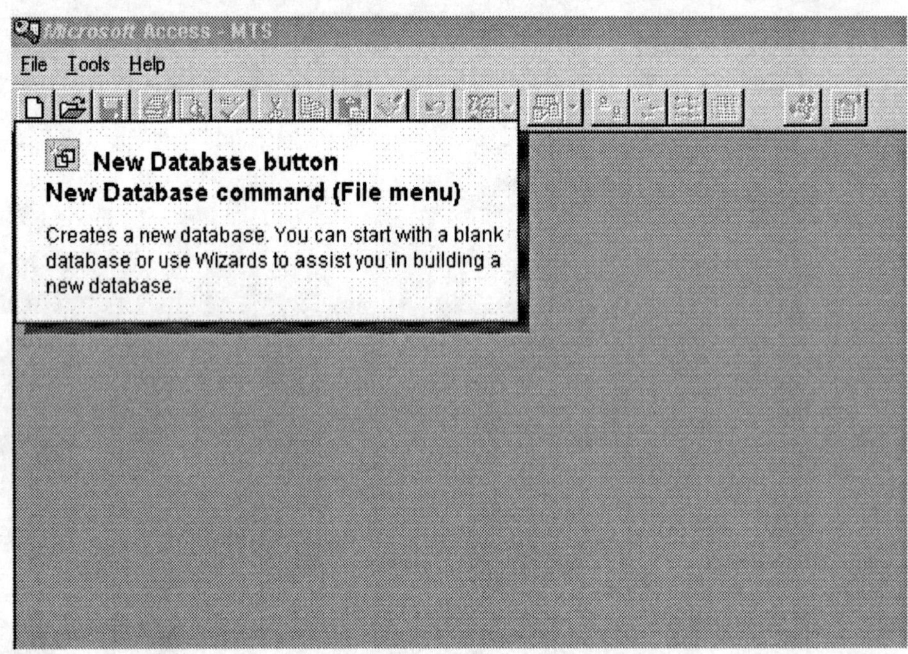

(c)

STEPS

If the *Help* button is not available, skip the following steps. Simply point to the item to receive a caption with its functions.

1 Click the *Help* button

The shape of the mouse pointer changes to an arrow superimposed over a question mark (similar to the image on the button).

2 Click the *New Database* button

A box like the one shown in Figure DB1-6c opens, which provides defining information about that button. Of course, if you need more detail, you can use the techniques previously described to search for more detailed Help screens.

To close the box,

3 Click any part of the screen [Esc]

CHECKPOINT

✓ Display the Access *Help* dialog box.
✓ Read the subtopic "What is a Database?" under the topic "Visual Introduction to Microsoft Access."
✓ Return to a blank desktop.

✓ Starting at the *Help* menu, display the *About Microsoft Access* dialog box.
✓ Display "System Info" and then return to a blank desktop.

THE ACCESS DATABASE FILE

Access has a variety of ways of storing and presenting data. Each of these ways is associated with a different kind of **object**. An object might be a database, a report, or a data entry screen. Objects are placed in the file by the user. You will soon be creating a number of objects. All objects associated with an application such as an inventory or a mailing list are contained in one file called a **database file**. The objects in a database file can be created, modified, copied, deleted, viewed, and managed from the file's **database window**, a view screen that shows you the contents of a database file. That is, the database window displays the names of the various objects that you have created and provides a menu and a toolbar for working with these objects.

By storing all the objects in one file, Access makes file management and backup very easy.

CREATING A DATABASE

Assume you want to create a table called CUSTOMER. Because you have, as yet, no data, you must first create the database file that will contain the table and other objects you are going to create. This is easily done by executing the following commands:

STEPS

1 **If needed, launch Access and press Esc**

2 **Click *File*, and then click *New Database*** [Ctrl + N]

You should see the *New* dialog box. It is asking you what *kind* of new object you wish to create. The choice you are offered is the only one that is available now—creation of a new database.

3 **Click *OK***

The *File New Database* dialog box has a number of features that are important to understand (refer to Figure DB1-7):

- The entire dialog box can be moved by pointing to the title bar, then clicking and dragging the box to another portion of the screen.
- There are two *command buttons:* clicking the *Create* button tells Access to execute the action with the settings currently appearing in the dialog box; clicking the *Cancel* button abandons the procedure and returns to the previous condition without executing any action.
- The three drop-down list boxes include the *Save in* list box, where you will select the drive and folder in which the database file is to be saved; the *File name* list box, where you will enter the filename of the database; and the *Save as type* list box, where you can select the file type.

FIGURE DB1-7 ■ THE *FILE NEW DATABASE* DIALOG BOX

This dialog box allows you to create a new database file.

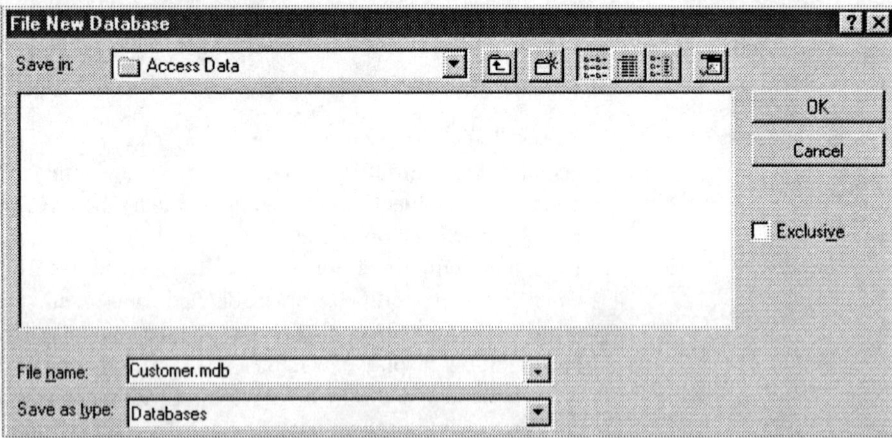

Tip: To enter text in any text box, point to it with the mouse and click. This places a text insertion point in it so that an entry, such as a filename, can be typed.

- A large rectangular area, which displays the names of folders and files in the current folder.
- A toolbar consisting of six buttons: the *Up One Level* button displays the contents of the parent folder; the *Create New Folder* button creates a new folder in the current folder; the *List* button displays file and folder names only; the *Details* button displays file and folder names, sizes, types, and dates modified; the *Properties* button displays file properties (more about properties later); and the *Commands and Settings* button permits you to control the sort order of files and folders in the display, the display of network drives, and so forth.

Tip: Access will display the name of each button if you point to it with the mouse.

To create an empty database file you need only indicate a filename, drive designation, and folder. For purposes of illustration, assume that you want to create a database in A:\Access Data. Fill out the dialog box in the following manner, using Figure DB1-7 as a guide. (Of course, you may alter the destination drive and folder to suit your own system.)

4 Click the drop-down arrow next to *Save In:*, then click the disk drive you will be using for data

Tip: There are two easy ways to indicate which drive you intend to use for data. One is the method described above. The other is to click the *Up One Level* button until you see the name of the folder or drive you intend to use.

5 Click the *3½" Floppy (A:) drive* icon

Tip: You can create a new folder by clicking the new folder button on the *File New Database* dialog box.

6 Click the *File name* text box, backspace over any existing text, and type CUSTOMER

7 Click the *Create* button

The object you next see displayed is the Customer: Database window. Because you just created the CUSTOMER database file, Access assumes you want to use it. Referring to Figure DB1-8, notice the features of the database window:

- Three command buttons are present: *New, Open*, and *Design.* At this time, only the *New* button is not dimmed. Because no objects exist in this database file, the only thing you can do is create new objects.
- Tabs are present for each of the Access object types: *Table, Query, Form, Report, Macro,* and *Module*. Clicking one of these tabs indicates that you wish to create objects of that type. Only one type of object can be selected at a time. If you have selected *Tables* as the object type, Access assumes, if you click the *New, Open,* or *Design* command buttons, that you want to create a new table,open an existing table, or modify the design of an existing table.

extension .MDB

FIGURE DB1-8 ■ THE DATABASE WINDOW

Clicking a selection button displays a list of the indicated type of object. The database is currently empty.

DB

To close the database window,

8 **Click *File*, then click *Close*** [Ctrl + W]

THE DATABASE WINDOW

You can now create a simple database table. In this exercise, you will name a table and describe its structure to Access. A *table structure,* identifies each data field to be included in the table, giving the field's name, type, and (in some cases) size.

OPENING THE DATABASE WINDOW. All Access objects must be contained by a database file. Before you can create a table, you must open the database window associated with that database file.

To open the database file you created in the last exercise,

STEPS

1 **Click *File*, and then click *Open Database...*** [Ctrl + O]

You will see the *Open* dialog box, where you identify the database file you want to open.

2 **If needed, click the drop-down button of the *Look In* box**

3 **Click the *3½" Floppy (A:) drive* icon**

4 **Click CUSTOMER on the filename selection list**

The filename should now be highlighted to indicate that it has been selected.

5 **Click the *Open* button**

The Customer database window appears, as you saw before (shown in Figure DB1-8). Note that, as before, there are six option tabs—one for each of the Access object types. Because you have selected the database file, Access now knows in which file to place the new object (table) you are about to design. To create a new table,

6 **Click the *Tables* tab (if necessary)**

7 **Click the *New* button**

The *New Table* dialog box appears and offers four choices: *Datasheet View, Design View, Table Wizard,* and *Import/Link Table.*

The Table wizard contains a number of standard table designs that you can use. Depending on the variety of data you need to enter, the Table wizard might save you some time. Several wizards are available in Access to help you design a variety of objects. We will explore some of them later in this text. Because the table you are about to design is not one of the types offered by the Table wizard,

8 Click *Design View*, then click *OK*

This choice indicates to Access that you intend to *design* a table. You should see the Table design screen (see Figure DB1-9a). In this screen you can define the structure of a new table. Later, you will use the same screen to modify the structure of an existing table.

FIGURE DB1-9 ■ THE TABLE DESIGN SCREEN 

(a) The screen is the design tool for creating new tables. (b) The first field has been completed.

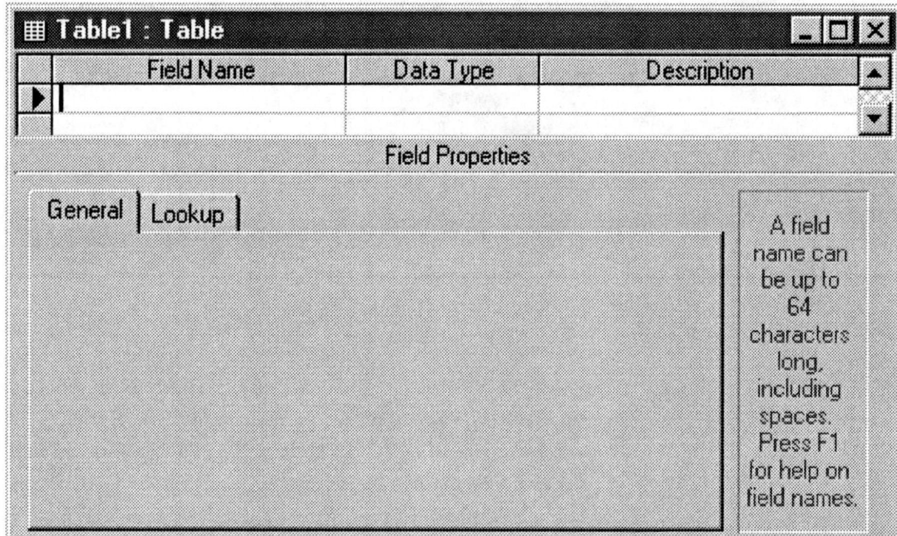

(a)

Table1 : Table

Field Name	Data Type	Description
Customer Number	Text	An identification code unique to this customer.

Field Properties

General | Lookup

Field Size	3
Format	
Input Mask	
Caption	
Default Value	
Validation Rule	
Validation Text	
Required	No
Allow Zero Length	No
Indexed	No

The label for the field when used on a form. If you don't enter a caption, the field name is used as the label. Press F1 for help on captions.

(b)

(continued)

FIGURE DB1-9 ■ *(continued)*

(c) The second field has been completed.

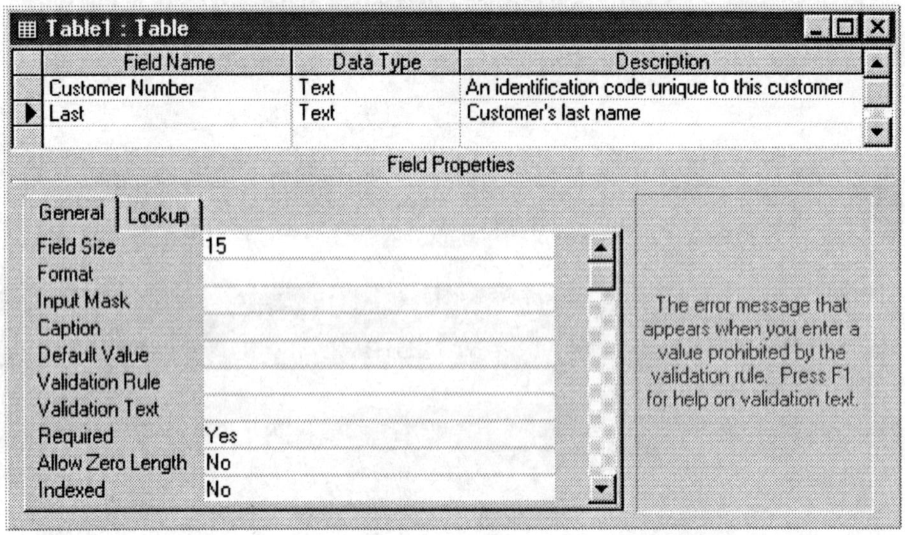

Table1 : Table

Field Name	Data Type	Description
Customer Number	Text	An identification code unique to this customer
Last	Text	Customer's last name

Field Properties

General | Lookup

Field Size	15
Format	
Input Mask	
Caption	
Default Value	
Validation Rule	
Validation Text	
Required	Yes
Allow Zero Length	No
Indexed	No

The error message that appears when you enter a value prohibited by the validation rule. Press F1 for help on validation text.

(c)

ADDING THE FIRST FIELD. The first step is to name a field. **Field names** may be up to 64 characters long. Field names may contain letters, spaces, numerals, or underline symbols. While spaces may be embedded in a field name (such as "GROSS PAY"), you cannot begin or end a field name with a space. Do not use square brackets ([ ]), an exclamation point (!), a period (.), or the back quote character (`}.

Tip: All Access objects follow these naming rules.

A *good* field name reminds you of the data that is to be stored in that field, so the total gross pay of an employee for the current pay period might be stored in a field named "GROSS", "GROSS_PAY", or "CURRENT GROSS PAY." Most punctuation marks are legal in a field name but they communicate little meaning. For example, "^~^#?{?t$" is a perfectly legal field name, but what does that name tell you about the data that might be stored in it? It is best to avoid using punctuation marks in field names unless you have a good reason to include them. When you first see the Table design screen, the text insertion point should be in the first row of the Field Name column. If you have moved it, return it to that location by clicking the first row of the Field Name column. Then,

STEPS

1 **Type Customer Number and press ↵**

Tip: If you make a mistake in typing, press Backspace to erase it. If you've already left the column, press the left arrow key to go back, and then reenter the field name. You may also use Insert or Delete to help fix errors.

CUSTOMER NUMBER appears in the Field Name column, and the cursor moves to the *Field Type* column.

You can now identify the *type* of **field values** (data) to be stored in this field. Notice that the cursor is in the **Data Type** column. Access has already entered Text as the default data type, and this is the correct type for this field. Text data consist of a string of characters that have no numeric value, such as a name, an address, a phone number, or a zip code.

Access offers eight data types, any or all of which can be used in the same table:

- Text (1 to 255 characters)—Contains any combination of letters, numbers, symbols, or other printable characters. Data in text fields have no numeric value.
- Memo—Extended comments, usually sentences organized into paragraphs. Can contain up to 64,000 bytes (characters).
- Number—**Format** choices consist of the following:

Byte	Numbers from 0 to 255; no fractions
Integer	−32,768 to 32,767; no fractions
Long integer	−2,147,483,648 to 2,147,483,647; no fractions
Single	Numbers from -3.4×10^{38} to 3.4×10^{38}
Double	Numbers from -1.79×10^{308} to 1.79×10^{308}

- Date/Time—Dates (like 11/15/95) and time (like 11:45am).
- Currency—Monetary amounts. Same as number except the currency symbol ($) is automatically inserted.
- AutoNumber—A numeric value, beginning with 1 and incremented by 1 for each record you add to a database.
- AutoNumber fields cannot be edited.
- Yes/No—Logical data containing yes/no, true/false, or on/off entries. Useful for data that can have only one of two values.
- OLE Object—An object containing binary, such as graphic images.
- Lookup wizard—Displays a list of values the user can choose from.

Tip: Some things called "numbers" should be regarded as text, not numbers. A phone "number," for example, has no numeric value. It is an identification code. The rule of thumb is if you're not going to use it in a calculation, it's not a number. In this case, *Customer Number* is an identification code, not a number.

DB

Since the correct data type has already been chosen,

2 Press ↵

The text insertion point moves to the Description column. This entry is optional. It should contain a descriptive line or phrase that describes the contents of the field. This line will be displayed later, during the data entry process, as a guide to the user. For now,

3 Type An identification code unique to this customer

Notice that the lower portion of the Table design screen contains an area where the properties of the field can be described. One of those properties has been filled in—**Field Size.** The size of a text field—that is, the maximum number of characters allowed—is under the control of the user. To change the size of this field to 3,

4 Place the text insertion point in the *Field Size* area by clicking it [F6]

5 Backspace over the default entry, then type 3 and press ↵

For now, leave the other properties at their default settings. Your screen should now look like Figure DB1-9b. To begin the entry of the second field,

6 Click the second row in the *Field Name* column

A text insertion point should appear there.

7 Type Last and press ↵

Again, text is the correct data type. To accept it,

8 Press ↵

In the *Description* column,

9 Type Customer's last name

It would be pointless to create a record without a last name, so it would be useful if Access were to force the user—whether it is yourself or a data entry clerk—to enter a last name for every record. This is an instance when adjusting the properties of this field is called for.

FIELD PROPERTIES

Before finishing the design of the table, a discussion of field **properties** is needed. Each field has certain properties attached to it. The properties vary with the type of field. By changing the properties of a field, you can control how the field behaves when it is displayed or printed, how much data can be entered, what kind of data must be entered, what kind of data will be refused, whether helpful instructions will be displayed for the user, and so on. The names of the properties are *Field Size, Format, Input Mask, Caption, Default Value, Validation Rule, Validation Text, Required, Allow Zero Length, Indexed, Filter Lookup*, and *Decimal Places.* Each can perform a potentially important function, depending, of course, on your application. However, not all of the properties will be used in the exercises you will be performing.

FIELD SIZE. Field size determines how many alphanumeric or numeric characters can be entered in the field. For *text* fields, type in a number between 1 and 255.

For *number* fields, use the arrow to open a drop-down list and select from among byte, integer, long integer, single, and double.

FORMAT. Number fields can display as *general number* (1234.5678), *currency* ($1,234.56), *fixed* (1234.56), *standard* (1,234.56), *percent* (23.32%), and *scientific notation* (1.23E+03). *Date fields* can be displayed in the following formats: *general date* (12/25/95 7:19:34 AM), *long date* (Monday, December 25, 1995), *medium date* (25–December–95), *short date* (12/25/95), *long time* (7:19:34 AM), *medium time* (7:19 AM), and *short time* (7:19).

INPUT MASK. The **input mask** automatically inserts literal characters into fields so that you do not have to type them. It can also restrict the characters that you are permitted to insert in any position in the field. For example, a mask for a phone number could be (999) 000-0000. "9" in a field mask means that only a numeral can be entered in that position, but entry is not required. "0" in a field mask means that only a numeral can be entered in that position, but entry *is* required. Access automatically provides the **literal** characters: the parentheses, the space, and the hyphen. Any user entering a phone number in such a field could only enter numerals, thus reducing the chances of typos. The area code would not be required, but all seven digits of the phone number would have to be entered. The mask for a social security number would be 000-00-0000. The input mask would provide the hyphens and would require 9 numerals. Access allows many other input mask characters. An Input Mask wizard is also available that can provide help in writing masks for data fields that are frequently needed, like phone numbers.

CAPTION. The **caption** is a descriptive word, phrase, or sentence that will be displayed instead of the field name when designing other Access objects. You will learn more about captions in Chapters 2 and 3.

DEFAULT VALUE. The **default value** property provides a value for the field, which the user can accept or overtype. For example, if you are maintaining a list of customers for your retail computer store, it is likely that most of your customers will be from your city. The default value property of the City field can automatically enter your city's name in the field. If a customer is from another city, you can simply overtype the value.

VALIDATION RULE. In some fields, it may be desirable to set limits on the data that can be entered. For example, no check written in a checking account can be for an amount greater than the balance. Perhaps no delivery date should be permitted to be more than two weeks after an order date because of store policy. Maybe the only legitimate grades are A, B, C, D, and F. A **validation rule** can be expressed that restricts the user's input to data permitted by the rule. For example, a validation rule requiring a check to be less than the available balance would be as follows:

[Check Amount]<=[Balance]

In this example, Check Amount and Balance are field names in a table. When used in validation rule expressions or formulas, the field name is enclosed in square brackets.

VALIDATION TEXT. **Validation text** provides the message displayed if the user attempts to enter a field value that violates the validation rule. An example of validation text would be as follows:

You have attempted to enter a check amount that is greater than the available balance. Please enter a lesser amount.

REQUIRED. As stated earlier, it would be pointless to create a customer record without entering a last name. The **required** property is a yes/no property. If it is set to yes, then you cannot create a record without entering valid data in that field. If it is set to no, then you may create a record without entering data in that field.

ALLOW ZERO LENGTH. The **Allow zero length** property applies to Text and Memo fields. It is another yes/no property. If Allow zero length is set to yes, then you will be permitted to enter strings with a size of zero—that is, two quote marks with nothing between them. This is sometimes useful in linking files.

INDEXED. The **indexed** property is used when you expect to sort data by the field or you expect to search for values in that field. The indexed property has three possible settings:

- No, do not create an index.
- Yes, create an index and do not allow duplicate entries.
- Yes, create an index and accept duplicate entries.

For example, you might index an INVOICE NUMBER field and prohibit the entry of duplicate invoice numbers. If you were to index on a LAST NAME field, you would not want to prohibit duplication, because you might have several customers named Smith or Gonzalez.

DECIMAL PLACES. In Number fields in which fractions are permitted (single and double) you may specify **decimal places,** that is, how many places are permitted to the right of the decimal (up to 15 places). Also, you may select Auto, allowing Access to determine how many decimal places to display based on the data entered in the field.

While the text insertion point is in a field, you may specify whatever properties you want to impose on the data that will be entered in that field. With the text insertion point in the LAST field,

STEPS

1 **Click the *Field Size* property box**

A text insertion point will appear in the box next to *Size.*

2 **Backspace over the default size and type 15**

3 **Click the *Required* property box**

A drop-down arrow will appear in the box next to *Required.*

4 **Click the drop-down arrow, then click *Yes***

This will prohibit the user from creating a record that has no last name. Whenever you place the text insertion point in a property line, you will have one of two options:

- If an ellipsis (...) appears in the property line, you can click the ellipsis to open a dialog box in which you can enter your preferences.
- If a drop-down arrow appears in the property line, you can click it and then click the desired value from a list of acceptable values.

Your screen should now resemble Figure DB1-9c. To return to the part of the dialog box that allows you to type in new field names,

5 Click the third row of the *Field Name* column

The highlight moves down to the next row so that a new field name may be entered.

COMPLETING THE TABLE STRUCTURE

Enter each of the field names and types as shown in Figure DB1-10. As you are entering the Amount field, set the number of decimal places to 2:

STEPS

1 Select the *Decimal Places* property box

2 Click the drop-down arrow and then select *2*

Then, impose a validity check so that no quantity greater than 5,000 may be entered. To do this,

FIGURE DB1-10 ■ STRUCTURE FOR THE CUSTOMER TABLE

Field Name	Data Type	Description	Field Properties
Customer Number	Text	An identification code unique to this customer	Width: 3
Last	Text	Customer's last name	Width: 15
First	Text	Customer's first name	Width: 10
City	Text	Customer's city	Width: 20
State	Text	Customer's state	Width: 2
Zip	Text	Customer's five-digit zip code	Width: 5
Amount	Currency	Amount owed by customer	Default Value: 0 Validation Rule: <=5000 Validation Text: "You must enter an amount less than or equal to $5,000.00"

3 **Select the *Validation Rule* property box**

This places the text insertion point in the box.

4 **Type <=5000**

If there is a validation rule, it is usually desirable to enter something in the Validation Text property box so the user will have some guidance if he or she violates the rule.

5 **Select the *Validation Text* property box**

6 **Type You must enter an amount less than or equal to $5,000.00**

SAVING THE TABLE STRUCTURE

Save the table after you have completed the table design. Until you have done this, the table design has not been written to the disk.

STEPS

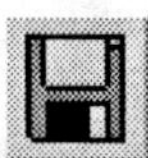

1 **Click *File*, then *Save*** [Ctrl + S]

Access will display a dialog box to prompt you for a table name.

2 **Type Customer List and select *OK***

Remember, this table is an Access object, not a file. Access will open a dialog box warning you that no key field has been selected and asking you if you want to create one. For now,

3 **Click *No***

DESIGN VIEW AND DATASHEET VIEW. Though the table design has been saved to your data disk, your screen still looks the same, except that the name you assigned to the table—CUSTOMER LIST—is now on the title bar. Access offers you two views of a table: **Design view** and **Datasheet view.** The view now on the screen is the Design view. It is from this screen that the table can be further modified: fields can be added or removed, their properties can be changed, and so on. To shift to the Datasheet view,

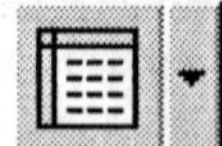

4 **Click *View*, then *Datasheet***

It is in the *Datasheet* view that data is entered, edited, deleted, sorted, and so on.

The table is now ready for data.

CHECKPOINT

- ✓ Create an empty database file on your floppy disk named Store.
- ✓ Create a new table that could contain a list of your employees.
- ✓ Save the table and return to the database window.
- ✓ Create a new table that could contain a list of your employees.
- ✓ Save the table and return to the database window.

EXITING AND REENTERING MICROSOFT ACCESS

Having accomplished this much, it is time for you to learn how to exit Access so that your data is saved to the disk, and then how to relaunch Access so that you can quickly open your data files and resume work.

CLOSING THE TABLE WINDOW AND THE DATABASE WINDOW

Access writes data to your data disk from time to time, but you cannot know how much of it has not been written. If you remove your disk or turn off the computer without properly saving all changes you have made to the design of objects and the data they contain, you may lose some or all of your data. As with most other Windows 95 applications, there are several ways to close your files. With the CUSTOMER LIST table still displayed,

STEPS

1 Click *File*, then click *Close* [Ctrl + W]

Tip : If you elect to close a window by clicking the *Close* button, be sure that you point your mouse to the correct one. Remember that every window has a *Close* button. The *Close* button that belongs to a window is to the right of that window's title bar. If you close a window containing other windows, you may close several windows at once. No data will be lost, because all Windows 95 applications will automatically save any data not yet saved (or will open a dialog box asking you if you want to save), but you can avoid a little time and frustration by closing the correct window.

The table window closes, revealing the database window that had been open all along but has been obscured by the table window. The same commands that closed the table window will close any Window. Choose a different one to close the database window.

2 Click the *Close* button

The database window closes, leaving you with an empty Access work area.

EXITING THE PROGRAM

To exit Access,

STEPS

1. **Click *File*, then click *Exit*** [Alt + F4]

LAUNCHING THE PROGRAM

If you exit Access, you must launch the program to use your files again. To do this,

STEPS

1. **Execute the necessary commands to start Windows 95**
2. **Click the *Start* button, point to *Programs*, and click Microsoft Access**

LISTING YOUR FILES

Access is a program designed to keep track of a lot of data: large inventories, mailing lists, customer lists, and so forth. Remember that all Access objects—tables, queries, forms, reports, macros, and modules—are contained within a single database file. Objects are not files. You should only place related objects within one database file. For example, you might have one database file for inventory, another for personnel, and so on. If all related objects are contained within one database file, then you will know where to find each object. The first step in seeing a list of your files is to see a list of database files. To do this,

STEPS

1. **Place your data disk in Drive A (or B)**

2. **Click the *Open an Existing Database* option, and then *OK***

You will see the *Open Database* dialog box, where you identify the database file you want to open.

3. **Click the drop-down button of the *Look In* box**
4. **Click the *3½" Floppy (A:) drive* icon**
5. **Click *CUSTOMER* on the *File Name* selection list**

FIGURE DB1-11 ■ THE DATABASE WINDOW DISPLAYING THE OBJECTS IN YOUR DATABASE FILE

CUSTOMER LIST is the only table in this database file.

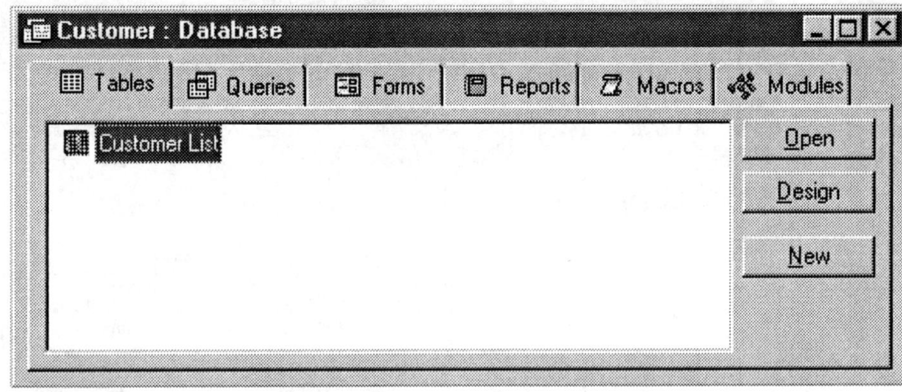

The *File Name* selection list displays a list of all the Access database files in the selected folder. Since you have only created one, you will see only CUSTOMER.DB. However, if you had created several database files and stored them in this folder, you would see a list of all of them here.

6 **Click the *Open* button**

The CUSTOMER database window appears. If you saved your table correctly, your screen should look like Figure DB1-11. Note that the table CUSTOMER LIST is displayed. Remember, from the database window, your options are described by the command buttons:

- *Open*—Open an existing object for use (in the table example it is found in the Datasheet view).
- *Design*—Open an existing object so that its design may be modified (this choice will take you back to the Design screen you saw when you first designed the table).
- *New*—Create a new object

Because there is only one table—CUSTOMER LIST—it is already selected. If there were several, you would have to select the table you wanted. To open the table,

7 **Click the *Open* button**

The table opens in the Datasheet view. Your screen should resemble Figure DB1-12a.

ENTERING RECORDS

This screen is really a blank table form awaiting new data to fill it in. The field names you created in the table structure appear at the top of each column, one column for each field. Notice that the buttons on the toolbar have changed to match the current operation.

FIGURE DB1-12 ■ THE DATASHEET VIEW OF CUSTOMER LIST

(a) The table contains no data. It is ready for the first record.
(b) The first record has been entered. Access has prepared a blank record #2.
(c) The first four records have been entered.

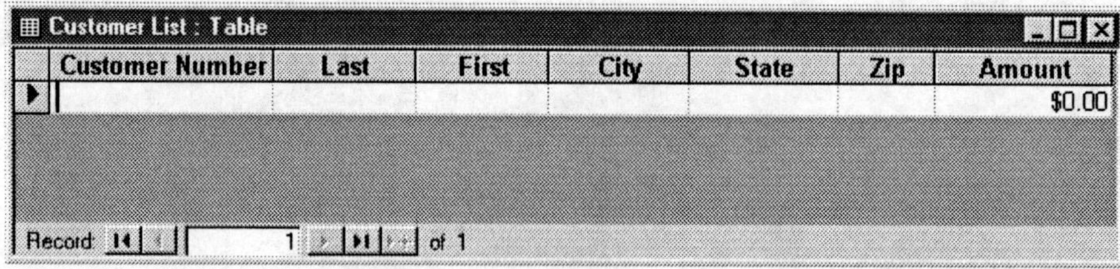

(a)

Customer List : Table

	Customer Number	Last	First	City	State	Zip	Amount
	670	Parker	Charles	Santa Fe	NM	87501	450.75
*							$0.00

Record: 1 of 1

(b)

Customer List : Table

	Customer Number	Last	First	City	State	Zip	Amount
	670	Parker	Charles	Santa Fe	NM	87501	$450.75
	101	Burstein	Jerome	San Jose	CA	95120	$230.45
	449	Laudon	Jane	New York	NY	10003	$230.45
▶	754	Martin	Edward	New York	NY	10001	$230.55
*							$0.00

Record: 4 of 4

(c)

THE DATA ENTRY SCREEN

Before entering any data at all, you should learn the rules of navigation for the table when viewed as a datasheet (columns and rows). First, of course, it is contained in a window, which follows the rules for all windows. It can be closed, resized, and moved like any other window. If the table has more data than can be displayed on the screen, then horizontal and/or vertical scroll bars will appear.

You can move the text insertion point, which is now in the CUSTOMER NUMBER field, in any of the following ways:

- Pointing to any column or field and clicking.
- Pressing Tab or → to move the insertion point to the right.
- Pressing Shift + Tab or ← to move the insertion point to the left.
- Pressing Pg Up or ↑ to move to previous records.
- Pressing Pg Dn or ↓ to move to subsequent records.
- Clicking the scroll buttons at the bottom of the table to cause the focus to move to the top of the file, to the previous record, to the next record, or to the last record.

ENTERING FIELD VALUES INTO A TABLE

Keep these pointers in mind while entering data:

- Type data into the field area and press Enter (or Tab or →). The highlight will move to the next field. Repeat this procedure for each field.
- Columns that extend past the right edge of the screen will come into view as you continue to enter data.
- Each row corresponds to one record. When you enter the last (right-most) column's data, the cursor returns to the left-most field on the next line so that it is in place when you are ready to enter a new record.
- Data are entered into each blank record (row) beneath the appropriate field name.

STEPS

1 Enter the data below for the first record

(This will be Record #1.)

Customer number	670
Last	Parker
First	Charles
City	Santa Fe
State	NM
Zip	87501
Amount	450.75

Note that when the text insertion point is in a field, the description you typed while designing the table is displayed on the status bar. This provides you with useful guidance. When entering data in the AMOUNT column, don't forget to place the decimal point in its proper position. Also, don't enter a "$" character in front of the Amount. Access will provide it automatically because the Amount column is already set for currency data type. Your screen should resemble Figure DB1-12b before you press Enter again. After you type the data for the amount,

2 Press ↵

Access always provides a new blank row, which is where you will type the next record. Notice that the status bar at the bottom shows *Record 2 of 2,* indicating that Access is currently pointing to the second record to be entered.

Tip: If you want to return to a previous row to correct an error in an entry, click the erroneous field value. Backspace over or delete the error, correct the entry, then press ↓ or point to the last record and click to return to the current row.

3 Type the following records into the table, each record on a separate row:

(This will be Record #2.)

Customer number	101
Last	Burstein
First	Jerome

City	San Jose
State	CA
Zip	95120
Amount	230.45

(This will be Record #3.)

Customer number	449
Last	Laudon
First	Jane
City	New York
State	NY
Zip	10003
Amount	230.45

(This will be Record #4.)

Customer number	754
Last	Martin
First	Edward
City	New York
State	NY
Zip	10001
Amount	230.55

Your screen should resemble Figure DB1-12c. Although you could continue to enter records into the table, you should also learn how to enter records into an individual record form as follows.

ENTERING DATA INTO A RECORD FORM

For this entry procedure that you will perform in the following exercises, you will switch from the Datasheet view, which displays several records horizontally in a table format, to one that shows each individual record, one per screen. Screen **forms** can be designed using standard formats provided by Access' Form wizard or you can design one yourself from scratch. If all you need is a quick form that places all the fields in a column with a description to their left, Access can provide it very quickly:

STEPS

1 Click the pull-down arrow next to the *New Object* button, then click the *Autoform* button

Clicking the *Autoform* button quickly produces a screen form similar to the one in Figure DB1-13.

> **Tip: Notice that the last *New Object* button you used remains on top of the stack. If you need to reuse that same button, it is not necessary to click the pull-down arrow again. Just click the button itself. You only need to use the pull-down arrow if you want to click a button that is not on top of the stack.**

FIGURE DB1-13 ■ USING FORM VIEW

This form presents one record per screen.

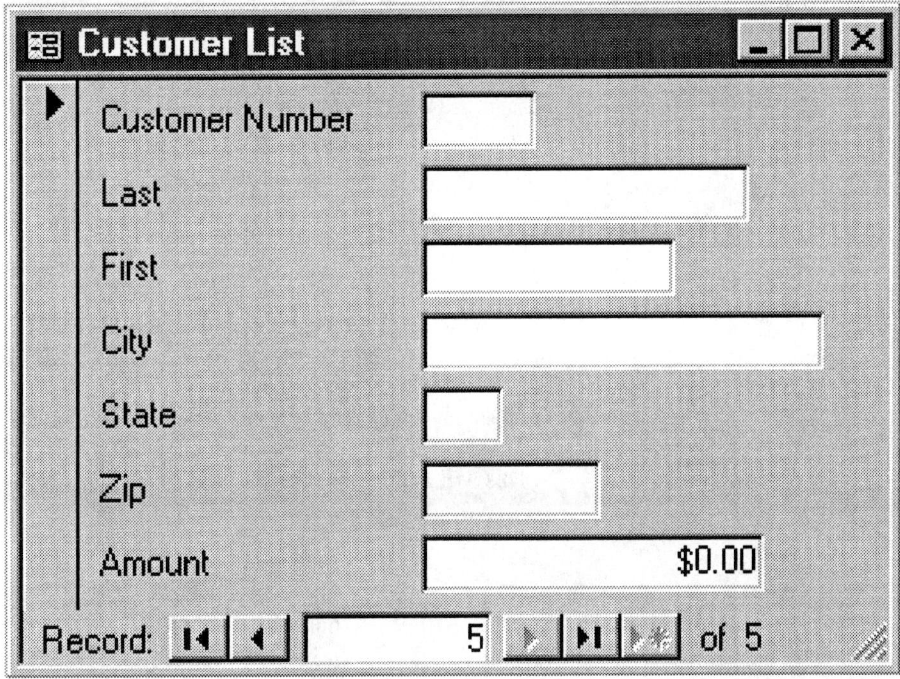

Although the entry procedure itself is similar, in this case the entry screen is now a blank record form awaiting new data to fill it in. The field names you created earlier appear at the left of the screen with a space for field values to the right of each. The highlight or text insertion point indicates the current field. (The record number and description of the current field appear on the status bar.)

As you enter the remaining records into the CUSTOMER LIST form, follow these guidelines:

- To enter data in the current field, type the data and press Enter.
- When you press Enter, the highlight moves down to the next field.
- When you enter the last (bottom) field's data and press Enter, Tab, ↓, or Pg Dn, Access advances to the next record.
- To jump quickly to the last (blank) record, click the *New Record* button.

Tip: To return to a previous record, press Pg Up. You can review or correct the entry. Then press Pg Dn to move forward to the next record form. If you are viewing the last record in the file, pressing Pg Dn will produce an empty record form.

If your screen is showing an existing record instead of a blank record,

2 Click the *New Record* button

Access will advance to the blank record at the bottom of the file.

DB

3 Enter the data below for the next record

The records that you will enter in CUSTOMER LIST are shown in Figure DB1-14 in the Datasheet view.

(This will be Record #5.)

Customer number	389
Last	Martin
First	Arthur
City	Flushing
State	NY
Zip	11367
Amount	65.30

Don't forget to place the decimal point in the AMOUNT column in its proper position as before. After you enter the amount, a new blank record form appears.

4 Add the remaining records to the table, each record in a separate form

(This will be Record #6.)

Customer number	176
Last	West
First	Rita
City	Chicago
State	IL
Zip	60601
Amount	$965.42

(This will be Record #7.)

Customer number	067
Last	Williams
First	DeVilla
City	Chicago
State	IL

FIGURE DB1-14 ■ USING DATASHEET VIEW

The datasheet view displays as many records as can appear on the screen.

Customer List : Table

Customer Number	Last	First	City	State	Zip	Amount
670	Parker	Charles	Santa Fe	NM	87501	$450.75
101	Burstein	Jerome	San Jose	CA	95120	$230.45
449	Laudon	Jane	New York	NY	10003	$230.45
754	Martin	Edward	New York	NY	10001	$230.55
389	Martin	Arthur	Flushing	NY	11367	$65.30
176	West	Rita	Chicago	IL	60601	$965.42
067	Williams	DeVilla	Chicago	IL	60601	$965.42
111	Hill	Karen	Chicago	IL	60605	$456.78
						$0.00

Record: 9 of 9

Zip	60601
Amount	965.42

If you make an error while typing a record, use the arrow keys to point to the error (or point to the field with your mouse and click) and type the correct data directly over the old data, using Backspace and Delete as needed. If the entire field value is selected (highlighted), as soon as you press a key, the entire field value will disappear so that you can enter the new correct value. If you want to be able to simply insert or delete individual characters, you must initiate the Editing mode by pressing F2 (or double-clicking the field with the mouse). This places an insertion point in the field that can be moved with the arrow keys. You can delete individual characters and insert new ones. The Editing mode is cancelled when you move the active area to another field or when you press F2 a second time.

You have now practiced entering field values in Datasheet (table) view and in Form view. To switch formats while viewing a form,

5 **Click *View, Datasheet***

> **Tip: To switch to Datasheet view using the toolbar, click the pull-down arrow next to the *View* button, then select the *Datasheet View* button. Note that there are three buttons corresponding to the three available views:**
>
> **Datasheet (table) view**
>
> **Form view**
>
> **Design view (more about Design view later)**

Access displays the data in Datasheet view. To switch back to Form view,

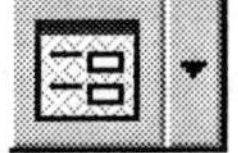

6 **Click *View, Form***

Use whichever method you prefer to enter records.

ENDING DATA ENTRY

When you have entered all the field values in your records, another blank record form (or row if you are in the table format) will appear on your screen. Note that the status bar shows *Record 8 of 8,* indicating that an eighth record is about to be added to the table. If you are not now in the Datasheet view,

DB

STEPS

1 **Click the *Datasheet View* button**

If all seven records are not displayed, it means that Access has not updated the table display. To command Access to do this,

2 **Click *Records*, then click *Remove Filter/Sort***

Access refreshes the display, showing records that have been added in the Form view (and displaying records that may have been added by another user on a network system). A complete view of the seven records is displayed on the screen for your review. To return to a blank work area, you will need to close three windows in succession:

- The newly created form
- The table CUSTOMER LIST
- The database window CUSTOMER

For each window,

2 Click the *Close* button

When you close the window containing the form, Access asks if you wish to save it. Because you can easily and quickly recreate this form with the *AutoForm* button, there is no reason to take up disk space saving it. When asked whether to save FORM1,

3 Click *No*

4 If desired, exit Access and shut down Windows

> **Tip: Access places data you have entered in the computer's primary memory (RAM). At intervals, it copies the data automatically onto your disk. Therefore, you must be sure never to remove a disk or turn off the computer until you have properly exited from Access. You have no way of knowing if Access is holding data in RAM that have not yet been written to the disk.**

DATA ENTRY MODE

Before examining your handiwork, finish the next brief section to discover another way to add records to your table. If your screen is filled with existing records, you can clear them away so that you have plenty of room to view new records. To do this, you must first open the CUSTOMER database:

STEPS

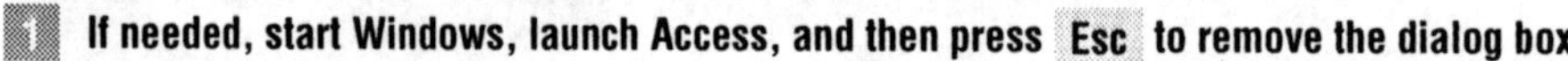

1 If needed, start Windows, launch Access, and then press Esc to remove the dialog box

2 Click the *Open Database* button

3 Click the drop-down button of the *Look In* box

4 Click the *3½" Floppy (A:) drive* icon

5 Click *CUSTOMER* on the *File Name* selection list

6 Click *Open*

The CUSTOMER database window appears. CUSTOMER LIST is the selected table.

7 Click *Open*

To activate the Data Entry mode,

8 **Click *Records, Data entry***

Access cleans the screen of existing records and jumps directly to the blank record at the end of the file.

9 **Type the following record**

(This will be Record #8.)

Customer number	111
Last	Hill
First	Karen
City	Chicago
State	IL
Zip	60605
Amount	456.78

To redisplay all records,

10 **Click *Records, Remove Filter/Sort***

Next, close all open windows. To close the CUSTOMER LIST table,

11 **Click the *Close* button**

To close the CUSTOMER database,

12 **Click the *Close* button**

To exit Access,

13 **Click the *Close* button**

CHECKPOINT

✓ In the DBTEST table, add a new record:

Name	TEST1	TEST2
Smith	78	92
Jones	65	75
Green	84	88

✓ Enter the two more records using the individual record form.
✓ Switch back to datasheet view.
✓ Add another record. Type your last name and test marks 85 and 95.
✓ Attempt to change Green's Test1 score to 125. Will Access let you do this?
✓ Return to a blank desktop and exit Access.

EXAMINING FIELD VALUES

Creating a table and entering field values are merely the preliminary steps to using a table. Once you have entered records into a table, you can invoke various commands to look at the data contained within them. Prepare for the next set of exercises as follows:

STEPS

1 **Launch Access**

2 **Open the CUSTOMER database**

3 **Open the CUSTOMER LIST table**

You will see the data that you previously entered into the CUSTOMER table. Access displays as much of the data as will fit on the screen. Your screen should now resemble Figure DB1-14.

You can use two methods to examine the data for certain records.

- You can scroll through the records using a combination of keystrokes or mouse actions, inspecting the records visually.
- You can find records containing certain field values without having to visually inspect records that do not contain those values.

You may also alter the order in which fields are displayed in your table so that they are presented in an order that is more useful to you.

SCROLLING THROUGH RECORDS

You can **scroll** through the records using the following features:

- Access provides vertical scroll bars if your table has more records than can be displayed on the screen (as in all windows).
- ↑ moves up one record.
- ↓ moves down one record.
- ← moves left one field (column).
- → moves right one field (column).
- Tab moves the highlight to the right.
- Shift + Tab moves the highlight to the left.
- Pg Up moves up one full screen.
- Pg Dn moves down one full screen.
- At the bottom of the datasheet or Screen Form window, you will see the **scroll buttons** (shown in Figure DB1-15). They allow you to move to the first record, up one record, down one record, or to the last record.

FINDING RECORDS

You will also notice a toolbar button displaying the image of a pair of binoculars. This button enables you to **find** records containing specific field values. As with other tool-

FIGURE DB1-15 ■ SCROLL BUTTONS

From left to right: go to first record, go to previous record, go to next record, go to last record.

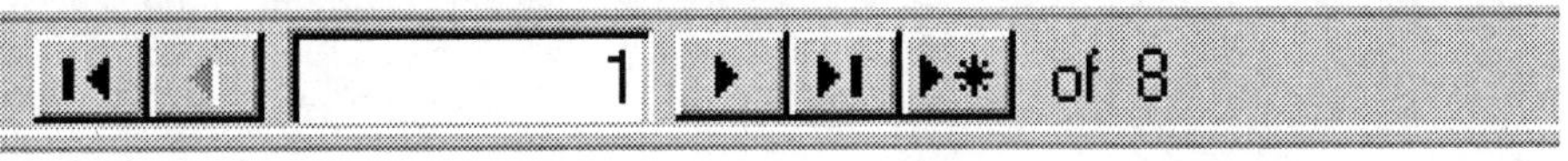

bar buttons, these offer quick ways to execute menu commands. To search for the first record containing a certain field value,

STEPS

1 Place the text insertion point (or highlight) on any record in the State field

To do this, of course, point to any location within the STATE column and click. Then,

2 Click *Edit, Find*

You will see the *Find* dialog box. In addition to the familiar features shared by other Access dialog boxes, this one enables you to enter the value for which you are searching. In Figure DB1-16, you see that "NY" has been entered in the *Find What* text box. "State" became the Current Field because that was the field containing the focus when the Find procedure was initiated. Take time to examine the features of this dialog box. Several options control how Access will conduct the search.

SEARCH OPTIONS. Access will confine its search to any of the following conditions:

- *Any Part of Field*—"ny" would match "many," "pony," and "Bunyon"
- *Match Whole Field*—"Kansas" would match only "Kansas," "kansas," or "Kansas" (depending on whether you checked the *Match Case* box), but it would not match Arkansas

FIGURE DB1-16 ■ THE *FIND* DIALOG BOX

The *Find* dialog box searches a table for a specific field value.

Find in field: 'State'
Find What: NY
Search: All
Match: Whole Field
Match Case
Search Fields as Formatted
Search Only Current Field
Find First
Find Next
Close

DB

- *Start of Field*—"ca" would match "California" but not "Chicago"

MATCHING VALUES. You can instruct Access to search for matching values in *All* records, *Down* (the current record and later records), and *Up* (the current record and previous records).

MATCH CASE. The field value must match your search value in characters *and* case. That is, the value "NY" would not match "ny" or "Ny" or "nY" because the case of one or more characters is different. If the *Match Case* box is not checked, then Access will compare characters but not case.

***FIND FIRST* COMMAND BUTTON.** When you choose this option, Access begins searching with the current record and moves in the direction you indicate until it reaches the first matching value or runs out of records.

***FIND NEXT* COMMAND BUTTON.** This option instructs Access to continue the current Find Search until it reaches the next matching value or runs out of records.

WILDCARDS. Access also allows you to use *Wildcard Characters* in your search. Wildcard characters can be inserted in the value typed in the *Find What* text box.

Two of the characters Access uses are the asterisk (*) and question mark (?), and they are used as they are in DOS commands or in Windows 95 Explorer. The asterisk substitutes for any group of characters and the question mark substitutes for any single character. For example, if you are searching through zip codes and want to find records for customers living in the region of west Texas where all zip codes begin with 799, then your search value could be entered as *799??,* meaning 799 followed by any two characters. *799** would match zip codes like 79924-0231, 79911, and 79901-6868 because the asterisk wildcard matches any number of characters.

Access also uses other wildcard characters:

- The pound sign (#) matches any single numeral, so 1#3 matches 123 and 183 but not 1R3.
- *Square brackets [ ]* are used to match any of several characters, so N[JY] matches NJ and NY but not NC.
- The *hyphen [-]* in square brackets is used to match a range of characters, so 799[01-05] would match zip codes 79901, 79902, 79903, 79904, and 79905 but not 79906.

For you to duplicate the Find procedure illustrated in Figure DB1-16, perform the following:

3 Enter NY in the *Find What* text box

4 Select *Match Whole Field*

5 Select the *Search Only Current Field* option button

We will not be using wildcard characters in this search.

6 Select the pull-down arrow next to *Search,* then select *Down* as the search direction

7 **Click the *Find First* command button**

The highlight should jump to the first value of "NY" in the State field. To find the next match,

8 **Click the *Find Next* command button**

The highlight jumps to the next matching value. If you repeat the procedure, Access finds each matching record in turn until the last one has been highlighted. When you attempt to find another match and no others are present, Access displays a dialog box asking if you want to restart the search at the beginning of the file. To close the *Find* dialog box,

9 **Click the *Close* command button**

Next,

10 **Close the table and database window**

This demonstration may not have seemed impressive when you are searching through only eight records, but imagine how useful it would be if you were searching through eight *thousand* customers!

CHANGING THE ORDER OF FIELDS

Using the mouse, you can easily change the order in which fields are presented in the CUSTOMER LIST table. If you place the mouse pointer on a field name at the top of a column of data, you will notice that the pointer changes shape, becoming a tiny arrow, pointing downward toward the values in the field. This area is called the **field selector**. If you click the mouse at this time the entire field (column) becomes selected.

While the field is selected, if you point again to the field name, you can drag and drop (that is, move the pointer while you are holding down the left mouse button) the field to another column position. When you release the button, the table rearranges itself so that the field you first selected has been moved to the column where the pointer was when you released the button. For example,

STEPS

1 **Open the CUSTOMER LIST table as you have before**

2 **Point to the column heading Last**

Note that the pointer changes to a small arrow pointing downward.

3 **Click the Last column heading**

The column should become highlighted as you see in Figure DB1-17a.

FIGURE DB1-17 ■ CHANGING THE ORDER OF COLUMNS IN A TABLE

(a) The Last column has been selected.
(b) The Last column has been repositioned.

Customer List : Table

Customer Number	Last	
670	Parker	Cha
101	Burstein	Jerc
449	Laudon	Jan
754	Martin	Edv
389	Martin	Artl
176	West	Rita
067	Williams	De\
111	Hill	Kar

Record: 1 of

(a)

Customer List : Table

Last	Customer Number	I
Parker	670	Cha
Burstein	101	Jero
Laudon	449	Jane
Martin	754	Edw
Martin	389	Arth
West	176	Rita
Williams	067	DeV
Hill	111	Kare

Record: 1 of

(b)

4 **Click and drag the Last column to the position occupied by Customer Number (all the way to the left)**

5 **Release the mouse button**

Observe that the *Last* column moved to occupy the column position formerly occupied by Customer Number (see Figure DB1-17b).

6 **Move the Last column back to its original position**

7 **Close the CUSTOMER LIST datasheet window**

8 **Close the CUSTOMER database window**

CHECKPOINT

- ✓ Open a database file of your choosing, then display any table.
- ✓ Scroll from record to record using the arrow keys, noting the behavior of the focus.
- ✓ Use the *Find* button to locate another field value.
- ✓ Use wildcard characters to locate another field value.
- ✓ Close the *Find* dialog box.

PRINTING RECORDS

Table records can also be generated in printed form using Access's quick print feature. With the CUSTOMER LIST table displayed on your screen (and with your printer on and ready, do the following:

STEPS

1 Open the CUSTOMER database and then the CUSTOMER list

2 Click the *Print* button

Access will design and print a quick report, which will basically be a copy of the CUSTOMER table that is on your screen. Note that the date of the report and the name of the file are automatically printed on the top of the page. The page number is on the bottom of the page.

Another way of generating a quick hard copy of the table is to

STEPS

1 Click *File,Print* [Ctrl + P]

You will see the *Print* dialog box, which allows you to express your preferences about the printing of your table (see Figure DB1-18). At the top of the box is the name of the destination printer. You may select from among three option buttons to indicate how much of the table you want printed.

- *All*—prints all records and all fields.
- *Pages*—prints only a certain range of pages (in larger tables).
- *Selected Records*—prints only the portion of the table that you have selected (highlighted).

2 Select *All*

3 Select *OK*

In this case, Access generates a report that looks like the first one. However, from the *Print* dialog box, you can select a printer other than the Windows 95 default printer, change printer settings, print a range of records or pages, and so on.

DB

FIGURE DB1-18 ■ PRINTING A TABLE

The *Print* dialog box gives you control over the printing of Access tables and other objects.

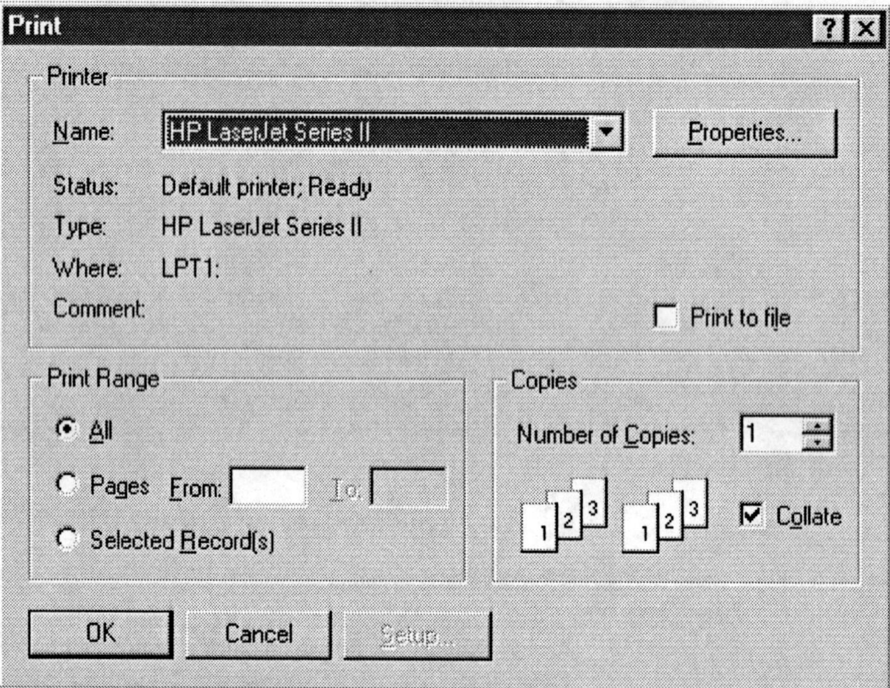

CHECKPOINT

- ✓ Display any table.
- ✓ Click the *Print* button.
- ✓ Open the *Print* dialog box by pressing CTRL + P.
- ✓ Click *OK*.
- ✓ Compare the two printouts.

CREATING QUERIES

Viewing the entire table (and scrolling through the fields and records) is fine for a quick review, but it may not be that helpful when you are looking for specific information. It may be more useful in this instance to create a **query.** A query is simply a question that is asked of the table. By using Access's Query feature, you can create a query that restricts the screen display to selected fields and (if you choose) display only those field *values* that meet search criteria.

Queries provide the true power in a database system. They allow you to view data from different perspectives, ask questions about data values, and manipulate field values into patterns that help you gain insight about your data. Queries can also be used to perform the following functions:

- Insert new values.

- Delete records that have certain field values.
- Modify field values.
- Perform calculations on field values.

Because of their importance, queries will be presented in some depth in the following exercises. At first, you will use the Query feature simply to restrict fields in a display; then you'll extend your search capabilities.

USING A QUERY TO RESTRICT FIELD DISPLAYS

To display only selected fields on the screen, display the CUSTOMER LIST table, then,

STEPS

1 **Click the *New Object* drop-down button at the right end of the toolbar**

> **Tip: The *New Object* button changes its symbol, depending on its last use. It is best to click its drop-down button, view the list, and then click on your desired choice. If in doubt, you can always point to each toolbar button to see its function.**

A dialog box will ask you to choose between the Query Wizard and New Query selections.

2 **Select *Design View,* then click *OK***

You will next see the Select Query design screen (see Figure DB1-19a). You can now indicate those fields that you want to include in the display by moving the mouse pointer to each field, then dragging and dropping the field name next on the Field row in the columns below. The following exercise will list only the last and first names in the table (use Figure DB1-19b as a guide):

3 **Drag and drop the last name to the field row of the first column**

4 **Drag and drop the first name to the field row of the second column**

If you place the wrong field in a column, backspace over the field name and repeat the procedure. Now the query can be executed:

5 **Click *Query,* then click *Run***

As shown in Figure DB1-19c, the field values for last and first name are displayed. The result of a query is called a **dynaset,** which looks and acts like a table, but it is really an extraction or a compilation of the data in an underlying table. Changes made to the dynaset are passed on to the table, so editing can be done on the records your queries find.

The query procedure can also search for selected field values and perform mathematical calculations on number fields, as you will see in the next portion of this exercise. To remove the dynaset from the screen,

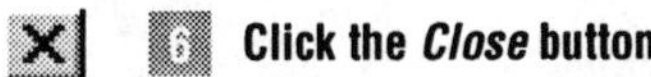

6 **Click the *Close* button**

Access will open a dialog box asking if you want this query to be saved so that it can be reused in the future.

7 **Click *No***

DB

FIGURE DB1-19 ■ USING THE SELECT QUERY DESIGN SCREEN

(a) The Select Query screen allows you to select the records and fields you want displayed in a dynaset.
(b) This query will display two fields: Last and First.
(c) The dynaset that is the result of the query shows only data from the two fields asked for.

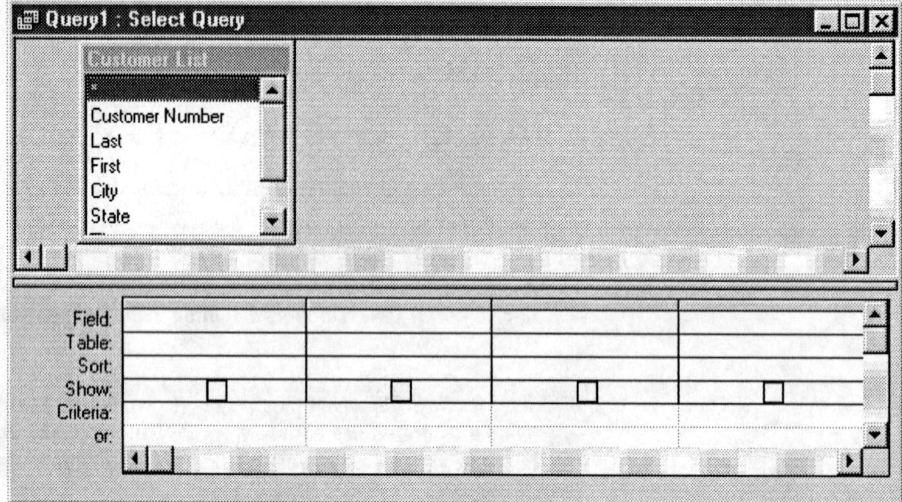

(a)

(b)

Query1 : Select Query

Last	First
Parker	Charles
Burstein	Jerome
Laudon	Jane
Martin	Edward
Martin	Arthur
West	Rita
Williams	DeVilla
Hill	Karen

(c)

USING A QUERY TO SEARCH FOR RECORDS

So far, the query procedure has restricted the fields shown in the dynaset but has not limited the number of records or field values selected from the CUSTOMER table. However, by adding a **conditional expression** to the Query, you can instruct Access to perform the command on *only those records that meet the stated condition* (criterion). Although criteria can be used to display particular field values, they can also modify the effects of many other Access commands, such as reporting, deleting, updating, replacing, and copying (as you will see).

Conditional searches fall into a number of categories. You can find records that match criteria exactly, fall within an acceptable range of values, fit a pattern, come close to search values, or are unlike the search criteria entirely. You can also combine criteria depending on your needs. The following exercises examine some of these techniques.

SELECTING RECORDS USING AN EXACT MATCH. To find records with field values that match a particular value, you simply select the fields you want displayed in the dynaset using the drag and drop method and then type the desired value in the criteria row of the appropriate field column. Any record that matches the query (or search) criteria will be displayed. Suppose you wanted to display name and address information about those customers whose state is New York. Display the CUSTOMER LIST table and do this:

STEPS

1 Click the *New Object's* drop-down button (at the right end of the toolbar)

Remember, Access leaves the button associated with the last type of object you created on top of the list of new objects. If the last object you created was a query, then the *New Query* button is still on top of the stack. If this is the case, you do not have to click the pull-down arrow next to the *New Object* button. Just click the button itself.

A dialog box will ask you to choose between the Query Wizard and New Query selections.

2 Click *Design View,* then click *OK*

You now see the empty Select Query design screen. Select the fields that you want to display in the answer—namely LAST, FIRST, CITY, and STATE (refer to Figure DB1-20a):

3 Click and drag Last to the field row of the first column

4 Click and drag First to the field row of the second column

5 Click and drag City to the field row of the third column

6 Click and drag State to the field row of the fourth column

So far, you've simply identified the field columns that will appear in the answer. Now you can restrict the records that will appear by specifying the search criteria as follows:

DB

FIGURE DB1-20 ■ SELECTING CUSTOMERS FROM NEW YORK STATE

(a) First, select the fields to be displayed. Then, enter NY as the selection criterion for State. (Note the double quotes that Access automatically inserts around alphanumeric criteria.)
(b) The resulting dynaset consists of only those records showing NY in the state field.

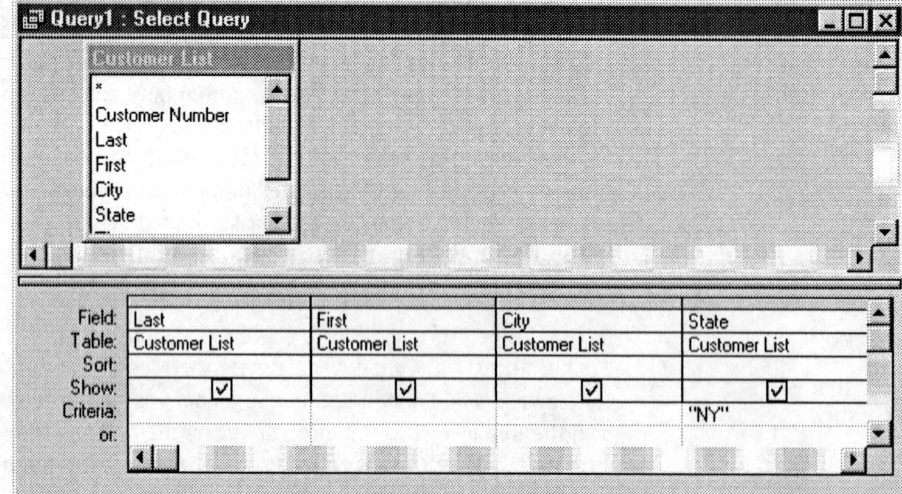

(a)

Query1 : Select Query

Last	First	City	State
Laudon	Jane	New York	NY
Martin	Edward	New York	NY
Martin	Arthur	Flushing	NY

Record: 1 of 3

(b)

7 Type NY in the criteria row of the State column

8 Click *Query, Run*

The answer to this query appears on your screen as in Figure DB1-20b. Note that only those records whose field value for STATE exactly matches the "NY" search criterion are listed. Note, too, that only the LAST, FIRST, CITY, and STATE fields are shown.

9 Close (but do not save) the query

It is easy to add additional criteria. Suppose we wanted to find a resident of New York state whose last name is "Martin." To ask Access to find any matching records for you,

10 Click the *New Object's* drop-down button

On the resulting dialog box,

11 Click *New Query,* then click *OK*

You again see the Select Query design screen.

12 Click and drag Last to the field row of the first column

13 Click and drag First to the field row of the second column

14 Click and drag City to the field row of the third column

15 Click and drag State to the field row of the fourth column

16 Type Martin in the criteria row of the Last column

17 Type NY in the criteria row of the State column

(If needed, use the scroll bar)

18 Click *Query, Run*

Now, only those records that match both criteria (LAST = "Martin" and STATE = "NY") are displayed.

19 Close all windows in the Access work area

SELECTING RECORDS WITHIN AN ACCEPTABLE RANGE. At times you will want to select records that fall within a *range* of values, not just one particular value. You can accomplish this by using a relational operator as part of the search criteria. A relational operator allows you to specify a range of criteria to be used in the search. Figure DB1-21 lists the relational operators used in queries.

To specify a range of values in a query, you simply enter an initial relational operator in the Field column, followed by the value to be searched. For example, to select records whose Amount field value is $200 or more, do this:

FIGURE DB1-21 ■ RELATIONAL OPERATORS USED IN ACCESS QUERIES

Operator	Example	Explanation
<	<500	Less than
>	>500	Greater than
=	=500	Equal to
<=	<=500	Less than or equal to
>=	>=500	Greater than or equal to
AND	>5 AND <10	Logical "and" connector; both conditions must be true
OR	>5 OR <0	Logical "or" connector; either condition must be true
NOT	NOT 500	Logical "not" expression; all values except 500

STEPS

1 Display the CUSTOMER LIST table, if necessary

2 Click the *New Object* drop-down button at the right end of the toolbar

On the resulting dialog box,

3 Click *Design View,* then click *OK*

You again see the Select Query design screen.

4 Click and drag Customer Number to the field row of the first column

5 Click and drag Last to the field row of the second column

6 Click and drag Amount to the field row of the third column

7 Click and drag State to the field row of the fourth column

8 Type >=200 in the criteria row of the Amount column

This last entry asks for only those records whose value in the amount is greater than or equal to $200. Note that you do not enter the currency symbol, nor would you enter commas to set off thousands in large amounts.

An additional feature offered by the Select Query screen is that of sorting. It would be reasonable to want the resulting dynaset to be sorted by customer number. To accomplish this,

9 Place the text insertion point in the Sort row of the Amount column

10 Click the drop-down button

The choices you will be given are Ascending, Descending, and not sorted.

11 Click *Ascending*

Compare your screen to Figure DB1-22a, then,

12 Click *Query, Run*

As shown in Figure DB1-22b, only those records whose field values for amount are 200 or more are listed. Note, too, that only the CUSTOMER NUMBER, LAST, and AMOUNT fields are shown and that the dynaset is sorted by CUSTOMER NUMBER.

13 Close the query, the CUSTOMER LIST table, and the CUSTOMER database without saving

COMBINING SEARCH CRITERIA. What if you want to include records whose amount meets or exceeds $200 but only if the value in the STATE field is "IL?" For such

FIGURE DB1-22 ■ ANOTHER SELECT QUERY

(a) This query asks for records whose amounts are greater than or equal to $200. It also specifies that the dynaset be sorted by Customer Number.
(b) The resulting dynaset contains 7 records. Only Arthur Martin has an amount less than $200.00.

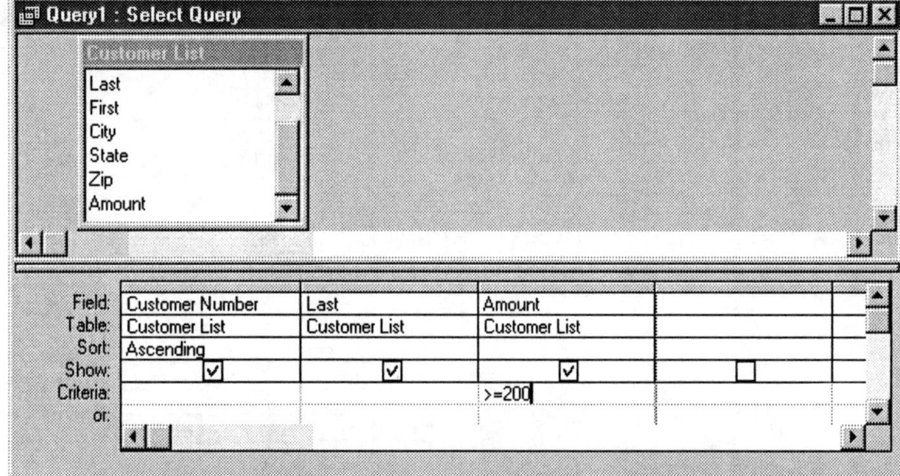

(a)

Query1 : Select Query

Customer Number	Last	Amount
067	Williams	$965.42
101	Burstein	$230.45
111	Hill	$456.78
176	West	$965.42
449	Laudon	$230.45
670	Parker	$450.75
754	Martin	$230.55
*		$0.00

(b)

needs, conditions can be combined with *AND* or *OR* connectors. Figures DB1-23a through DB1-23d show four different queries using AND or OR. Note that the AND connector finds records that meet both conditions, while the OR connector finds records that meet either condition. The first query uses an AND connector to find those records whose state equals IL and amount equals or exceeds 200. Try creating this query (shown in Figure DB1-23a) from a blank desktop as follows:

STEPS

1. **Display the CUSTOMER LIST table, if necessary**

2. **Click the *New Object* drop-down button (right end of toolbar)**

On the resulting dialog box,

FIGURE DB1-23 ■ USING *AND* AND *OR* CONNECTORS

(a) Illinois residents with amounts equal to or greater than $200.
(b) Amounts equal to or greater than $200 and less than $800.

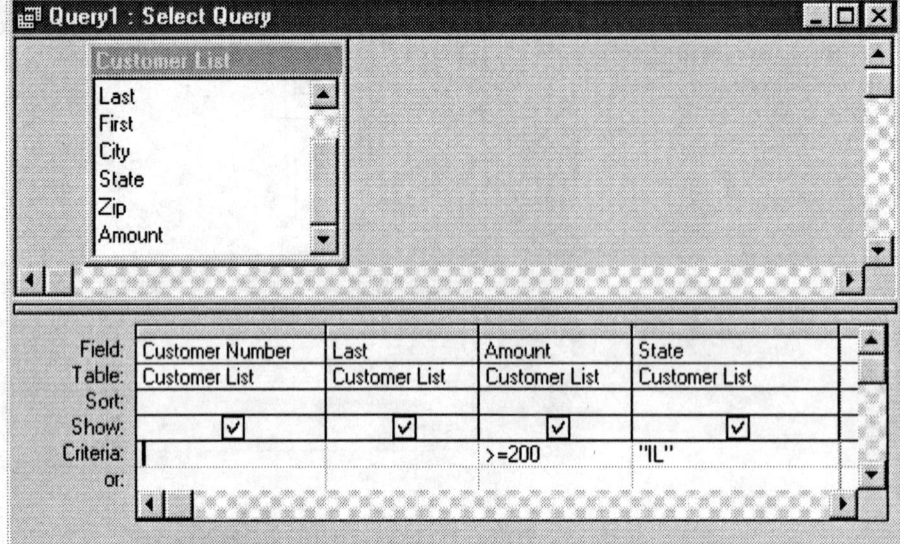

(a)

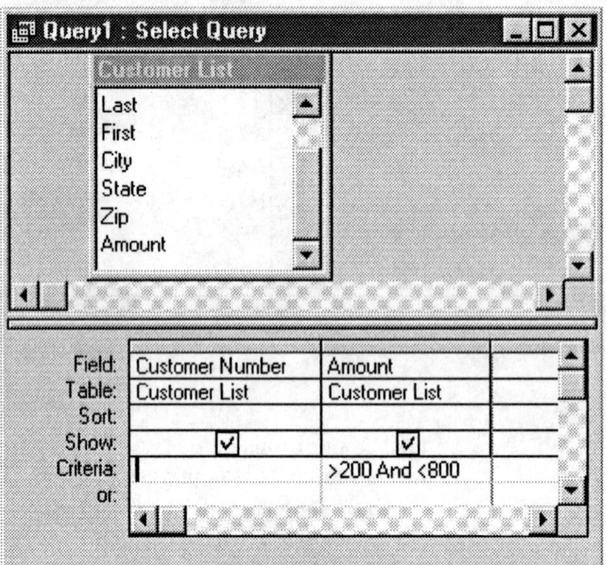

(b)

(continued)

3 Click *New Query, OK*

You again see the Select Query design screen.

4 Click and drag Last, First, Amount, and State to the field rows of the first four columns

5 Click the *Show* option buttons on the Amount and State columns

FIGURE DB1-23 ■ *(continued)*

(c) Amounts equal to or greater than $200 OR State is IL.
(d) Customers from Illinois or New Mexico.

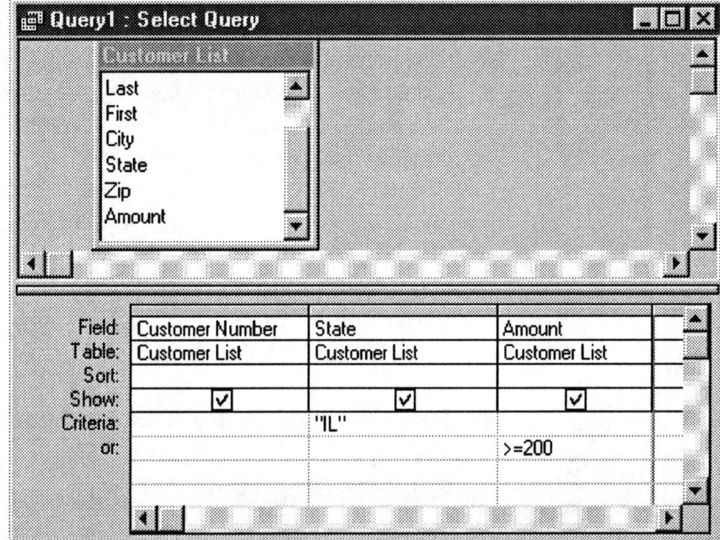

(c)

Query1 : Select Query

Customer List: *, Customer Number, Last, First, City, State

Field:	Last	First	City	State
Table:	Customer List	Customer List	Customer List	Customer List
Sort:	Ascending	Ascending		
Show:	✓	✓	✓	✓
Criteria:				"IL" Or "NM"
or:				

(d)

The "✓" in the box should be removed, meaning that these two columns will not be displayed in the dynaset.

6 **Type >=200 in the criteria row of the Amount column**

7 **Type IL in the criteria row of the State column**

8 **Type >=200 in the criteria row of the Amount column**

9 **Select *Ascending* in the Sort row of both the Last and First columns**

DB

Compare your screen to Figure DB1-23a. Then,

10 Click *Query, Run*

Only those records that match *both* criteria are displayed. Note, too, that fields used in criteria searches *need not appear in the dynaset.* Finally, note that the records in the dynaset are in same order as the underlying table, because no entries were made in the Sort row.

11 Close the Query window without saving

Now, using CUSTOMER NUMBER and AMOUNT as displayed fields, create queries to match the rest of the examples given. The first of these queries use an AND connector in the same field. This query finds records whose amount equals or exceeds 200 AND is less than 800.

Using Figure DB1-23b as a guide,

12 Type >=200 And <800 in the criteria row of the Amount column

13 Click *Query, Run*

Check to make sure each record in the dynaset conforms to the criteria.

14 Close the Query window

The next query uses an OR connector with two fields. In this example, records will be found whose state is IL OR whose amount equals or exceeds 200.

15 Open the Select Query window

Use CUSTOMER NUMBER and AMOUNT as displayed fields. The STATE field used to express criteria will not be displayed. Create the query using Figure DB1- 23c as a guide:

16 Type IL as criteria for the State column

17 Type >=200 as criteria for the Amount column

Note that the criteria for the Amount column should be typed on a different row than the criteria for the State column. This is the way the OR connector is expressed between values found in different fields.

18 Click *Query, Run*

19 Close the Query window

The last query uses an OR connector within *one* field to list records whose value in the State field is either IL or NM. Using Figure DB1-23d as a guide,

20 Create and execute the query

21 Close all windows in the Access work area

As you have seen in these four queries, AND connects two criteria in the same field column, as does the OR connector. When combining criteria in different fields, those on the same row indicate an AND connector, whereas those on separate rows indicate an OR connector.

PATTERN SEARCH. You can also search for patterns or a series of characters. Access provides the same wildcard characters for queries that are used in the Find procedure discussed earlier. Assume, for example, that you want to see records whose City field value starts with an "S." Try this query:

STEPS

1. **Open the Select Query design screen**

2. **Select the Last and City fields to be included in the dynaset**

3. **Type S* in the criteria row of the City column**

When the active area is moved, Access automatically changes the display to read *Like "S*"*. Compare your screen to Figure DB1-24a, then

4. **Click *Query, Run***

Those cities that begin with an "S" (San Jose and Santa Fe) will be shown. Add this change to search for records whose CITY field value starts with an "S" but also includes a "t":

5. **Close the Query window**

Re-create the same query, but this time

6. **Type S*t* in the criteria row of the City column**

Compare your results with Figure DB1-24b, then

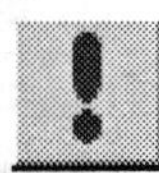

7. **Click *Query, Run***

Now only one city (Santa Fe) matches the modified criteria. Pattern searches are useful when you are looking for particular phone area codes (as in 718*) or dates in a certain year (as in ??/??/94) or month (as in 11/??/??). You can devise many other possibilities once you know how to use patterns to search records.

8. **Close all windows in the Access work area**

CHECKPOINT

- ✓ Using DBTEST, display only the student names in the table.
- ✓ Now list those records whose TEST2 score meets or exceeds 90.
- ✓ Create a list to display records whose TEST1 score is less than 80 and whose TEST2 score exceeds 50.

FIGURE DB1-24 ■ USING WILDCARD CHARACTERS IN SELECT QUERIES

(a) This query finds any city beginning with the letter *S*.
(b) This query finds any city beginning with the letter *S* and containin a *t*, like Santa Fe.

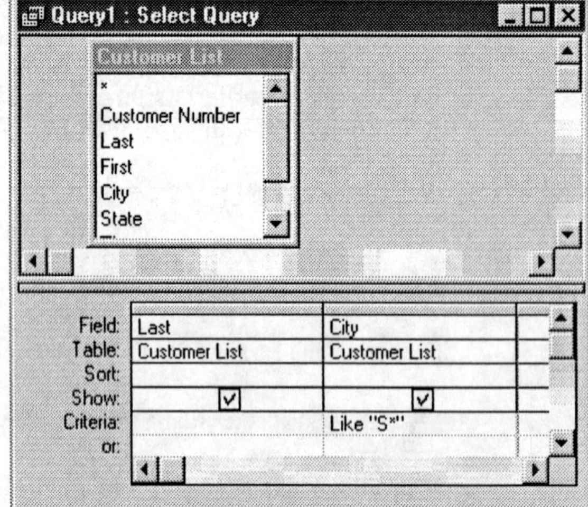

(a)

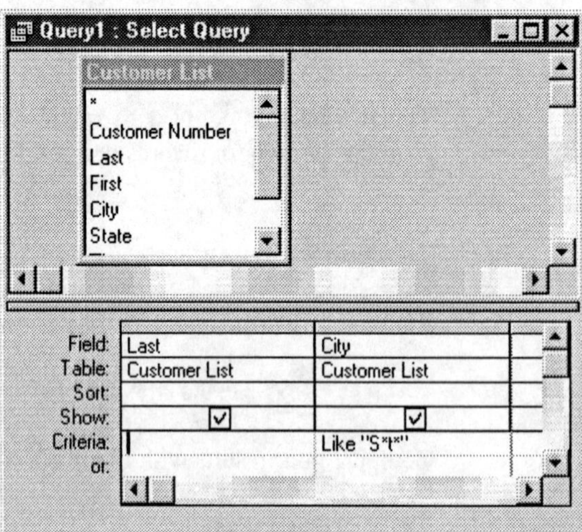

(b)

- ✓ Display only those records whose TEST1 scores are less than a particular student's score.
- ✓ Display only those records whose name comes after (Hint: read "is greater than") a particular student's name in the alphabet. Then exit Access.

DELETING RECORDS

Deleting records is frequently necessary to keep a table current. Records can be deleted individually or as part of a query procedure

DELETING INDIVIDUAL RECORDS

Permanently deleting individual records is easy to do. To prepare for this exercise,

STEPS

1. **Execute the necessary commands to start Windows 95**
2. **Click the *Start* button, point to *Programs,* and then click *Microsoft Access***
3. **Open the CUSTOMER LIST table for use**

After the table appears,

4. **Press ↓ to move to Record 5**
5. **Click the row selector to highlight the row as in Figure DB1-25a**

The row selector is a rectangular area to the left of the row. It contains a small triangle.

6. **Press Delete**

A dialog box asks you to confirm the deletion.

7. **Click *Yes***

The record is permanently removed from the table. The only way to recover the deleted record is from a backup copy of the table.

8. **Close all windows in the Access work area**

DELETING MULTIPLE RECORDS WITH A QUERY

You can also delete a group of records by using a Delete Query window. Records that match the specified criteria in the query will be removed from the table. Try deleting the group of records whose STATE field value is "NY," using a conditional expression in a Query screen as follows:

STEPS

1. **Open the CUSTOMER LIST table**
2. **Open the Query design screen (click the *New Object* drop-down button, then click *New Query, OK)***
3. **Click the drop-down arrow next to the *Query Type* button, then click *Delete***

FIGURE DB1-25 ■ DELETING RECORDS

(a) Click the row selector to select the record, and then press the Delete key to remove it.
(b) This query will delete all records whose State value is "NY."

Customer List : Table

Customer Number	Last	First	City	State	Zip	Amount
670	Parker	Charles	Santa Fe	NM	87501	$450.75
101	Burstein	Jerome	San Jose	CA	95120	$230.45
449	Laudon	Jane	New York	NY	10003	$230.45
754	Martin	Edward	New York	NY	10001	$230.55
389	Martin	Arthur	Flushing	NY	11367	$65.30
176	West	Rita	Chicago	IL	60601	$965.42
067	Williams	DeVilla	Chicago	IL	60601	$965.42
111	Hill	Karen	Chicago	IL	6605	$456.78
*						$0.00

Record: 5 of 8

(a)

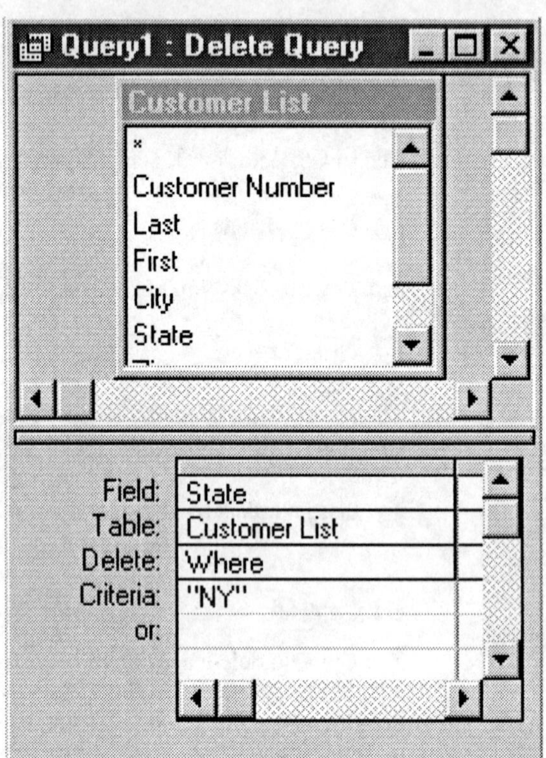

(b)

4 Select the State field to be included in the dynaset (drag State to the field row of the first column)

5 Type NY in the criteria row of the State column

Compare your screen with Figure DB1-25b, then

6 Click *Query, Run*

Access opens a dialog box to warn you that two rows are about to be deleted. These are two records with NY in the STATE field. Instead of permitting Access to proceed,

7 **Click *No***

This aborts the deletion process.

8 **Close all windows in the Access work area**

9 **Exit Access and shut down Windows**

CHECKPOINT

- ✓ Create a database file named Politics.
- ✓ Create a table named Presidents with the following fields and data:

Name	Party	Year
Truman	D	1948
Eisenhower	R	1952
Kennedy	D	1960
Johnson	D	1964
Nixon	R	1968
Carter	D	1976
Reagan	R	1980

- ✓ Create a query which will delete the Republican presidents. Run the query.
- ✓ Individually delete the records of those presidents elected before 1960. Create a query that will delete those presidents elected before 1975. Run the query. (Only the Carter record should remain.)

SUMMARY

- A database management system (DBMS) allows you to organize data so that they can be easily stored, accessed, modified, and maintained.
- Data can be categorized in a hierarchy composed of a database, table (file), record, and field.
- In Access, a popular DBMS, tables display data in a two-dimensional array with records forming the rows and fields shown in columns.
- The main menu screen is composed of (1) the title bar, (2) the menu, (3) the toolbar, (4) the work area, and (5) the status bar
- A table is one kind of Access object.
- Objects are contained in a file called a database file. When the database file has been opened, the names of objects in the file are displayed in the Database window.
- In creating new tables, a structure is designed that includes a field name, type, and sometimes size.
- There are eight field types. The most important ones are Text, Number, Currency, and Date/Time.

- The *File, Exit* command closes all open windows and exits to the Windows 95 environment. Failure to exit properly can result in lost or damaged files.
- Once a table is identified for use, records can be added to the file. Records are added to the end of the table.
- Records can be added in either table or single-record form. Table form presents data in rows and columns, whereas record form displays one record on each screen.
- A table can be quickly printed by selecting the *Print* button while viewing a table or form.
- A query is another type of Access object. Selected fields can be shown by the query procedure. Field names are placed in query columns using the drag and drop procedure.
- Conditional searches using relational operators in a query can restrict displayed records to those that meet the stated condition.
- Deleting a single record can be accomplished by selecting a record and pressing Delete, which irretrievably removes the highlighted record from the table.
- The Query window can be used to delete records that meet a condition or set of conditions.

KEY TERMS

Shown in parentheses are the page numbers on which key terms are boldfaced.

Allow zero length (DB28)
Button (DB3)
Caption (DB27)
Clicking (DB5)
Conditional expression (DB51)
Context sensitive (DB12)
Data type (DB25)
Database (DB2)
Database file (DB19)
Database window (DB19)
Datasheet view (DB30)
Decimal places (DB28)
Default value (DB27)
Design view (DB30)
Dialog box (DB3)
Double-clicking (DB5)
Dynaset (DB49)
Field (DB3)
Field name (DB24)
Field selector (DB45)
Field size (DB26)
Field value (DB25)
Find (DB42)
Format (DB25)
Forms (DB36)
Graphical user interface (DB3)
Icon (DB3)
Indexed (DB28)
Input mask (DB27)
Literal (DB27)
Menu bar (DB8)
Mouse (DB5)
Mouse pointer (DB5)
Object (DB19)
Pointing (DB5)
Properties (DB26)
Query (DB48)
Record (DB3)
Required (DB28)
Scroll (DB42)
Scroll buttons (DB42)
Shortcut keys (DB7)
Status bar (DB11)
Table (DB3)
Title bar (DB8)
Toolbar (DB11)
Validation rule (DB27)
Validation text (DB27)
Windows (DB3)

QUIZ

TRUE/FALSE

___ 1. Access is mainly a menu-driven program.
___ 2. The status bar appears at the bottom of the Access window.

___ 3. The Database window is used only to create a new table.
___ 4. Telephone numbers should be stored in a number type field.
___ 5. There is no direct Save command in Access
___ 6. Data is an equivalent term to field value.
___ 7. Records must be entered into record forms.
___ 8. Queries can not be used to delete records.
___ 9. To change data in a table manually, you must press F2.
___ 10. Deleting records with Ctrl+Delete irrevocably removes them from the table.

MULTIPLE CHOICE

___ 11. Which switches between table and record form screens?
a. *Form View* button
b. Insert
c. F1
d. S

___ 12. To execute a menu command without the mouse, you must first press the ______.
a. Tab
b. Escape
c. Alt
d. Delete

___ 13. Which of the following field types must include a width?
a. Text
b. Number
c. Date
d. Currency

___ 14. Which menu command ensures that windows are properly closed?
a. *File, Exit*
b. *File, Close*
c. *End*
d. Ctrl + X

___ 15. To edit the contents of a field, you must activate (the) _______.
a. Field edit
b. Edit mode
c. Shortcut key mode
d. None of the above

___ 16. What does an ellipsis (...) after a menu command mean?
a. A dialog box follows.
b. Another menu follows.
c. The command will be executed immediately.
d. An error message will follow.

___ 17. When you want to close a table window, you first
a. Press Alt + F4
b. Press Shift + F10
c. Press Ctrl + F4
d. Press F1

___ 18. Which connector requires that both conditions be met for record selection?
a. OR

b. NOT
c. AND
d. +

___ 19. Which of these conditions is an example of a pattern search?
a. M..n
b. LIKE Martin
c. NOT LIKE Martin
d. > 400

___ 20. When deleting records using a query, which step actually results in the removal of the records?
a. Selecting the *Run* button
b. Selecting the *Create Query* button
c. Pressing F9
d. Pressing F2

MATCHING

Select the term that best matches each feature indicated on the Access desktop screen shown in the figure.

___ 21. *Close* button
___ 22. Toolbar

FIGURE DB1-A ■ MATCHING EXERCISE

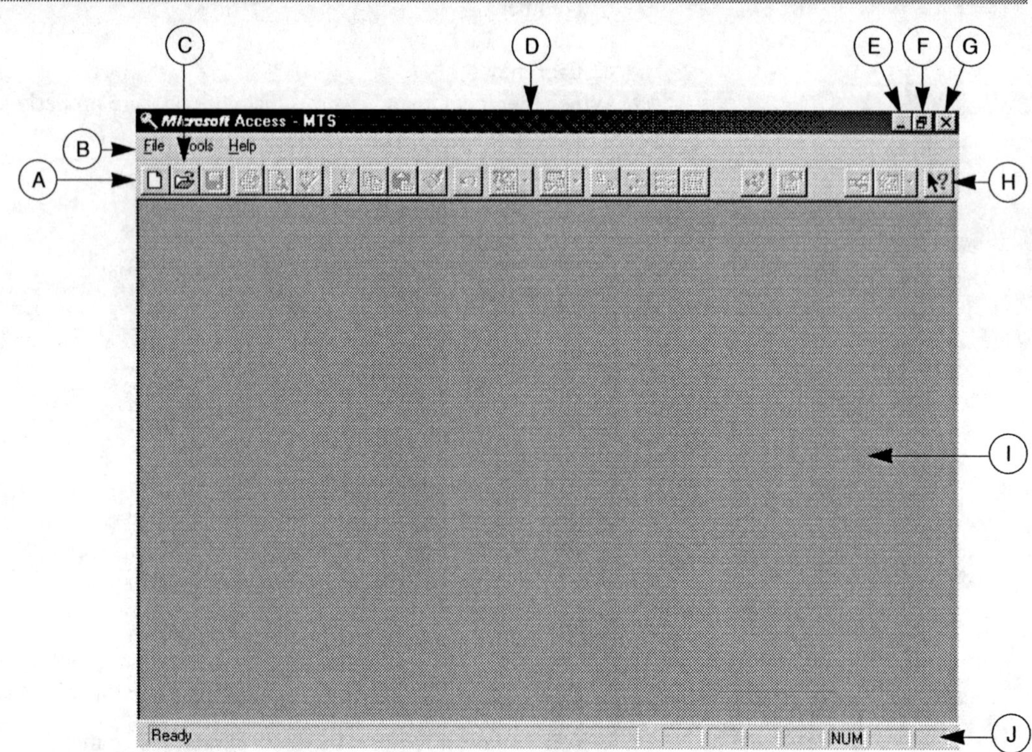

___ 23. *Maximize* button
___ 24. Menu bar
___ 25. *Minimize* button
___ 26. *Open Database* button
___ 27. Status bar
___ 28. Title bar
___ 29. *Help* button
___ 30. Work area

ANSWERS

True/False: 1. T; 2. T; 3. F; 4. F; 5. T; 6. T; 7. F; 8. F; 9. T; 10. T
Multiple Choice: 11. a; 12. c; 13. a; 14. a; 15. d; 16. a; 17. c; 18. c; 19. a; 20. a
Matching: 21. g; 22. a; 23 f; 24 b; 25. e; 26. c; 27. j; 28. d; 29. h; 30. i

EXERCISES

I. OPERATIONS

Provide the Access sequence of actions required to do each of the operations shown below. For each operation, assume a system with a hard disk designated as Drive C, the Access program properly installed, and a data disk in Drive A. A table called ADDRESS is contained on your data disk.

1. Launch the Access program.
2. Create a new database file named ADDRLIST on A:\.
3. Create a table structure named ADDRESS with these fields : Last, First, Address, Zip, Phone, and Salary.
4. Add five records to the table.
5. Display all the records in the ADDRESS table; then print them.
6. Add two records to the ADDRESS file : one at the end and one before Record 6.
7. List only the LAST field values in the ADDRESS table.
8. List LAST and ZIP fields for those records whose zip code starts with 113.
9. List LAST and FIRST fields for records whose zip code starts with a one and contains a zero.
10. Create a query to display those records whose SALARY field exceeds $25,000 and whose name starts with "Sm."
11. Remove the fourth record from the table.
12. Prepare a query that will delete records that have the word "Road" somewhere in the ADDRESS field.
13. Execute the query described in item 12 above.

14. Retrieve the deleted records back into the table.
15. Close all open windows and exit from Access.

II. COMMANDS

Describe fully, using as few words as possible in each case, what action is initiated or what is accomplished in Access by pressing each series of keystrokes or executing each series of menu commands given below. Assume that Access is running and that each exercise part is independent of any previous parts. If the series of commands is not complete, indicate what action should be taken to finalize the command.

1. Pressing F1
2. Clicking the *New* button on the database window
3. Clicking *File, Exit*
4. Clicking *Open database* button
5. Pressing F7
6. Clicking *Design View*
7. Clicking the *Find* button
8. Pressing F2
9. Pressing Tab while editing a table
10. Using OR in a query
11. Using Sno* in a query
12. Pressing Delete while a record is selected
13. Selecting the *Print* button
14. Moving the mouse pointer to a button on the toolbar
15. Pressing Ctrl + F4

III. APPLICATIONS

Perform the following operations using your computer system. You will need a system with Access on it and a data disk to store the results of this exercise. In a few words, explain how you accomplished each operation and describe its result. If you want to continue these exercises later, be sure to exit properly after each operation. Note that these exercises should be performed in sequence. Make sure you label each printed result with the exercise number, your name, and your class.

APPLICATION 1: NOTES ON LOUIS XIV

1. Launch Access and create a new database named FRANCE.
2. Create a table named LOUIS with the following fields:

Field Name	Field Type	Width
Last	Text	15
First	Text	10
Born	Number	
Died	Number	
Comment	Text	40

3. Enter these five records into the table:

Rec	Last	First	Born	Died	Comment
1	Villars	Claude	1653	1734	Marshall of France
2	Le Tellier	Michel	1603	1685	Secy of State & War, later chancellor
3	Fouquet	Nicolas	1615	1680	Supt. of Finance, imprisoned 1661
4	Adelaide	Marie	1685	1712	Wife of Louis, mother of Louis XV
5	Stuart	Charles II	1630	1685	King of England

4. Print the table, then add the following records:

Rec	Last	First	Born	Died	Comment
6	Colbert	Jean-Baptiste	1619	1683	Minister of Commerce
7	Louis XIV		1638	1715	King of France 1643–1715, the "Sun King"
8	Richelieu		1585	1642	Cardinal, favorite minister
9	Turenne	Henri	1611	1675	Marshall of France
10	Villeroi	Francois	1644	1730	Marshall of France

DB

5. Delete the record containing Charles II of England. (What is an Englishman doing in this list anyway?)
6. Print a list of all records and fields.
7. List the individuals born before Louis XIV. Save and print the output.
8. Create a query that will include all people who became Marshall of France. List the LAST, FIRST, and BORN fields using this query. Save and print the output.
9. Create a query (using the "example" procedure) to limit searches to people who outlived Louis XIV. Use the query to list these people, showing all fields.

10. Use a query to delete all records for individuals who lived after 1700.
11. Print a list of the remaining records.
12. Exit Access.

APPLICATION 2: DEGREE PLAN

1. Launch Access.
2. Create a table named DEGREE with the following fields:

Field Name	Field Type	Width
Course	Text	5
Number	Text	5
Grade	Text	1
Completed	Yes/No	

3. Enter these five records into the table:

Tip: Yes/no records are true/false. Just click to select or de-select.

Rec	Course	Number	Grade	Completed
1	CIS	3102	B	True
2	CIS	3200	A	True
3	ENG	3101	C	True
4	MATH	3210		False
5	SPAN	4101	B	True

4. Add Records 6, 7, and 10 to the end of the file. Insert Records 8 and 9 before Record 3.

Rec	Course	Number	Grade	Completed
6	ACCT	3313		False
7	PE	3304	A	True
8	MATH	3213	I	False
9	HIST	3214	C	True
10	MUSIC	3333		False

5. Delete the record pertaining to Music 3333.
6. Print a list of all records and fields.
7. List the courses with a grade of A. Print the output.
8. Create a query that will include all CIS courses. List the COURSE, NUMBER, and GRADE fields using this query.
9. Create a query to limit searches to courses with no grade. Use the query to list these courses, showing all fields. (**Hint:** Use the "Is Null" criteria.)
10. Use a query to delete all records with no grade.
11. Print a list of the remaining records.
12. Print a list of the resulting table.
13. Exit Access.

APPLICATION 3: VIDEO COLLECTION

1. Start Access and set the directories.
2. Create a table named VIDEO with the following fields:

Field Name	Field Type	Width
Volume	Text	3
Start	Text	4
Subject	Text	25
Type	Text	2
Time	Number	

3. Enter these eight records into the table:

Rec	Volume	Start	Subject	Type	Time
1	101	0000	The Rough-Face Girl	C	30
2	101	0650	Will's Mammoth	C	25
3	102	0000	Magic of the 90s	M	120
4	102	1500	Star Trek XXV	SF	128
5	102	3000	Star Warts : Space Frogs	SF	147
6	103	0000	Terminator 15	A	132
7	104	0000	Japanese Ghost Stories	C	45
8	104	4000	Computerized Magician	M	60

4. Add Records 9 through 12.

Rec	Volume	Start	Subject	Type	Time
9	105	0000	Using Today's Software	I	125
10	106	0000	Lotus Made Easy	I	90
11	106	1575	The Magic of Show-Biz	M	120
12	104	1250	Animal Dreaming	C	90

5. Add a record with a volume of 108, a start of 0100, your last name as the subject, I for type, and 100 for time.
6. Print the entire table.
7. Use a query to display the volumes, starts, and subjects for those tapes that are coded as C type. Generate a report of the answer table and print it.
8. Create a query that will include all subjects whose length exceeds 60 minutes. List the volume, subject, and time using this query and print it.
9. Create a query to limit searches to subjects that are coded as M types. Use the query to list these tape entries, showing all fields and print it.
10. Using a query, prepare to delete the record whose subject is "Lotus Made Easy." Close the query screen without performing the query.
11. Using a query, prepare to delete the record whose time is 132 minutes. Perform the deletion.
12. View the answer table and print it.
13. Exit Access.

APPLICATION 4 : PERSONAL INVENTORY

1. Launch Access and set the directories.
2. Create a table named SOUNDS with the following fields:

Field Name	Field Type	Width
Item	Text	30
Category	Text	10
Year	Number	
New_Cost	Currency	
Source	Text	20

3. Enter these five records into the table and adjust the column widths as needed:

Rec	Item	Category	Year	New_Cost	Source
1	Stereo	Elec	1991	$875.33	Al's Stereo Shop
2	Super Woofer Set	Elec	1992	$210.35	Woofer City
3	TV	Elec	1990	$313.95	Al's Stereo Shop
4	Entertainment Center	Furn	1988	$285.00	Furn-a-Mundo
5	Bookshelf Speakers	Elec	1992	$50.00	Hock-a-Rama

4. Print the table. Add Records 6 through 10 .

Rec	Item	Category	Year	New_Cost	Source
6	Microwave	Appl	1991	$211.13	Al's Stereo Shop
7	Washing Machine	Appl	1988	$75.00	Hock-a-Rama
8	Gas Dryer	Appl	1988	$50.00	Hock-a-Rama
9	Fire Extinguisher (for dryer)	Misc	1988	$17.50	World-Mart
10	Gorilla Banana Printer	Elec	1991	$25.00	Hock-a-Rama

5. Delete the record containing the Gorilla Banana Printer (Author's note: There really was a printer sold under that name in the early 1980s.)
6. Print a list of all records and fields.
7. List the records for items worth less than $100. Print the output.
8. Create a query that will include all appliance items. List the ITEM, NEW_COST, and SOURCE fields using this query. Save and print the query.
9. Create a query to limit searches to items that cost more than the woofers. Use the query to list these records, showing all fields. Save and print the query.
10. Delete the record for the fire extinguisher (you hocked it).
11. Print a list of the resulting table.
12. Exit Access.

APPLICATION 5 : PAYROLL

1. Launch Access and set the directories.
2. Create a table named PAYROLL with the following fields:

Field Name	Field Type	Width
Name	Text	25
Dept	Text	5
Hours	Number	
Rate	Currency	

3. Enter these four records into the file:

Rec	Name	Dept	Hours	Rate
1	Brown, Larry	Sales	45	10.25
2	White, Eileen	Sales	37	9.75
3	Silver, Steven	Acctg	39	8.75
4	Gold, Paul	Prsnl	35	8.25

4. Print the table, then add Records 5 through 8 to the end of the file.

Rec	Name	Dept	Hours	Rate
5	Brown, Phil	Acctg	35	7.50
6	Black, Susan	Prsnl	42	8.25
7	Green, Caryn	Acctg	38	6.75
8	Indigo, Jessica	Prsnl	43	5.25

5. Add a record with your name to the end of the file. Assume you are an employee in Prsnl who worked 41 hours at a rate of $9.75.
6. List all records and fields. Print the table.
7. Create a query with the names and rates of employees whose department is Prsnl and who worked more than 40 hours. Save and print the query.
8. Create a query that will screen out all records except those in Sales. List employees' names and departments using this query.

9. Create a query to limit searches to employees in Acctg whose rate is $7.50 or more. Use the query to list those employees, showing all fields. Save and print the query.
10. Delete Caryn Green's record.
11. Delete records for the sales department using a query.
12. Print the entire table.
13. Exit Access.

APPLICATION 6 : SALES

1. Launch Access and set the directories.
2. Create a table named SALES with the following fields:

Field Name	Field Type	Width
Customer	Text	6
Item	Text	20
Quantity	Number	
Price	Currency	

3. Enter these five records into the table adn adjust the column widths as needed:

Rec	Customer	Item	Quantity	Price
1	MAR-75	Screen, Super VGA	1	250.00
2	PAR-15	Disk Drive, 3.5" HD	2	89.00
3	MAR-75	Cable	1	35.00
4	WIL-11	Keyboard, 101 keys	5	49.95
5	PAR-15	Disk, 3.5" HD	100	.59

4. Add the following records to the end of the file:

Rec	Customer	Item	Quantity	Price
6	MAR-75	Printer, Ink Jet	1	495.00
7	PAR-15	Trackball	1	59.95
8	WIL-11	Screen, VGA	5	199.95
9	PAR-15	Disk, 3.5" DD	150	.39

5. Add a record with the first three letters of your last name followed by "-55" (for example, if your name is Garcia, type Gar-55). Assume you ordered two super VGA screens at $199.95 each.
6. Print a list of all records and fields.
7. Create a query that will list the customers and quantities for those people who ordered two or more screens. Save and print the query.
8. Create a query that will include all orders for MAR-75. List the customers, items, and quantities using this query. Save and print the query.
9. Create a query to limit searches to customers who ordered items whose unit price exceeds $200. Use the query to list these customers, showing all fields. Save and print the query.
10. Use a query to delete all records for WIL-11.
11. Print a list of the remaining records.
12. Remove the record for MAR-75's cable order.
13. Print a list of the remaining records.
14. Exit Access.

MASTERY CASES

The following mastery cases allow you to demonstrate how much you have learned about this software. Each case describes a fictitious problem or need that can be solved using the skills you have learned in this chapter. Although minimum acceptable outcomes are specified, you are expected and encouraged to design your response (files, data, lists) in ways that display your personal mastery of the software. Feel free to show off your skills. Use real data from your own experience in your solution, although you may also fabricate data if needed.

These mastery cases allow you to display your ability to

- Start the program.
- Create a file (or table).
- Enter data.
- Print records.
- Use a query or search.

CASE 1. TRACKING YOUR DEGREE PROGRAM

You want to keep track of your progress toward graduation. Create a file, or table that will store the following data for each course that you must take to complete your degree : department, course number, credits, semester in which course was (or will be) taken, grade, and instructor's name. Include additional fields that you deem important. If you are not enrolled in a degree program, create fictitious data for one of the degree programs offered in your school. Enter data for all courses required for your degree, completing all data as appropriate. Print two lists: one that displays data for all courses and one that displays only the courses you've completed.

CASE 2. TRACKING YOUR MUSIC COLLECTION

You want to create a catalog to keep track of your music collection. Create a file or table that will include the following data for each music selection in your collection: selection title, artist, album title, type of music (rock, classical, jazz, etc.), and type of media (tape, CD, LP, etc.). Enter data for at least 20 selections representing a mix of different albums, music, and media types. Print two lists displaying the most important data about your collection: one showing all selections and listing only the CDs in your collection.

CASE 3. TRACKING THE CLIENTELE FOR A BUSINESS

A friend who owns a hair salon asks you to help her keep track of her upscale clientele. Create a file or table that will contain data for each client's name, address, home phone, work phone, date of last visit, service(s) performed, amount charged, name of cosmetologist who performed work, and date of next appointment. Enter data for 15 clients. Print two lists: one that displays all clients and another that lists only the clients served by one specific cosmetologist.

2

Enhancing the Database: Rearranging, Reporting, and Editing

OUTLINE

OBJECTIVES

After completing this chapter, you will be able to

1. Modify a table structure to insert, delete, or change fields.
2. Explain and demonstrate the difference between sorting in the same table and into a new table.
3. Create report forms and print reports on the screen and printer.
4. Modify existing report forms to insert and delete columns, change titles, and use subtotals.
5. Edit records individually and globally.
6. Restrict the screen display and reports to records that meet specified criteria.
7. Use math operators on records to calculate Sum, Average, and Count using conditions.

OVERVIEW

This chapter expands on the basic database skills you learned in the previous chapter by presenting techniques to modify table structures, rearrange records, and use formal reports. The chapter begins with an explanation of table structure modifications—changing, adding, and deleting data fields. Techniques for sorting records follow. The chapter then examines methods to create, use, and modify reports in both basic and grouped formats. Commands to locate records and edit their contents are presented next, followed by an examination of summary math commands.

MODIFYING A TABLE STRUCTURE

Prepare to perform the exercises to follow.

STEPS

1. **Launch Access**
2. **In the *Microsoft Access* dialog box, click the *Open an Existing Database* option, *OK* (or by Menu bar, press Esc to remove the *Access* dialog box, and click *File, Open)***
3. **Click the *Look in* drop-down button, and then the *3½ Floppy (A:)* drive icon**
4. **Click the *CUSTOMER* icon in the Open list box and then the *Open* button**
5. **Click the *CUSTOMER LIST* icon, and then the *Design* button**
6. **Us the arrow keys to move to the Amount row**

   Your screen should now look like Figure DB2-1a.

THE TABLE DESIGN SCREEN

This is the Table Design screen. It looks just as it did when you finished designing the CUSTOMER LIST table. It is from this screen that you can continue the design process. You can add fields, delete fields, or change the properties of fields to correct past errors or to adapt to new needs.

ADDING NEW FIELDS

STEPS

1. **Click the CITY field row selector (the fourth field) to select it**

(Remember, the row selector is the box on the left of the field name CITY. The entire row containing CITY should become highlighted.

2. **Press Insert (or click *Insert, Field)***

A new blank row appears. Now simply complete the field parameters as follows:

3. **Place a text insertion point in the Field Name column of the new row (point to it with the mouse and click)**
4. **Type Address and press ↵**

The highlight moves to the Data Type column. Text is the default data type, and that happens to be the correct choice for this field.

FIGURE DB2-1 ■ THE TABLE DESIGN SCREEN

(a) This screen shows the current design of the Customer List table.
(b) A new blank row has been inserted where the Address field is to be placed in Customer List.
(c) The completed Address field has been inserted in the table's design.

(a)

Field Name	Data Type	Description
Customer Number	Text	An identification code unique to this customer
Last	Text	Customer's last name
First	Text	Customer's first name
Address	Text	Customer's address
City	Text	Customer's city
State	Text	Customer's state
Zip	Text	Customer's five digit zip code
Amount	Currency	Amount owed by customer

Field Properties

General | Lookup

Format	Currency
Decimal Places	2
Input Mask	
Caption	
Default Value	0
Validation Rule	<=5000
Validation Text	You must enter an amount less than or equ
Required	No
Indexed	No

A value that is automatically entered in this field for new records

(b)

Field Name	Data Type	Description
Last	Text	Customer's last name
First	Text	Customer's first name
Address	Text	Customer's address
City	Text	Customer's city
State	Text	Customer's state
Zip	Text	Customer's five digit zip code
Amount	Currency	Amount owed by customer
Paid	Currency	Customer payment
Form	Text	

Field Properties

General | Lookup

Field Size	5
Format	
Input Mask	
Caption	
Default Value	
Validation Rule	
Validation Text	
Required	No
Allow Zero Length	No
Indexed	No

The maximum number of characters you can enter in the field. The largest maximum you can set is 255. Press F1 for help on field size.

(c)

Custo	Last	First	Address	City	State	Zip	Amount	Paid	Form
670	Parker	Charles		Santa Fe	NM	87501	$450.75		
101	Burstein	Jerome		San Jose	CA	95120	$230.45		
449	Laudon	Jane		New York	NY	10003	$230.45		
754	Martin	Edward		New York	NY	10001	$230.55		
176	West	Rita		Chicago	IL	60601	$123.45		
067	Williams	DeVilla		Chicago	IL	60601	$965.42		
111	Hill	Karen		Chicago	IL	60605	$456.78		
*							$0.00	$0.00	

5 **Press** ↵

6 **Type** **Customer's address**

DB

7 Move the text insertion point to the Field Size row by pointing and clicking, delete the default width, type 25 , and press ↵

The new field is completed as shown in Figure DB2-1b. Fields can also be added at the end of the structure. To add a currency field called PAID at the end,

8 Place the text insertion point in the Field Name column in the blank row beneath the AMOUNT field

Tip: If that row is not visible, use the vertical scroll bars to bring it into view.

A new field is about to be added.

9 Type Paid and press ↵

10 Use the drop-down arrow to select CURRENCY as the field type and press ↵

In the Comments column,

11 Type Customer Payment

To move the text insertion point to the next row,

12 Press ↵

Add another field—FORM—as follows:

13 Type Form and press ↵

Text is the correct data type, so

14 Press ↵

Leave the Comments area blank, but set Field Size to 5.

15 Move the text insertion point to the Field Size column by pointing and clicking, delete the default width, type 5 , and press ↵

The completed table is shown in Figure DB2-1b. Although you can save the modified form whenever you want, wait until you finish a few more changes before you try it. To display the modified table so that you can compare your work to Figure DB2-1c,

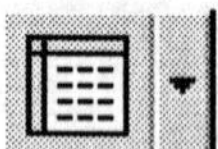

16 Click *View, Datasheet*

You will be asked whether you want to save your work.

17 Click *Yes*

18 If needed, change the Amount for Customer number 176 (west), from 965.42 to 123.45

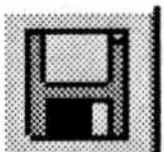

19 Click *File, Save* to resave Ctrl + S

CHECKPOINT

- ✓ Create a new database file named Books.
- ✓ Create a table in that file named Library with the following structure:

Title	Text	25
Author	Text	25
Due Date	Date	

- ✓ Add five library books to the table, filling in imaginary data. Print the table's records.
- ✓ Revise the structure of the table in the following ways:
  - Change Author to Major Author.
  - Add a text field for Publisher.
- ✓ Print the table's records.

REARRANGING THE TABLE

SORTING INTO A NEW TABLE

Sorting is a process that changes the order of records in a table. Sometimes, sorting physically rewrites the table—or creates a new table—which is in the desired order. For example, our list of customers might meaningfully be sorted into last name order, city order, or zip code order.

Access also permits you to create a new table that has the same records in a different order. To do this,

DB

STEPS

1 Open the CUSTOMER LIST table, if necessary

2 Click the *New Object* drop-down button (right side of toolbar) for its list

3 Click *New Query, OK*

A number of query types are available. You are already familiar with Select queries. To make a new table that contains all our data but in a different order, we will need to use the Make Table query type. On the resulting dialog box,

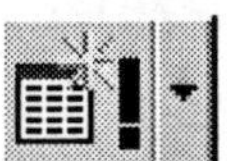

4 Click *Query, Make Table*

Tip: This button is found in a stack of buttons labeled *Query Type.* If necessary, click the pull-down arrow next to the stack, then select the *Make Table* button. As with the *New Object* stack, if the *Make Table* button happens to be on top of the stack, you need only click the button.

You will see a dialog box that asks you to name the destination table for the sort.

5 Type Customer ID and click *OK*

The next screen is the Make Table query design screen. You need to tell Access which fields you want copied to the new table. In this exercise, all fields will be copied to the new table. To select all field names and then copy them to a new table:

6 Click *Customer Number* in the Field List window, and then press Shift + End to select all fields

7 Point to the highlighted field names, and drag the list of field names to the Field row of the first column.

When you release the mouse button, all field names should have been copied to the Make Table query design screen. Next,

8 Click the Sort row of the Customer Number column to place the insertion point there

9 Click the drop-down arrow, then click *Ascending*

Your screen should now look like Figure DB2-2a. To execute the query,

10 Click the *Run* button

If you have followed these steps correctly, Access will inform you that seven records will be copied to the new table. To confirm the action,

11 Click *Yes*

It is at this point that Access creates the new table. It will copy the fields you indicated (all of them) to the target table you specified in ascending order by customer number. Next, let's verify that the sort was successfully performed. To open the new CUSTOMER ID table,

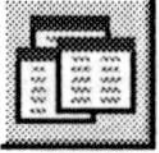

12 Click the *Show Database Window* button

13 Click the *Table* tab, if necessary, to display a list of tables in the database window

You should see CUSTOMER ID on the list.

14 Click the CUSTOMER ID table icon and click the *Open* button

FIGURE DB2-2 ■ SORTING TO ANOTHER TABLE

(a) This Make Table Query will sort to another table named Customer ID.
(b) The resulting table has been sorted.

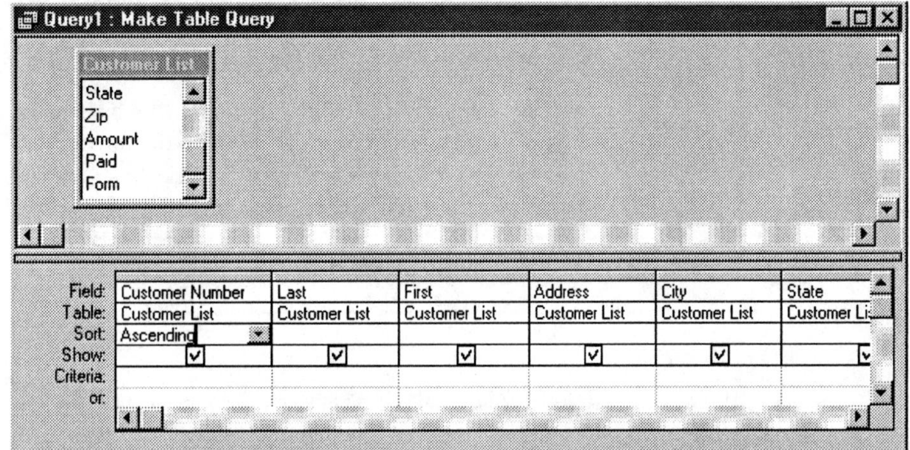

(a)

Customer ID : Table

Customer Num	Last	First	Address	City	State	Zip	Amount	Paid
067	Williams	DeVilla		Chicago	IL	60601	$965.42	
101	Burstein	Jerome		San Jose	CA	95120	$230.45	
111	Hill	Karen		Chicago	IL	60605	$456.78	
176	West	Rita		Chicago	IL	60601	$123.45	
449	Laudon	Jane		New York	NY	10003	$230.45	
670	Parker	Charles		Santa Fe	NM	87501	$450.75	
754	Martin	Edward		New York	NY	10001	$230.55	

Record: 1 of 7

(b)

Your results should resemble Figure DB2-2b.

Close the sorted table:

15 Click the *Close* button

If the Query Design screen is not displayed,

16 Click *Window,* then click *Query1: Make Table Query*

Next, close the Query Design screen.

17 Click the *Close* button

18 Click *No* when asked if you wish to save the query

If the CUSTOMER LIST table is not displayed,

19 Click *Window*, then click *Table: Customer List*

Don't close the CUSTOMER LIST table, because it will be used in the next exercise.

SORTING IN THE SAME TABLE

Access also permits the user to display records temporarily in an order other than the one in which they were entered. In this procedure, the records will be *displayed as if* the table had been rewritten into the new order, but they will actually remain in the same order that you entered them. To select the Last and First columns as in Figure DB2-3a:

STEPS

1 Click the *Last* column selector (the box on top of the column containing "Last")

Access will presume that these are the columns you intend to use for the sort.

2 Press and hold Shift while clicking the *First* column selector

FIGURE DB2-3 ■ SORTING THE CUTOMER LIST TABLE

(a) Select columns by clicking the column selector.
(b) The records have been rearranged into the desired order.

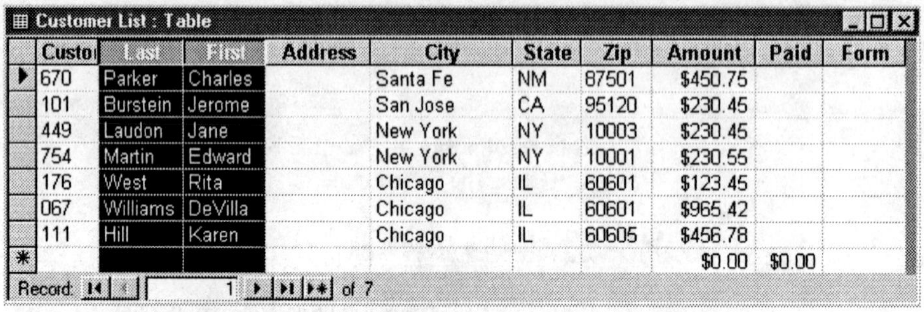

Customer List : Table

Custo	Last	First	Address	City	State	Zip	Amount	Paid	Form
670	Parker	Charles		Santa Fe	NM	87501	$450.75		
101	Burstein	Jerome		San Jose	CA	95120	$230.45		
449	Laudon	Jane		New York	NY	10003	$230.45		
754	Martin	Edward		New York	NY	10001	$230.55		
176	West	Rita		Chicago	IL	60601	$123.45		
067	Williams	DeVilla		Chicago	IL	60601	$965.42		
111	Hill	Karen		Chicago	IL	60605	$456.78		
*							$0.00	$0.00	

Record: 1 of 7

(a)

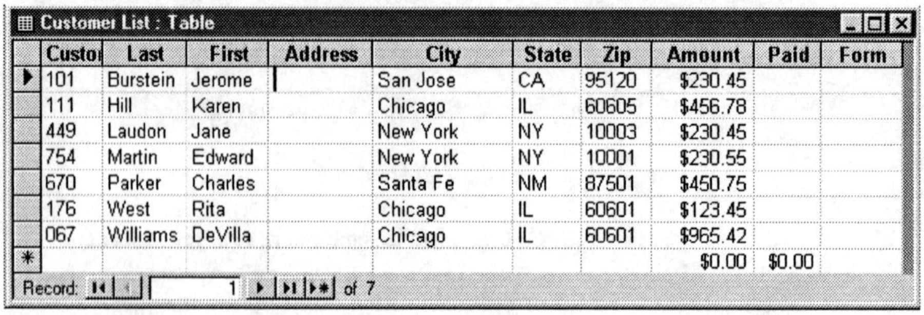

Customer List : Table

Custo	Last	First	Address	City	State	Zip	Amount	Paid	Form
101	Burstein	Jerome		San Jose	CA	95120	$230.45		
111	Hill	Karen		Chicago	IL	60605	$456.78		
449	Laudon	Jane		New York	NY	10003	$230.45		
754	Martin	Edward		New York	NY	10001	$230.55		
670	Parker	Charles		Santa Fe	NM	87501	$450.75		
176	West	Rita		Chicago	IL	60601	$123.45		
067	Williams	DeVilla		Chicago	IL	60601	$965.42		
*							$0.00	$0.00	

Record: 1 of 7

(b)

3 Click *Records, Sort, Ascending*

Access reorders the records so that they are in alphabetical order by last name (see Figure DB2-3b) because the Last column was selected at the time of the sort. If there had been two or more people with the same last name, Access would have sorted those two records by first name, since the First column was also selected. Access sorts from left to right when more than one column is selected. However, Access is merely *displaying* the records as *if* they had been sorted. The records remain in the file in the same order.

To return the table to **natural order** (the order in which they were entered),

4 Click *Records,* then click *Remove Filter/Sort*

The records return to their original order. To close the table window,

5 Click the *Close* button, *No*

6 Close all windows in the Access work area by clicking its *Close* button (Do not close Access)

CHECKPOINT

- ✓ Sort the records in the DBTEST table by name into a new table called DBNAME.
- ✓ Print a quick report by clicking the *Print* button.
- ✓ Sort the records in the DBTEST table by TEST1 into a new table called DBTEST1.
- ✓ Sort the records in the DBTEST table by TEST2 into the same table (DBTEST).
- ✓ Print DBTEST by clicking the *Print* button while the table is displayed.

REPORT FORMS

Viewing (that is, just looking at the table on the screen) and querying your data are fine for quick looks at table records, but Access also offers more formalized reports that give you extended control over titles, columns, and their contents.

To use a report, you must first create a report specification, or **report form,** into which Access will place data from the current table. Once the form is created, it can be recalled whenever you desire a report.

A report form is like a skeleton—it contains a structure that will be filled in with data from its corresponding table. In the following exercise, you will create a report form called "Customer Report #1."

DESIGNING A REPORT FORM

STEPS

1 Start from a blank Access work area

DB

2 Open the Customer database window

3 Click the *Reports* tab

4 Click the *New* button

On the *New Report* dialog box (shown in Figure DB2-4a)

5 Click the drop-down arrow next to *Choose the Table...*, then click CUSTOMER LIST

Here, you are telling Access what table will be used to provide the data for this report. At this point, we will only be using data from one table, but in Chapter 3 you will learn how to include data from two or more tables on the same report.

6 Click *Report Wizard*, and then *OK*

Other choices on this dialog box take you to other ways of creating different kinds of reports. If you were to choose *Design View*, you will be led to a completely blank screen on which you can design any kind of report that Access is capable of. It is the more flexible choice, but it requires more work on your part. Other choices automatically design report types that will be discussed later.

The Report Wizard takes the data from the file you have indicated—in this case CUSTOMER LIST—and places it in one of several standard formats. The Report Wizard will probably satisfy most of the report needs you will have. Also, the Report Wizard's output can be modified later if it is not exactly what you want.

This report will be a tabular report (columns and rows of data). It will have five columns:

- Last
- First
- Customer Number
- Amount
- Paid

Access displays the *Report Wizard* dialog box so that you can choose the fields for your report (see Figure DB2-4b). The *Available Fields* box lists of all the fields in the CUSTOMER LIST table.

7 Click *Last* in the Available Fields box, then click the > button

The Last selection jumps to the *Selected Fields* box, indicating that it is going to be included on the report. By repeating this procedure, you can select the fields you want in your report. The order in which they appear in the *Selected Fields* box is the order in which they will appear in your report. Continue the process by selecting the other fields. If you accidentally select a field you do not want on your report, deselect it by clicking <.

8 Select each of the desired fields in the order shown in Figure DB2-4 by first clicking the Field and then the > button

9 Click the *Next* button

FIGURE DB 2-4 ■ THE REPORT WIZARD

(a) Here you indicate that you want a report using data from the Customer List.
(b) Select the fields you want in the desired order.

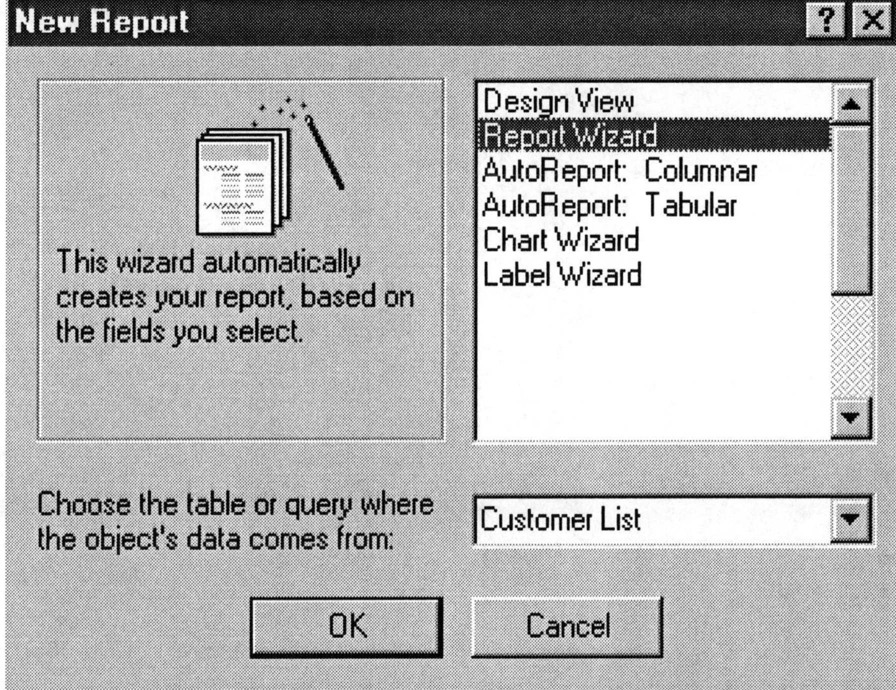

(a)

Report Wizard

Welcome to the Microsoft Access Report Wizard.
Which fields do you want on your report?
You can choose from more than one table or query.

Tables/Queries:
Table: Customer List

Available Fields:
Address
City
State
Zip
Form

Selected Fields:
Last
First
Customer Number
Amount
Paid

Cancel < Back Next > Finish

(b)

(continued)

DB

FIGURE DB2-4 ■ *(continued)*

(c) Next, select *Ledger* style and *Portrait* orientation.
(d) Choose style that you prefer.

Report Wizard
How would you like to lay out your report?
Layout
Vertical
Tabular
Orientation
Portrait
Landscape
Adjust field width so all fields fit on a page
Cancel
< Back
Next >
Finish

(c)

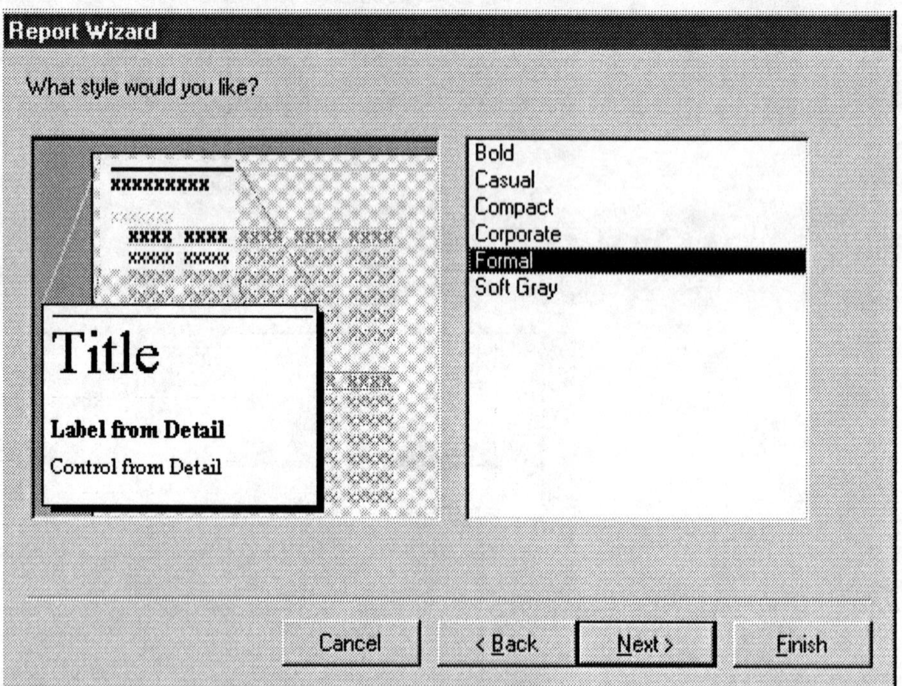

(d)

The next dialog box asks for the field or fields you want to group by. Grouping will be discussed in more detail later in this text. For now,

10 Click the *Next* > button, and then the *Next* > button

The next dialog box (Figure DB2-4c) asks about report layout. A **tabular report** is a column and row table; each column containing a field, each row containing a record. A **vertical report** contains one record per page, with the field names and values arranged vertically. For this report,

11 Click *Tabular*

You are also asked whether you want the report to have a *portrait* or *landscape* orientation. **Portrait orientation** means that the report will be printed so that the shorter edges of the page will be the top and bottom of the report, like this:

Landscape orientation will result in reports that are wider than they are tall, like this:

12 Click *Portrait*, then click the *Next* button

The next dialog box in this series asks about report style—that is, the size and shape of the alphabetic and numeric characters in your report. In Figure DB2-4d, the Formal style was selected. The appearance of your report will depend on which printer you are using and which fonts are available on your system. Although you can choose the style that suits your own taste, for now,

13 Click *Formal*, and then the *Next* > button

The next dialog box, shown in Figure DB2-5a, is the final one in this series. It asks you to type in the report's title (the table name (CUSTOMER LIST) is inserted as the default title).

14 Type Customer Report #1

15 Click *Preview the Report*, then click *Finish*

Depending on the speed of your system, there may be a short delay for processing. Then, the completed report is displayed on your screen just as it would appear on the page if printed. Your report should look like Figure DB2-5b. If a printer is available, you can generate a hard copy of the report.

16 Click the *Print* toolbar button

Notice that the report presents the title you typed in, *Customer Report #1,* field values from all records for the fields selected, and the date and page number are at the bottom of the page. To exit this Print Preview screen:

Close

17 Click the *Close* button

Access now displays the Report Design screen (see Figure DB2-6). It contains the report that was designed for you by the Report wizard. The Report Design screen contains many features that will enable you to design very sophisticated and attractive reports in the future.

One of the very useful features Access offers is the ability to display—at any stage of development—what the report would look like if printed. The toolbar for this screen contains a *Print Preview* button. Clicking this button causes Access to display a facsimile of the report on the screen as it would appear on the page if printed at that stage of development. However, before further modifying the report, you should save your work.

SAVING THE REPORT DESIGN. Access normally saves a report using its title (as in step 14 above) as its file name after clicking the *Finish* button (step 15). If your version of Access did not save the report, do the following:

STEPS

1 Click *File*, then click *Close*

FIGURE DB2-5 ■ FINISHING THE REPORT

(a) Enter the title.
(b) The final product.

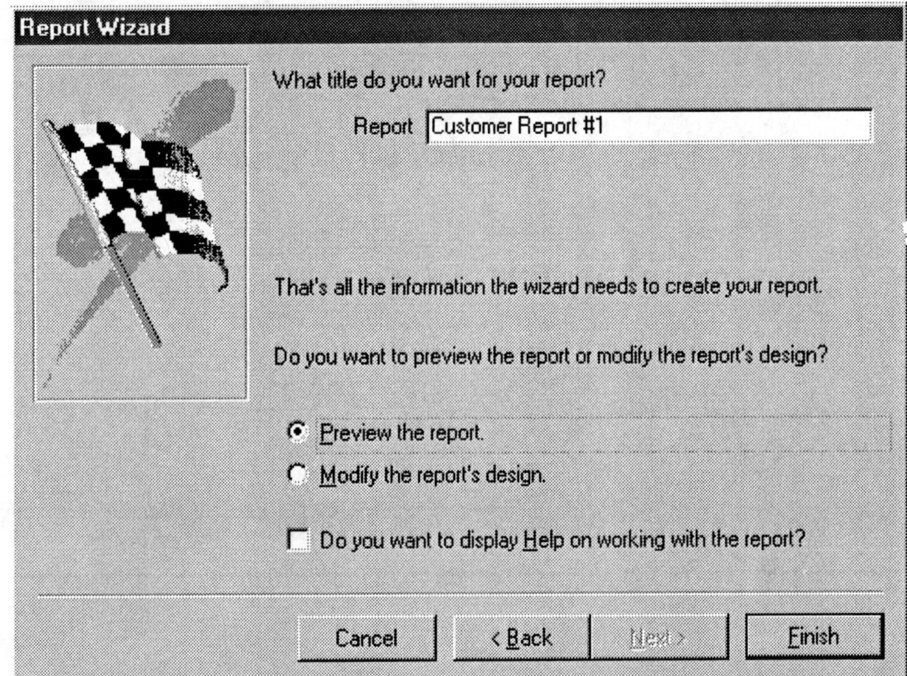

(a)

Customer Report #1

Customer Report #1

Last	First	Customer Number	Amount	Paid
Williams	DeVilla	067	$965.42	
Burstein	Jerome	101	$230.45	
Hill	Karen	111	$456.78	
West	Rita	176	$123.45	
Laudon	Jane	449	$230.45	

Page: 1

(b)

If the report design has been changed since the last time you saved it or if the report has never been saved, Access will display a dialog box asking if you want to save the report. Since this is the first time the file has been saved, it has been assigned no name as

FIGURE DB2-6 ■ VIEWING THE REPORT IN DESIGN MODE

This is the report designed for you by the Report Wizard

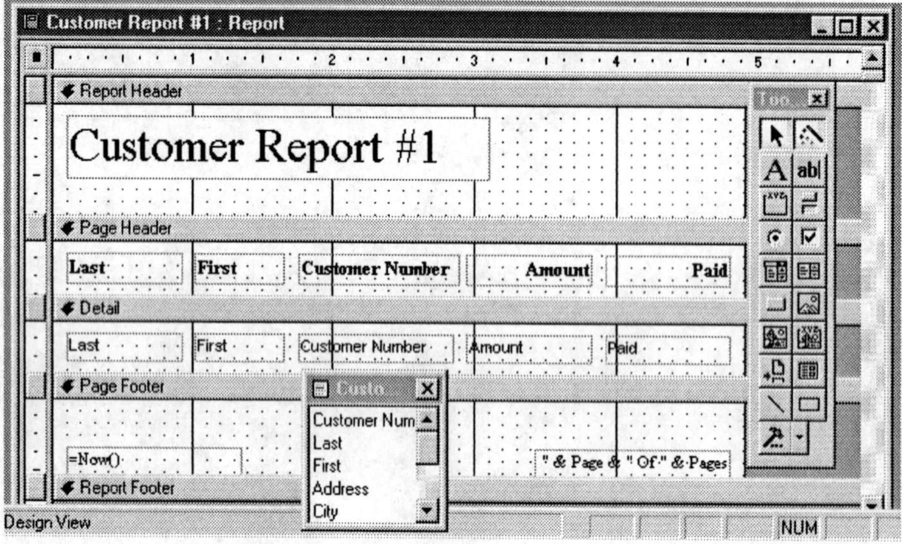

yet. Access presents a *Save File As* dialog box so that you can assign a filename to this report design. The report's title line—*Customer Report #1*—is suggested as the object's name.

2 Type CUSTOMER REPORT #1 as the new report name, then select *OK*

To close the database window,

3 Click *File*, then click *Close*

Access returns to a blank work area.

CONTINUING THE REPORT DESIGN PROCESS. Open the report CUST01 and continue with the design process.

STEPS

1 Open the Customer database window

2 Click the *Reports* tab

3 Click *Customer Report #1*, and click the *Design* button

The Report Design screen should return, displaying the design of Customer Report #1 just as it was saved. Continue examining the features of this screen.

4 If needed, rearrange your screen as in Figure DB2-6 (Remember, to move a window, drag its title bar. To resize a window, drag one of its walls or corners.)

Notice that the image of the report is divided into *bands*—namely *Report Header, Page Header, Report Footer, Page Footer,* and *Detail.*

Tip: You may have to maximize the window containing the Report Design screen and use the vertical scroll bars to view all of the features referred to on this screen.

This **banded report** style is typical of many current database management programs. **Bands** define the different components of the report. Each band is separated from others by a narrow line at its top and bottom, with an identifying title on the separator lines.

- The **Report Header band** and **Report Footer band** form the base layer of the report. Items in these bands print only once in the entire report. Items placed in the top portion of the band appear in the report header—at the start of the report; items in the lower portion appear in the report footer at the end of the report.
- The **Page Header band** and **Page Footer band** print once on each page. Items placed in the top portion of the band appear in the page header—at the top of each page; items in the lower portion appear in the page footer at the bottom of each page.
- A **Group band** is an optional band created when records are grouped within the report. Group identification is typically placed at the top of the band; summary statistics are placed at the bottom. (There is no group band in the CUST01 report at this point.)
- The **Detail band** forms the body of the report. When the report is generated, the report design is filled with data from the table associated with the report.

Each band contains the various *objects* that make up the report. Note that each object is enclosed in a rectangular box. The boundaries of the rectangle show the size and position of the object. A *label* object displays a descriptive title. A *field* object displays field data. In a *Report Wizard* dialog box, you could have changed the order of the columns by changing the order of the field names. It is also possible to achieve those same functions easily in this Report Design screen.

CHANGING THE ORDER OF COLUMNS. You may have second thoughts about the order of columns after you have closed the *Design Layout* dialog box. Suppose you wanted to change the order of columns and move the Customer Number column to another position. First, you have to select the area you intend to change.

Figure DB2-6 shows what your screen should look like at the beginning of this exercise.

DB

STEPS

1 In the Page Header band, click the label object *Customer Number* (the rectangular box containing the text "Customer Number")

2 Shift-click (press and hold Shift while clicking) the field object *Customer Number* in the *Detail* band

Both objects should have been selected; that is, they became outlined, as you see in Figure DB2-7a.

FIGURE DB2-7 ■ MOVING A COLUMN

(a) Objects associated with the fields First and Last have been selected.
(b) Objects associated with the fields First and Last have been dragged to their new positions.

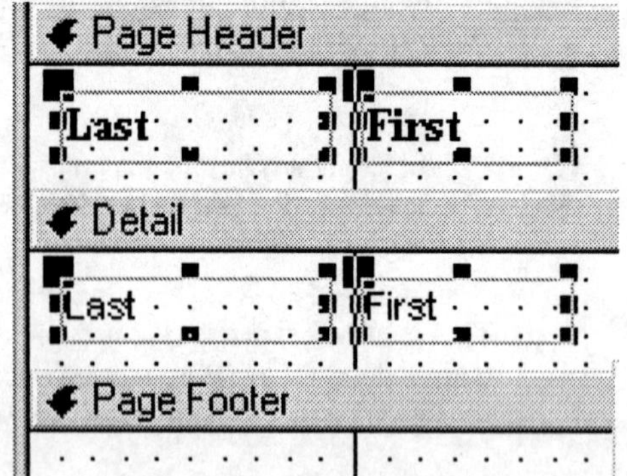

(a)

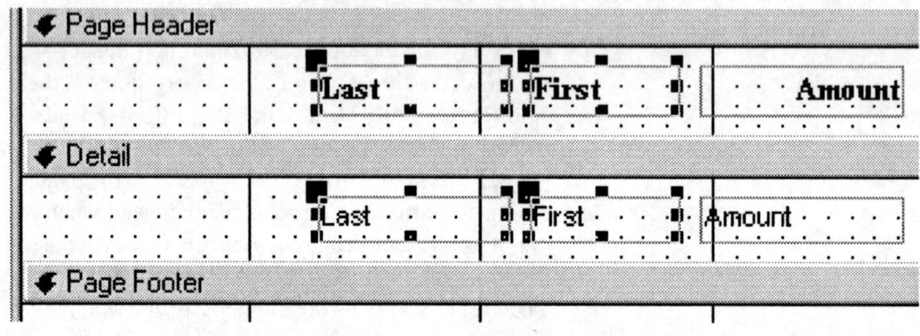

(b)

(continued)

3 Click *Edit, Cut* **Ctrl + X**

The selected objects disappear, but they have been copied to the Windows Clipboard. To change the order of columns, you will move column headings in the Page Header band and move field objects in the Detail band. You will use a Select and drag procedure:

- Move the mouse pointer to the object to be relocated.
- **Select** (click) a single object. (It will become outlined.)
- Shift-click multiple items. (Each object will become outlined as you click it, and all the objects can be moved, deleted, cut, copied, and so forth as one unit.)
- Move the mouse pointer along the boundary of the selected object(s) until the pointer changes shape to that of an open hand.
- Press *and hold* the left mouse button.
- Move the pointer to the desired position, dragging the object with the pointer.

Now, using shift-click to select multiple objects,

4 Select the label objects *Last* and *First* in the Page Header band and the field objects *Last* and *First* in the Detail band (Remember, click the *Last* object and then shift-click each additional object.)

The objects should look like Figure DB2-7a. Next, using Figure DB2-7b as a guide,

FIGURE DB2-7 ■ *(continued)*

(c) A new field object—Customer Number—has been inserted in the detail band, and a corresponding column heading is in the page header band.
(d) The revised report.

(c)

(d)

Customer Report #1

Customer Number	Last	First	Amount	Paid
670	Parker	Charles	$450.75	
101	Burstein	Jerome	$230.45	
449	Laudon	Jane	$230.45	
754	Martin	Edward	$230.55	
176	West	Rita	$123.45	
067	Williams	DeVilla	$965.42	
111	Hill	Karen	$456.78	

5 Drag and drop all four objects rightward until the FIRST field is next to the AMOUNT field

The next step is to insert the CUSTOMER NUMBER field object in the Detail band. Using Figure DB2-7c as a guide,

6 Point to the future location of Customer Number in the Page Header band and click

This tells Access where the field is to be pasted.

7 Click *Edit, Paste* Ctrl + V

The objects are now in place. To inspect the results of your work,

8 Click *File, Print Preview*

Your screen should look like Figure DB2-7d. If one of the objects you have moved or inserted is not properly aligned, try this:

DB

- Return to the Report Design screen.
- Select the object.
- Move the mouse pointer to the boundary of the object so that it changes to an open hand.
- Adjust the object's position using the drag and drop technique.
- Check the results of your work by clicking the *Preview* button.

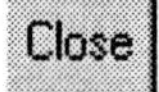

9 Click the *Close Window* toolbar button and then the *Close* button of the Customer Report #1 window

When asked if you want to save changes to Customer Report #1,

10 Click *Yes*

REMOVING A COLUMN. Even after you have been presented with an opportunity to remove field names in the earlier *Report Wizard* dialog box, you might still want to remove columns. To remove the Customer Number column,

STEPS

1 Open *Customer Report #1* in the Design mode

2 Select (shift-click) the Customer Number label object in the Page Header band and the Customer Number field object in the Detail Band

3 Press Delete

The Customer Number column has disappeared. It will now be necessary to move the other columns to the left.

4 Select each of the objects in the Page Header and Detail bands

Use Figure DB2-8a as a guide,

5 Drag all the objects to the left

6 Click outside the selection to deselect

7 Click *File, Print Preview*

Compare your results to Figure DB2-8b. If some objects are not properly aligned, return to the Report Design screen, select them, and move them until you are satisfied.

8 Click *View, Report Design*

MOVING AND RESIZING OBJECTS. You can also move and resize objects to make room for new objects.

FIGURE DB2-8 ■ DELETING A COLUMN

(a) Customer Number has been deleted, and all remaining objects have been moved leftward.
(b) The sample preview of the report.

(a)

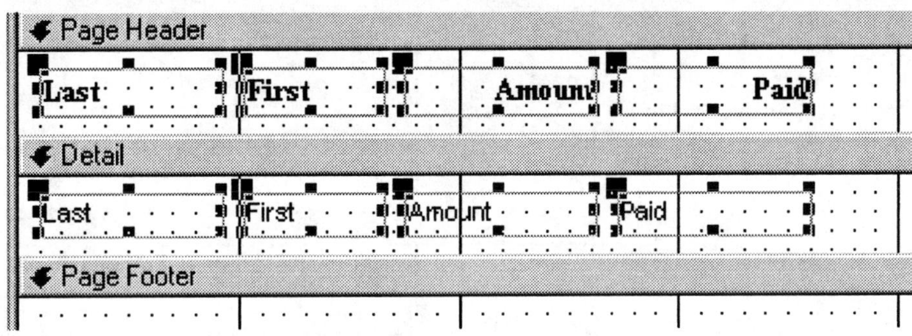

(b)

Customer Report #1

Last	First	Amount	Paid
Parker	Charles	$450.75	
Burstein	Jerome	$230.45	
Laudon	Jane	$230.45	
Martin	Edward	$230.55	
West	Rita	$123.45	
Williams	DeVilla	$965.42	
Hill	Karen	$456.78	

STEPS

DB

1. **Select the Amount and Paid label objects in the Page Header band and the AMOUNT and PAID fields in the Detail band**

2. **If needed, move the Toolbox and Field List windows by dragging their title bars**

3. **If needed, click the *Maximize* button of the Customer Report #1 window to enlarge its view**

4. **Drag all selected objects to the right as in Figure DB2-9a against the 5″vertical guideline (use the scroll bar to reposition the view area)**

The Report Design screen should resemble Figure DB2-9a. A blank space has now appeared in the report. There are no objects in this area because you have not placed any there. However, you can free more room for additional data by making the Amount and Paid field objects in the Detail band narrower. The numbers in the AMOUNT field do not require that much room. As yet, there are no values in the PAID field. An object can be made narrower (or wider) by this procedure:

FIGURE DB2-9 ■ MOVING AND RESIZING OBJECTS

(a) The report thus far in design mode.
(b) Existing objects have been dragged to the right to make room for new objects.
(c) The sample preview of the report.

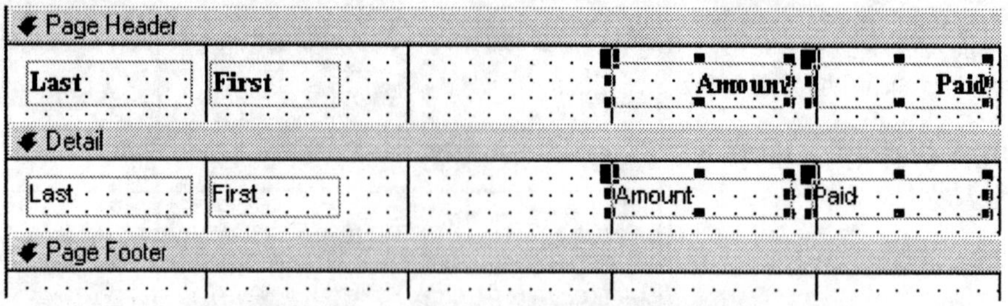

(c)

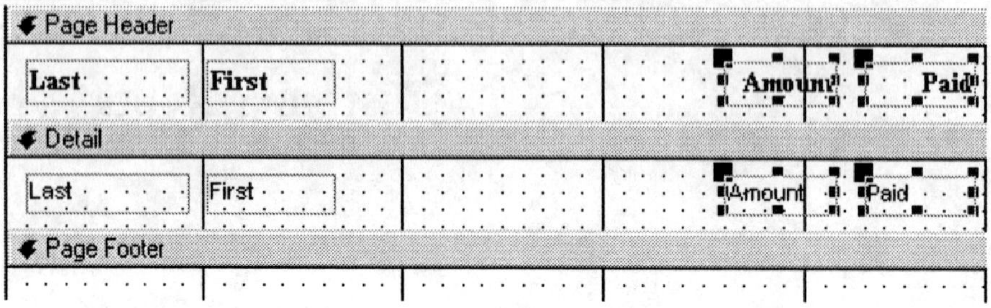

Last	First	Amount	Paid
Parker	Charles	$450.75	
Burstein	Jerome	$230.45	
Laudon	Jane	$230.45	
Martin	Edward	$230.55	

- *Select the Object.* It will become outlined as you have seen. On the boundary of the selected object you will see little black rectangles called **handles.**
- *Position the mouse pointer over a handle.* The mouse pointer will change shape to that of a double arrow, pointing in the directions that the handle can be moved (up/down, left/right, or diagonally).
- *Drag-and-drop the handle to resize the object.*

Using Figure DB2-9b as a guide,

5 Click any open space outside the selection to deselect

Using Figure DB2-9b as a guide, resize the Amount and Paid objects:

6 Select the Paid objects in the Page Header and Detail bands by clicking the *Paid* label object in the Page Header band and then press and hold Shift while clicking the *Paid* field object in the Detail band

7 **Point to the center left wall *selection handle* (small square) of either selected object until the pointer changes to a horizontal double arrow, and then drag right until the objects are resized similar to Figure DB2-9b**

8 **Select the *Amount* objects in the Page Header and Detail bands using the same technique as in Step 6**

9 **Drag the *Amount* objects right to align them closer to the *Paid* objects**

10 **Repeat Step 7 to resize the *Amount* objects**

11 **Click any open space outside the selection to deselect**

12 **Click *File, Print Preview***

Your screen should now resemble Figure DB2-9c.

13 **Click *View, Report Design***

PLACING A FIELD. You can now place fields into the new blank area. Placing a field includes inserting column headings in the Page Header band, inserting field objects in the Detail band, and, if needed, adjusting the size of the object. The first step is to place the field object properly. In the following exercise, you will place the CUSTOMER NUMBER field to the right of the customer's first name. Later, the customer's City will be placed to the right of the CUSTOMER NUMBER field.

To insert the CUSTOMER NUMBER field object in the Detail band,

STEPS

1 **Resize the Last and First objects in the Page Header and Detail bands to resemble Figure DB2-10**

2 **If the Field List and Toolbox windows are not opened, click *View, Field List* and then *View, Toolbox***

3 **Click *Customer Number* in the Field List window and then drag and drop it into the Detail band to the right of the First field object**

If two Customer Number objects appear, the left object is a label box and the right, a text box. Remember, a label object displays descriptive text, whereas a field object displays field data. Only the field object is needed in the Detail band for this exercise.

4 **If needed, to delete the Customer Number label object (left), click outside the objects to deselect, click only the *Customer Number* label object, and then press Delete**

5 **Move the *Customer Number* field object in the Detail band to the right of the *First* field object by dragging, and then resize it to resemble Figure DB2-10 (Remember, to resize an object, drag one of its selection handles.)**

FIGURE DB2-10 ■ INSERTING THE ID FIELD

(a) The new objects have been inserted.
(b) The sample preview of the report thus far.

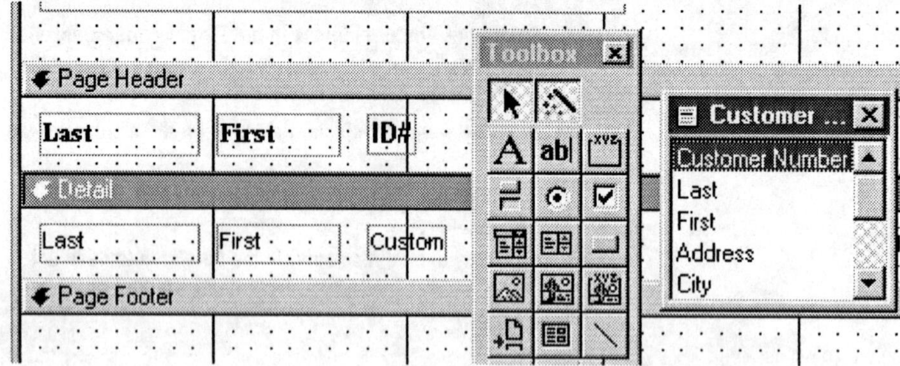

(a)

Last	First	ID	Amount
Parker	Charles	670	$450.75
Burstein	Jerome	101	$230.45
Laudon	Jane	449	$230.45

(b)

To place the label "ID#" in the Page Header band as in Figure DB2-10a,

6 **Click the *Label* button in the toolbox window (your pointer should now resemble +A)**

7 **Point the position where the top left corner of the label object should appear and then drag as needed to draw the box**

8 **Type ID# and press ↵**

9 **Click outside the selection to deselect**

Now, to preview the additional field as in Figure DB2-10,

10 **Click *File, Print Preview***

11 **Click the *Close* toolbar button and then click *File, Save***

Next, to add the City objects as in Figure DB2-11:

12 **Repeat Steps 3 through 9 to add the City objects to the report**

13 **Click *File, Print Preview***

Close

14 **Click the *Close* toolbar button**

FIGURE DB2-11 ■ ADDING THE CITY COLUMN

Objects associated with the City field have been inserted in the report.

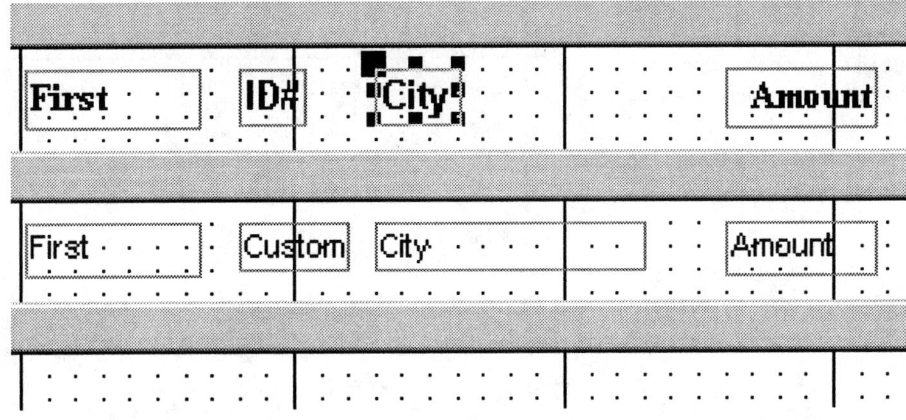

If objects are out of place, realign them or resize them. (Of course, you must consider not just the size of the data that is currently in the table but also the size of the data that *might* appear in some future version of the table.) The ultimate test of a report is the eyeball test. If the report is pleasing to the eye and the information that the user is looking for is easily and naturally found, then the report passes the test. Next,

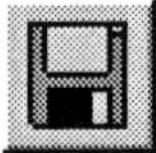

15 Click *File*, *Save* to resave [Ctrl + S]

Warning: If a column is too small to display an entire number, then Access will print a partial number, like "4.55" instead of "234.55." A poorly designed report could mislead a user. Exercise appropriate caution.

ADDING CALCULATED FIELDS AND SUMMARY OBJECTS. Columns can also contain expressions that perform calculations on numeric fields. For example, the following exercise calculates the difference between the AMOUNT and PAID fields and places the result in the last column with a heading of "Due." This is a multistep procedure.

- The City column will be deleted to make room.
- The Amount and Paid columns will be moved.
- An object will be inserted in the Detail band that describes the calculation that you want Access to make each time the report is printed (Amount – Paid).
- An appropriate column heading will be inserted.

STEPS

1 Select the City objects in the Page Header band and Detail band

2 Press Delete

FIGURE DB2-12 ■ INSERTING A CALCULATED FIELD

(a) A new object is placed in Detail band.
(b) The properties of the new object are adjusted.

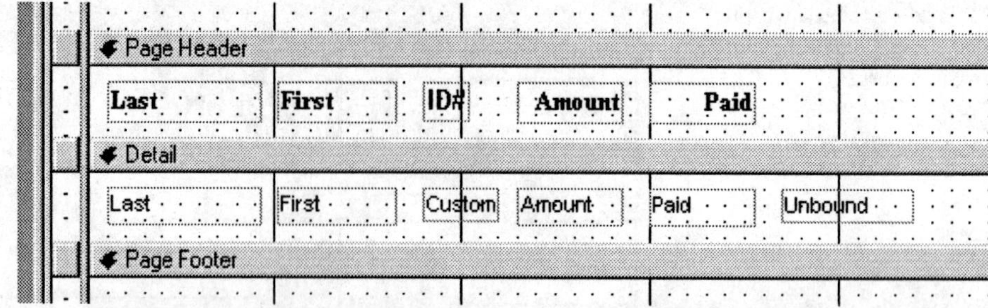

(a)

Text Box: Due

Format | Data | Event | Other | All

Name	Due
Control Source	=[Amount]-[Paid]
Format	Currency
Decimal Places	2
Input Mask	
Visible	Yes
Hide Duplicates	No
Can Grow	No
Can Shrink	No
Running Sum	No
Left	3.7"
Top	0.0833"
Width	0.7"
Height	0.1667"

(b)

(continued)

The City column should have disappeared.

3 Select the Amount and Paid objects in the Page Header and Detail bands

Using Figure DB2-12a as a guide,

4 Drag these objects leftward to make room for the new column

5 Click the *Text Box* button on the toolbox (your pointer changes to a "+abl")

6 Position the "+" portion of the pointer where the top left corner of the field object should appear and then click

FIGURE DB2-12 ■ *(continued)*

(c) A column heading is placed in the Page Header band.
(d) An object is placed in the Report Footer band.

(c)

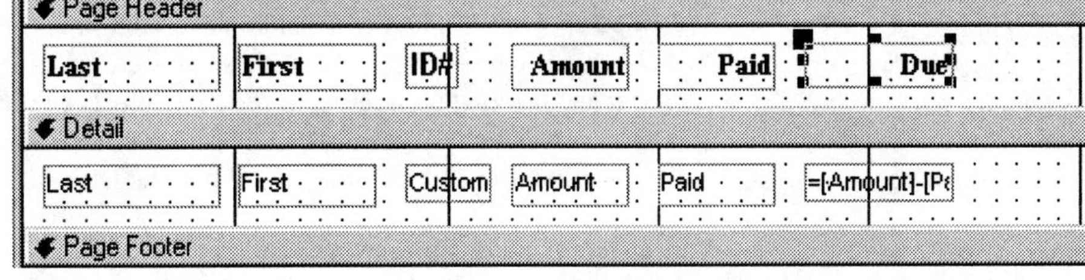

(d)

Two objects should now appear, a label object (left) displaying "Text#" and a field object displaying "Unbound" (right). Unbound simply indicates that the object is currently not associated with (bound to) any field in the table. This will be changed shortly by adjusting this new object's *properties.* An object's properties are its characteristics or behavior. Before bounding a field to this object, do the following to delete the "Text#" label object:

7 Click outside the selected objects to deselect, click only the "Text#" label object and then press Delete

8 If needed, position the "Unbound" field object as in Figure DB2-12

Now to open the field object's properties dialog box,

9 If needed, select the object by clicking it

10 Click *View, Properties* for its dialog box

Soon you will adjust this object's properties to resemble Figure DB2-12b. Note that an objects properties dialog box contains several tabs. Each tab's function is described next.

- *Format.* This group of properties controls the way the object appears on the screen or page, determining font name, font size, format, and so forth.

DB

- *Data.* This group of properties controls the data that the object displays, where the data comes from or how it is calculated, how many decimal places are displayed, and so forth.
- *Event.* These properties are used by advanced users developing more sophisticated applications that will not be covered in this text.
- *Other.* The most important of these properties is *Name,* which allows an object to be named so that it can be referred to in subsequent calculations or procedures.
- *All.* Clicking this tab causes all properties to be displayed in order of importance so that the user can scroll up and down the list adjusting any of the properties.

You can click the various tabs one by one until you understand how you can restrict the list of properties or display all properties. To change a property, point to the value and click. Then, you may have to do one of three things:

- Delete the existing value and type in the desired value.
- Click a button displaying a drop-down arrow so you can select from a list of available values.
- Click a button displaying an ellipsis (...) to display the Access *Expression Builder* dialog box, which is used to create fields that are the results of calculations.

Then, make the following changes to the properties of the new unbound object:

11 In the object's name row, type Due and press ↵

12 In the Control Source row, type =[Amount]-[Paid]

Access field names are enclosed in square brackets in expressions. This is a formula: Due=Amount-Paid. Next, indicate to Access that this value is to be displayed as currency.

13 Click the *Format* row, then click the drop-down arrow

14 Click *Currency* on the list of formats (use the scroll bar if necessary)

15 Click the decimal places row, and type 2

Your data should resemble Figure DB2-12b.

16 Close the *Properties* dialog box by clicking the *Properties* button

Next, place a label object with the caption "Due" in the Page Header band, as in Figure DB2-12c.

17 Click the *Label* button on the toolbox

18 Click the upper left corner where the label should appear in the Page Header band and type Due

19 Resize the label object and then click the *Align Right* toolbar button

Finally, it will be necessary to place an object in the Report Footer band that will sum the Amount, Paid, and Due columns. Use Figure DB2-12d as a guide for placement. Repeat steps 20 through 28 for the Amount, Paid, and Due sums.

FIGURE DB2-13 ■ LIST OF PROPERTIES FOR THE SUMMARY OBJECTS IN CUST01

Name	Control Source	Format	Decimals	Font Weight
Grand_Total_Amount	=Sum([Amount])	Currency	2	Bold
Grand_Total_Paid	=Sum([Paid])	Currency	2	Bold
Grand_Total_Due	=Sum([Amount])-Sum([Paid])	Currency	2	Bold

20 **Click the *Text Box* button on the toolbox and place an object in the Report Footer band beneath the appropriate column (Remember to delete any object to the left of the "Unbound" field object)**

Tip: If the Report Footer band is not visible on your screen, use the vertical scroll bars to scroll downward until you see it.

Adjust the properties of the new object using Figure DB2-13 as a guide.

21 **If needed, click the object to select it**

22 **Click *View, Properties***

The properties dialog box for the object is displayed. Make the following changes:

23 **Change the Amount object's name**

24 **Change the Control Source**

Next, indicate to Access that this value is to be displayed as currency.

25 **Click the *Format* row, click the drop-down arrow, then click *Currency* on the list of formats (use the scroll bar if necessary)**

26 **Click the Decimal Place row and type 2**

We want the totals to be displayed in bold type, so,

27 **Use the scroll bar to move to *Font Weight* and then click it, click the drop-down arrow, then click *Bold***

28 **Close the *Properties* dialog box by clicking the *Properties* toolbar button**

When you have inserted all three objects,

29 **Click *File, Print Preview* to check your work**

FIGURE DB2-14 ■ VIEWING THE REPORT

The print preview of the report.

Customer Report #1

Last	First	ID	Amount	Paid	Due
Parker	Charles	670	$450.75	$0.00	$450.75
Burstein	Jerome	101	$200.45	$0.00	$200.45
Laudon	Jane	449	$200.45	$0.00	$200.45
Martin	Edward	754	$200.55	$0.00	$200.55
West	Rita	178	$120.45	$0.00	$120.45
Williams	DeVille	087	$965.42	$0.00	$965.42
Hill	Karen	111	$458.78	$0.00	$458.78

At this point, no values are showing in the Paid and Due columns of the Detail band because no values have been placed in the PAID field as yet—not even zeroes—so no calculation is possible. This is easily fixed.

30 **Click the *Close* toolbar button and then the *Database Window* toolbar button**

31 **Click *Table, Customer List,* then click the *Open* button**

32 **Type 0 (zero) in the PAID field for each customer**

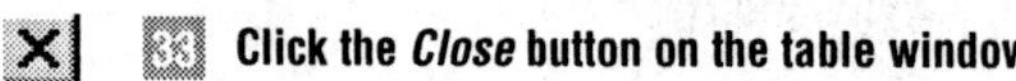

33 **Click the *Close* button on the table window**

To return to the Report Design screen,

34 **Click *Window,* then click *Customer Report1: Report***

35 **Click *File, Print Preview***

Compare the results of your efforts to Figure DB2-14. If necessary, return to the Report Design screen and adjust the location and size of objects.

Access is capable of performing calculations at print time and placing the results of those calculations in the report. In this case, Access can subtract Paid from Amount and place the result in the Due column. Then, the sum of all Paid values can be subtracted from the sum of all Amount values. This would be displayed in the Report Footer band. The following chart shows examples of formulas that might be used in calculated fields.

Examples of Calculated Fields

Column Expression	Explanation
[AMOUNT] * .08125	Multiply AMOUNT times .08 (as in calculating tax, in this case 8.125%
100 * [PAID]/[AMOUNT]	100 times PAID divided by AMOUNT—useful to calculate percentage of the full AMOUNT paid
[AMOUNT] + 2	Add 2 to AMOUNT
([AMOUNT] – [PAID]) * .1	10% of the difference between AMOUNT and PAID—useful to calculate finance charges
IF([AMOUNT] > 500, [AMOUNT] * .9, [AMOUNT])	A logical IF statement that returns two possible answers based on the truth of the first expression. In this case, if AMOUNT exceeds 500, the column will show 90% of the AMOUNT; otherwise, the full AMOUNT will be shown.

To save your work and leave the Report Design screen,

36 Click the *Close* button on the report window

When asked if you want to save changes to Customer Report #1,

37 Click *Yes*

To close the database window

38 Click the *Close* button on the database window

Access will write your changes to the disk and return to a blank desktop.

ADDING TEXT TO THE REPORT. The report now contains the data and summary fields. Access's wizard has automatically inserted the date, page number, and title. However, the report could still be improved. For this report, we will add the following:

- The report title line will be centered.
- The word "Totals:" will be placed in the report footer.

Note: The report date, page number, and title lines are placed in the *page* header or footer because we want them to print each time a *page* is printed. The word "Totals:" will be placed in the *report* footer because the totals only print once per *report*—not once per page.

Access has already inserted one object in the Page Header band: a text box with the report title in it. The first task is to center the report title. For this exercise, use Figure DB2-15a as a guide.

FIGURE DB2-15 ■ MODIFYING THE CUST01 REPORT

(a) The report title is being changed.
(b) The word "Totals:" is being inserted in the Report Footer band.
(c) This is what the modified report will look like when printed.

(a)

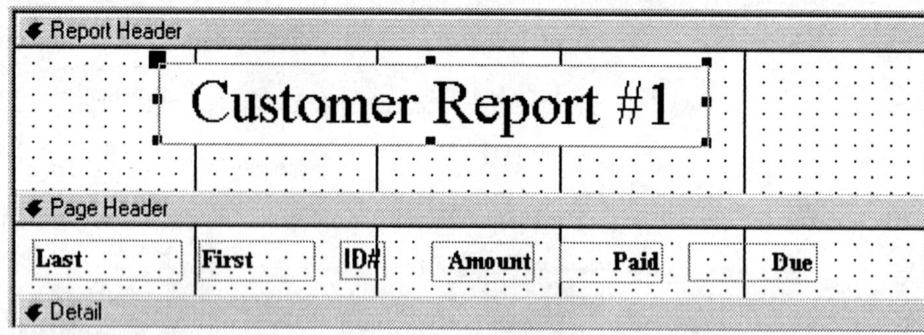

(b)

=Now()
" & Page & " Of " & Pages
Report Footer
Totals:
=Sum([Amc
=Sum([Paid
=Sum([Amour

(c)

Customer Report #1

Last	First	ID	Amount	Paid	Due
Parker	Charles	670	$450.75	$0.00	$450.75
Burstein	Jerome	101	$230.45	$0.00	$230.45
Laudon	Jane	449	$230.45	$0.00	$230.45

STEPS

1. **Open the *Customer Report #1* report in Report Design view**

2. **Click the label object containing "Customer Report #1" to select it**

> **Tip: An alternate way to get to the *Properties* dialog box of an object is to right-click the object, then select *Properties* on the menu that appears. Once the properties dialog box is displayed, you do not need to close it to view the properties of another object. Just click the other object, and the properties of that object will be displayed in the *Properties* dialog box.**

To change the Text Align property to Center,

3 Click the *Center Align* toolbar button

The report title should have centered itself when you changed the Text Align property. This causes the text that you type in the object to be centered within the boundaries *of the object,* which is not the same as being centered on the page. The *object* must be centered on the page for the text in it to be centered on the page. The next task is to drag the object containing the report title rightward until it is centered over the data.

4 If needed, click the object containing the report title to select it

Observe that the handle (little black rectangle) at the upper left corner of the object is larger than the other handles. The larger handle is called the *move* handle. The other handles are *sizing* handles. One easy way to change the position of a selected object is to position the mouse pointer over the move handle. The pointer will change shape to that of a hand with extended forefinger. If you press the left mouse button and hold it down while you move the mouse, the object will move on the design screen. This process is called *drag and drop.*

5 Drag and drop the report title object to a position that is centered over the data

Finally, insert an object that will contain the word "Totals:" to the left of the totals on the report. Again, use Figure DB2-15b as a guide:

6 Use the scroll bar to adjust the display of the Report Footer band as in Figure DB2-15b

7 Click the *Label* button on the toolbox

8 To place an object in the Report Footer band, click the desired position in the band

9 Type Totals: and press ↵

10 If needed, click the *Bold* (B) toolbar button

Check your work thus far:

11 Click *File, Print Preview*

If the objects are not properly aligned, return to the Design screen and make adjustments.

The report would be more attractive if the title lines were boxed.

12 Click the *Close* toolbar button to return to the Report Design view

13 Click the object containing the report title to select it

14 Click *View, Properties*

15 Change the Border Style property to *Solid* and the Border Width property to *2 pt*

This means a width of two points. *Points* are a measure of line thickness. One point is equal to 1/72″, so 2 points would indicate a thickness of 1/36″. The larger the number of points, the thicker the line. This will place a box around the object at the object's boundary lines. Access offers a variety line widths and styles. You may wish to experiment with them.

15 Click *File, Print Preview*

Compare your results to Figure DB2-15c. Make adjustments if necessary. Then, when you are satisfied with the report, save the work you have done:

16 Click the *Close* toolbar button

When asked if you want to save changes to the report,

17 Click *Yes*

If your report needs some final touches, you can move or resize objects. Don't forget to save any final changes you make in the report design.

18 Close all windows in the work area

USING A REPORT FORM

Reports can be generated on screen or in print. To generate the report,

STEPS

1 Open the Customer database window

2 Click the *Report* tab

3 Click *Customer Report #1*

4 Click the *Preview* button

Access displays the report on the screen. Then, if you want a hard copy,

5 Click the *Print* button on the toolbar to print the report

> **Tip: If you are sending a report to the printer, be sure to verify that the printer is on, online, and filled with paper. If something is wrong with your printer, then Window's *Printers* folder will superimpose itself over Access with an error message. Take whatever corrective action is appropriate, then click *Retry* on the *Printers* folder dialog box.**

When you preview the report, the records from the CUSTOMER table are incorporated into the report form. Note, too, that Access automatically inserts the current date and correct totals.

Of course, most reports will be longer than can be displayed on the screen at one time. When you generate a screen report in Access, you are provided with new buttons on the toolbar which allow you to move freely throughout the report and examine all of its pages. Those buttons are reproduced in Figure DB2-16. These buttons, in order, move to

- The first page

- The previous page
- The next page
- The last page

Also, you can place a text insertion point in the text box where the page number is located, backspace over the number, and type a new value. Access will advance to that page.

Notice also that the Preview Screen toolbar contains a *Print* button that sends the report immediately to the printer without having to return to the database window or the Report Design screen. Clicking this button causes the entire report to be sent to the printer immediately. If you click *File, Print,* the *Print* dialog box appears for you to indicate which pages you want printed, how many copies you want, and so on.

If you sent the report directly to the printer, you will be returned to the blank desktop after the report has been sent to the Windows print queue (even if the printer is still printing).

If you are viewing the report on screen, you will need to close Customer Report #1 to return to a blank desktop.

6 **Click the *Close* toolbar button on the Preview screen**

7 **Close the database window**

REPORTS WITH QUERIES. At times, you will want to prepare reports that include only a specific portion of your table records. You can do this by first preparing a query to select records and then using its answering dynaset in the report. For example, the following exercise restricts Customer Report #1 (CUST01) to those customers whose amounts exceed $400.

STEPS

1 **Open the Customer database window if necessary**

2 **Click the *Query* tab**

3 **Click *New***

A dialog box asks if you want to use the Query wizards. This query is easily done without the wizards.

4 **Click *OK***

Access asks what table you wish to add; that is, from which table will data be drawn. Previously, this step had been unnecessary because the query was designed for the table that was open at the time.

DB

FIGURE DB2-16 ■ REPORT PREVIEW SCROLL BUTTONS

These buttons move, in order from left to right, to first page, previous page, next page, and last page.

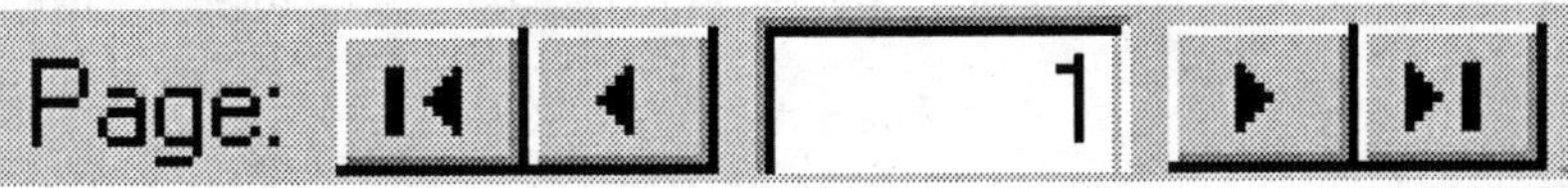

5 **Click *Customer List*, click *Add*, then click *Close***

First, using Figure DB2-17a as a guide, create the query as you have learned:

6 **Drag and drop the following fields to the field name boxes: LAST, FIRST, CUSTOMER NUMBER, AMOUNT, and PAID**

FIGURE DB2-17 ■ PRINTING A REPORT FROM A QUERY

(a) Create a Select Query that asks for records with Amounts greater than $400. You need only include the fields that are needed in the report.
(b) The dynaset that results from the query.
(c) The Cust01 report displaying data from Amounts >400.

(a)

Query1 : Select Query

Customer List: City, State, Zip, Amount, Paid

Field:	Last	First	Customer Number	Amount	Paid
Table:	Customer List	Customer List	Customer List	Customer List	Customer List
Sort:					
Show:	☑	☑	☑	☑	☑
Criteria:				>400	
or:					

(b)

Query1 : Select Query

Last	First	Custo	Amount	Paid
Parker	Charles	670	$450.75	$0.00
Williams	DeVilla	067	$965.42	$0.00
Hill	Karen	111	$456.78	$0.00
			$0.00	$0.00

(c)

Customer Report #1

Last	First	ID	Amount	Paid	Due
Parker	Charles	670	$450.75	$0.00	$450.75
Williams	DeVilla	067	$965.42	$0.00	$965.42
Hill	Karen	111	$456.78	$0.00	$456.78
		Totals:	$1,872.95	$0.00	$1,872.95

Of course, the answer table must contain all the fields that the CUST01 report needs: LAST, FIRST, AMOUNT, and PAID. (Remember, "DUE" is calculated at the time the report is generated. It is not part of the table's data.)

7 Type >400 in the Criteria row of the Amount column

8 Click the *Run* button

This query creates a temporary table (dynaset) on your screen, which should look like Figure DB2-17b. This query needs to be saved to the disk so that a report can be generated from it.

9 Click the *Close* button

When Access asks if you want to save changes to the query,

10 Click *Yes*

When Access asks for a name for the query,

11 Type Amounts > 400 and click *OK*

Remember, this is not a filename. It is an Access object that will become a part of the CUSTOMER database file. Now that the query has been saved that can generate the desired data, the report can, in turn, be generated from it. When you saved the query, Access should have returned you to the database window.

12 Click the *Report* tab

13 Click *Customer Report #1*, then click the *Design* button

The Report Design screen containing Customer Report #1 appears. If the report were printed now, it would draw data from the CUSTOMER LIST table as you designed it to do. To attach it, instead, to the Amount > 400 query, do the following:

14 Right-click the gray area beneath the report footer

15 Click *Properties* on the resulting menu

You will see a list of the report's properties looking like Figure DB2-17b. The pertinent choice here is *Record Source*. This is the property that determines where the report will get its data.

16 Click *Record Source*, then click the drop-down arrow that appears

17 Click *Amounts > 400*

18 Click the *Properties* button

The window closes. The report is now attached to the Amounts > 400 query instead of the CUSTOMER LIST table.

19 Click *File*, *Print Preview*

Your results should resemble Figure DB2-17c.

> **Tip: It is a good practice to examine report results on the screen first, to avoid the possible waste of time and paper. Check to see that the layout and contents appear as expected.**

Note that there are only three records and that all of them have Amounts in excess of $400. Send the report to your printer next:

20 Select the *Print* button on the toolbar

Once the report has printed,

21 Close all windows in the Access work area without saving

By not saving, the changes remain attached to CUSTOMER LIST.

MODIFYING A REPORT FORM

As you have seen, report forms are as flexible as table structures—they can be modified to change existing settings, add new columns, or delete old ones.

COPYING A REPORT FORM. Although you can modify a report form directly when you need to correct errors, sometimes you will want to create a modified version of the original report. In this case, you can copy the report form into a new file and then modify the new report. This leaves the original report form intact for future use. This exercise demonstrates the procedure by copying the CUST01 report into CUST02. Use this technique whenever you want to copy a report form before modification. From a blank desktop,

STEPS

1 Open the Customer database window

2 Click the *Report* tab

3 Click *Customer Report #1*, if necessary

4 Click *Edit*, *Copy* [Ctrl + C]

This indicates that you wish to copy the selected object.

5 Click *Edit*, *Paste* [Ctrl + V]

This indicates that you wish to insert a duplicate of the object at the current location, namely the Customer database window. You will see a Paste as dialog box.

6 **Type Customer Report #2 and click *OK***

The report form has been copied from Customer Report #1 into Customer Report #2 and is now available for use. You should see the name Customer Report #2 on the database window immediately.

CHANGING THE REPORT. Access allows you to open a report form to alter its contents, as you have seen. A report form can be redesigned from the same screens used to design it in the first place. The process of modifying a report is very similar to the process of designing one: inserting new objects, deleting existing objects, repositioning objects, and changing the properties of objects. The following exercises review some techniques you have learned and examine a few additional illustrative procedures. To start the process,

STEPS

1 **Open the Customer database window if necessary**

2 **Click the *Report* tab, click *Customer Report #2,* and click the *Design* button**

The Report Design screen appears. As you can see, Customer Report #2 is a faithful copy of Customer Report #1. You can now alter the design of Customer Report #2, making whatever modifications you wish and saving them. The original report, Customer Report #1, was unchanged by the copy process.

Tip: Another easy way to copy the report into the same or another database file is to use the File, Save As command from the Report Design screen. For example, the Customer Report #2 report could now be saved as Customer Report #3, and it could be saved into the CUSTOMER database or another database.

CHANGING PAGE DATA. Practice changing the report title and left margin. First, change the title line of the report from "Customer Report #1" to "Customer Report #2."

STEPS

1 **Click the label object containing the title "Customer Report #1"**

2 **Place the text insertion point in the object by clicking it while it is selected**

3 **Retype #1 as #2 and press ↵**

The margin for the report is set at 1 inch. If it were changed to 1.5 inches, the report would be more attractively centered on the page.

4 **Click *File, Page Setup***

The *Page Setup* dialog box appears (see Figure DB2-18). There are many page settings that can be changed from this dialog box. Notice the four margin settings (Left, Right, Top, and Bottom) in this dialog box.

FIGURE DB2-18 ■ THE *PRINT SETUP* DIALOG BOX

Margins can be changed from this dialog box.

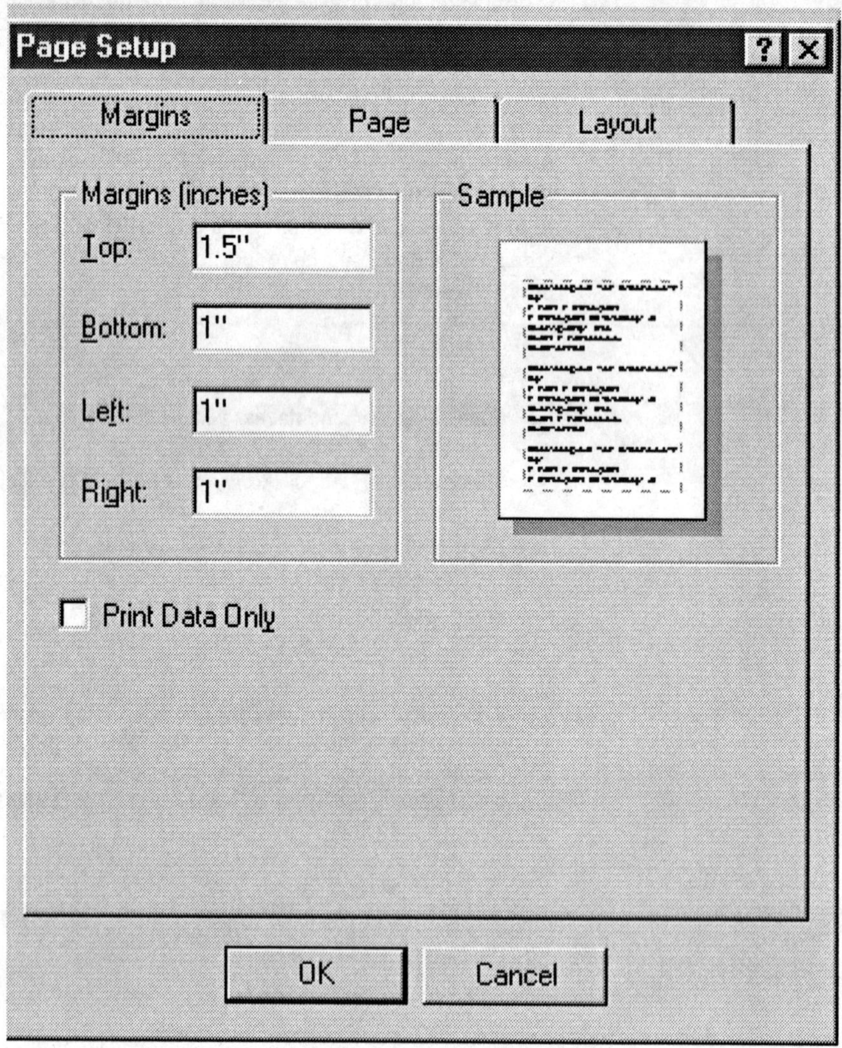

5 **Place the text insertion point in the Left margin area by clicking it**

6 **Change 1.0 to 2.0**

7 **Click *OK***

The change is not immediately apparent. The horizontal ruler on the Report Design screen measures the distance *from the margin,* wherever it is set. To see the effects of this change,

8 **Click *File, Print Preview***

After you have examined the report on the screen (you will probably have to use the horizontal scroll bars to see all of the report as it should extend beyond the right edge of your screen), you will want to be sure to save your work.

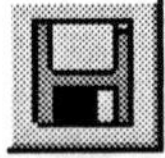

9 Click *File, Save* **[Ctrl + S]**

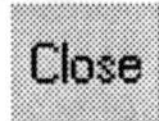

10 Click the *Close* toolbar button

DELETING COLUMNS. As you have seen earlier, columns can be removed by selecting the objects involved and pressing Delete. The next exercise will again delete the Customer Number column so that different data can be place in that position.

STEPS

1 Select the *ID #* object in the Page Header band and the *Customer Number* object in the Detail band

2 Press Delete

The objects should disappear.

INSERTING COLUMNS. Columns can also be inserted by creating objects for column headings, field objects, and summary objects (if desired) and placing them in the proper alignment.

STEPS

1 Display the toolbox and Field list if necessary

2 Click the *Label* button on the toolbox

Using Figure DB2-19a as a guide (note that the title in the Report Header band and the City Header band will be adjusted later):

3 Draw a rectangle in the Page Header band and type Zip

4 Click the ZIP field on the Field list window (use the scrollbar, if needed)

5 Drag the ZIP field to a position in the Detail band under the Zip Code column heading

6 Delete the Zip label object and then resize the ZIP field object as in Figure DB2-19a

7 Click *File, Print Preview*

8 Click the *Close* toolbar button

DB

FIGURE DB2-19 ■ INSERTING COLUMNS

(a) The City name will be printed in the City Header band, and summary objects have been placed in the City Footer band.
(b) The print preview of the report grouped by city.

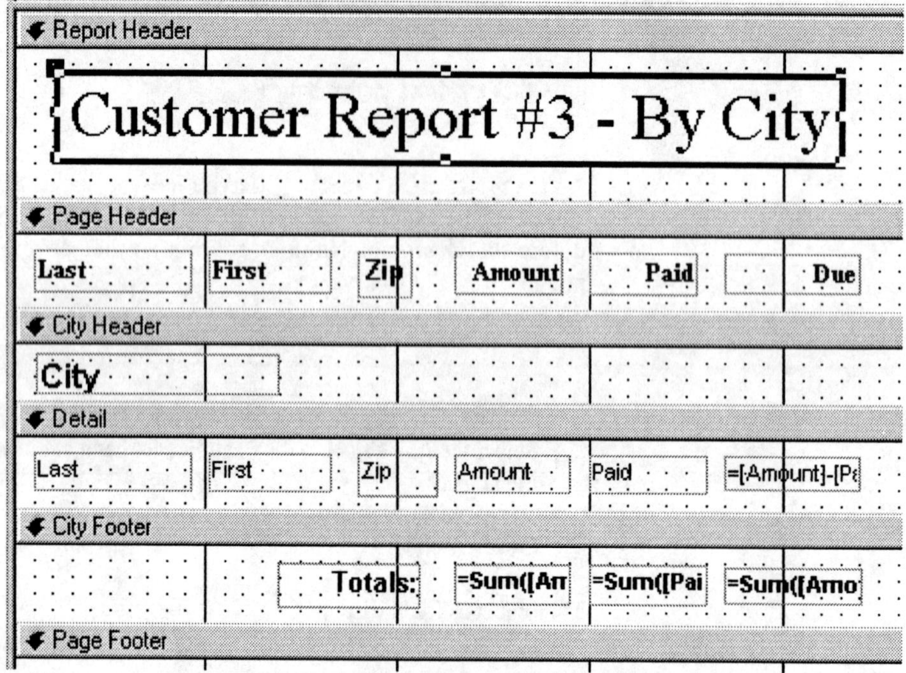

(a)

Customer Report #3 - By City

Last	First	Zip	Amount	Paid	Due
Chicago					
Hill	Karen	60605	$456.78	$0.00	$456.78
Williams	DeVilla	60601	$965.42	$0.00	$965.42
West	Rita	60601	$123.45	$0.00	$123.45
		Totals:	**$1,545.65**	**$0.00**	**$1,545.65**
New York					
Martin	Edward	10001	$230.55	$0.00	$230.55
Laudon	Jane	10003	$230.45	$0.00	$230.45

(b)

REMOVING SUMMARY OBJECTS. If you no longer want to display summary statistics for specified columns (such as Amount or Paid), simply delete those objects as follows:

STEPS

1 Select all the objects in the Report Summary band

This includes the object containing the word "Totals" and the three objects that sum the Amount, Paid, and Due columns. Remember, to select multiple objects, use shift-click until they are all selected. When all the objects have been selected,

2 Press Delete

RESAVING THE REPORT. When you've made all your changes, you can save the modified report form:

STEPS

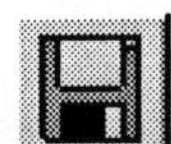

1 Click *File, Save* [Ctrl + S]

2 Close all windows in the Access work area

FIGURE DB2-20 ■ REMOVING SUMMARY OBJECTS

ADVANCED REPORTS

Reports need not merely provide lists of records. Records can also be grouped with subtotals automatically generated by the Access. The following exercise demonstrates how to modify your report to regroup and subtotal your report by one field. To prepare for this exercise,

STEPS

1. **Launch Access if necessary**
2. **Open the Customer database window**
3. **Click the *Report* tab**
4. **Copy report *Customer Report #2* to *Customer Report #3* (Hint: Use the *Copy* and *Paste* buttons)**
5. **Click *Customer Report #3* and click the *Design* button**
6. **Change the title line to read "Customer Report #3—By City"**
7. **Deselect the title**

GROUP REPORTS. A table can be rearranged in a report by one or more fields so that records that contain the same data (in that field) can be displayed as a group. These groups can then be subtotaled separately. This example will group and total all customers in the CITY field. (Of course, you could group by any field you wanted.)

STEPS

1. **Click the *Sorting and Grouping* button**

The *Sorting and Grouping* dialog box (see Figure DB2-21) appears, providing an opportunity to indicate by which field the report is to be grouped.

2. **Click the first row of the Field column**
3. **Click the drop-down arrow and click *City***

The default **sort direction** is ascending, which is what you want.

4. **Click the *Group Header* property row, click the resulting drop-down arrow, and click *Yes***
5. **Click the *Group Footer* property row, click the resulting drop-down arrow, and click *Yes***
6. **Click the *Close* button in the *Sorting and Grouping* dialog box**

The dialog box closes. The Report Design screen reappears, but new bands have been inserted in the report. The effects of the changes you made in this dialog box on the performance of the CUST03 report are as follows:

FIGURE DB2-21 ■ GROUPING THE REPORT'S OUTPUT

Indicate that City is the field to be used for grouping.

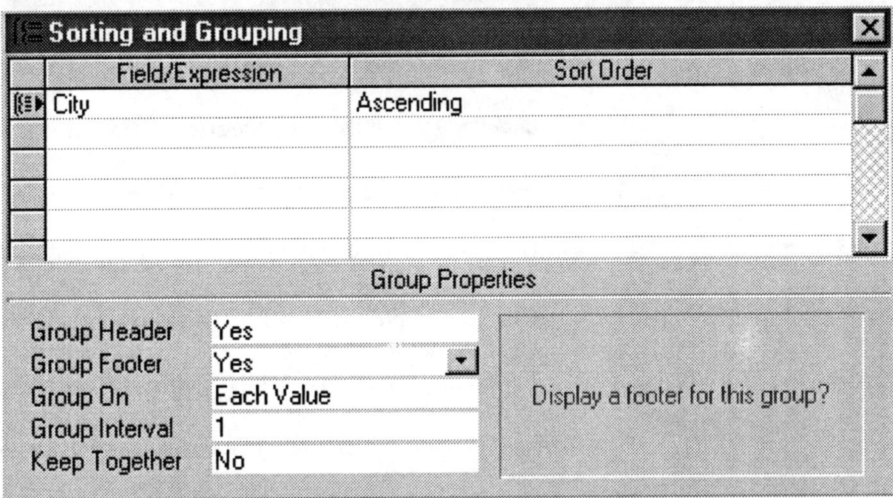

- Records will be printed in city order in the Detail band.
- Objects in the City Header band will print whenever a new City value is encountered.
- Objects in the City Footer band will print whenever all the records for a particular City value have been printed.

You may need to use the scroll bars to view the City Footer band. You are going to insert several objects in these bands:

- A field object, which displays the name of the city in the City Header band.
- Summary objects, which sum Amount, Paid, and Total for each city in the City Footer band.

7 Display the Field list, if necessary

8 Drag and drop *City* to the City Header band as in Figure DB2-19a (Delete the City label object, leaving only the City field object.)

9 Display the *Properties* dialog box for the new object

10 Change the font size to *12*

11 Change the font weight to *Bold*

12 Close the *Properties* dialog box

13 Display the toolbox if necessary

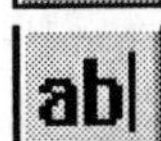

14 Click the Text box button on the toolbox and click in the City Footer band beneath the Due column (Delete the "Text #" label object.)

DB

Tip: If you inadvertently place an object in the wrong band, you can solve your problem by selecting it and pressing Delete.

An *unbound* object is displayed. As you recall, this is an empty object which has no assigned purpose. To make the box display totals, you must change its properties.

15 Click the *Unbound* field object to select it and then click *View, Properties*

Remember, to change properties on the properties dialog box,

- Use the scroll bars, if necessary, to bring the property into view.
- Click the property you want to modify.
- Click the drop-down arrow that appears.
- Click the setting that you desire.
- Repeat the process until all the pertinent properties have been adjusted.

Control Source is the property that determines where the data comes from that will be displayed in the box.

16 Click *Control Source* and type =Sum([Amount]) – Sum([Paid])

This formula means "Subtract the sum of the PAID field from the sum of the AMOUNT field." Because this object is in the CITY FOOTER field, its value will be zeroed out each time a new city is encountered in the data. Remember that the field names are enclosed in square brackets [fieldname].

17 Change format to *Currency*

18 Change font weight to *Bold* and leave the Properties dialog box open

19 Click the *Text Box* button on the toolbox and draw a rectangle in the City Footer band beneath the Paid column (Again, remember to delete the "Text #" label object)

Note that the *Properties* dialog box did not disappear. It is now displaying the properties of the selected object, which is the unbound text box you just drew.

20 Click *Control Source* and type =Sum([Paid])

21 Change format to *Currency*

22 Change font weight to *Bold*

23 Click the *Text Box* button on the toolbox and draw a rectangle in the City Footer band beneath the Amount column (Delete the "Text #" label object)

24 Click *Control Source* and type =Sum([Amount])

25 Change format to *Currency*

26 Change font weight to *Bold*, and then close the Properties dialog box

27 Click the *Label* button on the toolbox and draw a rectangle in the City Footer band to the left of the summary objects

28 Type Totals: and press ↵

29 If needed, click the *Align Right* toolbar button

Your screen should resemble Figure DB2-19a.

30 Click *File, Print Preview*

Don't forget to save your work:

31 Click the *Close* toolbar button

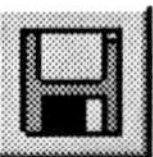

32 Click *File, Save* **[Ctrl + S]**

> **Tip: If an undesired amount of blank space appears in the report in the City Header or City Footer, remove it by moving the group band's boundary using drag and drop. A group band can be made wider or narrower.**

You may want to generate this report on your printer. You may also want to display a subset of the records—for example, records whose city starts with any letter from A to R (before the letter S). To do this, you could use the query technique you examined earlier (set City column criteria to < S..) to limit the number of records that appear in the report.

33 Close all windows in the Access work area

CHECKPOINT

- ✓ In the DBTEST table, create a report called DBRPT1 that shows Name, Test1, Test2, and Test3 with no totals.
- ✓ Modify the report form to delete Test3 and add a column named "Average" calculated as =([Test1] + [Test2])/2.
- ✓ Reinsert Test3
- ✓ Change the Average column so that it calculates the average of all three exams.
- ✓ Print the report.

MODIFYING RECORD CONTENT

Modifying (changing) record data is the primary way to keep a table current. The changes may be necessary for a number of reasons. Data originally typed into a field may be incorrect, or conditions may have changed since they were entered—perhaps a customer moved or made a new payment. New fields may have been created in the table that now require data entry. Whatever the reason, editing allows you to change the field values contained in any record.

The first step in editing data is locating the record you want to modify. You can do this directly in a table or record form screen by moving the cursor to the desired record (the Down and Up arrow keys in a table form or the scroll buttons in a record form) or by conducting a record search to locate a particular record.

LOCATING RECORDS

If you plan to *edit*—that is, change field values in—most of your records, it is probably easiest to position Access's record counter at the top of the file and then move the pointer sequentially through each record (either in table or record form). However, if you want to edit a particular record (or group of records), then you should position the pointer at the desired record (or first one in the group). This eliminates the need to move through other records in order to find the one you need, which is important in large tables. The following exercise demonstrates the major techniques used to reposition the record pointer to locate records. To prepare for the exercise,

STEPS

1. **Launch Access**
2. **Open the Customer database window**
3. **Open the CUSTOMER LIST table**

Next, sort the CUSTOMER LIST table into Last and First name order.

4. **Select the Last and First columns (Remember to click the Last column selector and shift + click the First column)**

5. **Click *Records, Sort, Ascending***
6. **Click *File, Save***

The table should be arranged as expected. Although you can use these techniques in either table or record form, it is easier to conduct searches in the table format and then switch to record form if desired for actual editing.

BY ARROW KEYS. The easiest way to locate a record in a small table is to press the Down or Up arrow keys to move the cursor to the desired row. In single record format, use the scroll buttons to move from page to page.

BY RECORD NUMBER. In a larger table, it may be easier to reposition the pointer directly at a specific record by referring to its record number. To position the cursor in record #6 of the CUSTOMER LIST table,

STEPS

1. **Click the Record text box at the bottom of the Customer List window containing the record number**

2 **Delete the default record number**

3 **Type 6 and press ↵**

BY CONDITION. Access can also position the record pointer at the first record that meets a specified condition. The condition is expressed as it is in queries. For example, the next exercise positions the pointer at the first record whose CITY field is "Chicago." First, it is helpful if the cursor is located in the City column:

STEPS

1 **Select any value in the City column**

2 **Click the *Edit, Find* button** [Ctrl + F]

You will see the *Find* dialog box. Fill it out as you see in Figure DB2-22.

3 **Click the *Find What* box to place the insertion point there, and then type Chicago**

Access knows that you want to search through the CITY field because a value in that field had been selected.

4 **Click the *Find First* button**

Access highlights the first occurrence of the value "Chicago" in the CITY field.

FIGURE DB2-22 ■ THE *FIND* DIALOG BOX

Finding records with the value "Chicago" in the City field.

Custo	Last	First	Address	City	State	Zip	Amount	Paid	Form
101	Burstein	Jerome		San Jose	CA	95120	$230.45	$0.00	
111	Hill	Karen		Chicago	IL	60605	$456.78	$0.00	
449	Laudon	Jane		New York	NY	10003	$230.45	$0.00	
754	Martin	Edward		New York	NY	10001	$230.55	$0.00	
670	Parker	Charles		Santa Fe	NM	87501	$450.75	$0.00	
176	West	Rita		Chicago	IL	60601	$123.45	$0.00	
067	Williams	DeVilla		Chicago	IL	60601	$965.42	$0.00	
							$0.00	$0.00	

Find in field: 'City'

Find What: Chicago

Search: All

Match: Whole Field

Match Case

Search Fields as Formatted

Search Only Current Field

Find First

Find Next

Close

DB

5 Click the *Find Next* button

Access highlights the next occurrence of the value "Chicago" in the CITY field.

You can continue to select the *Find Next* button and Access will continue to locate succeeding occurrences of the same value until no more remain.

6 Click the *Close* button on the *Find* dialog box

Of course, any *conditional* expression can be typed as the search criterion, even ranges or pattern searches. Now, try these:

- Find the first record whose last name starts with "W."
- Find the first record whose zip code is 10003.
- Find the first record whose state is IL.

USING FILTERS

Access has the capability of suppressing the display of all records except those you want to see. Suppose, as you did in the previous exercise, you are interested in customers who live in Chicago. You can instruct Access to display only those records in which the State value is "IL" by using Access's filtering feature.

STEPS

1 If needed, open the Customer table

Next, indicate any cell containing the value that you want to filter by.

2 Click (or tab to) the State value in West's record

3 Click *Records*, then *Filter*, then *Filter by Selection*

Access displays only those records whose State value is identical to the value that was selected when the filter command was executed. You should see a table containing only those three records—West, Williams, and Hill—in which "IL" is the value in the STATE field. Records can be edited, deleted, or printed using the methods you have already learned, but only those records that pass the test imposed by the filter will be displayed on the screen or printer. The filter remains in effect until you cancel it by clicking the *Apply Filter* button to deselect it.

4 Click *Records*, and then click *Remove Filter/Sort*

All seven records are again displayed. Access remembers the last filter that you used, and it can be applied again at any time. To reimpose the same filter condition as before,

5 Click *Records*, then click *Apply Filter/Sort*

As before, you see the filtered table using the same condition (STATE=IL). To print the filtered table,

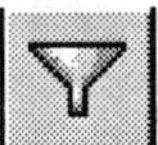

6 Click *File, Print, OK* button

Then, remove the filter:

7 Click the *Apply Filter* button or *Records, Remove Filter/Sort*

Remember, the *Apply Filter* button acts as a toggle. If a filter is active, clicking this button again will deactivate the filter.

More complicated filters are also possible. Suppose you wanted to view only those records whose zip begins with "1" (like Laudon and Martin) or "6" (like Hill, West, and Williams). This will require more than simply pointing to the value you want to use as a filter condition. To accomplish this,

8 Click *Records*, then *Filter*, then *Filter by Form*

Access will display a blank table in which you can enter sample values for the records you want to see, edit, or print. Refer to Figure DB2-23a for Steps 9 and 10.

9 Place the text insertion point anywhere in the Zip column by clicking it

10 Type 1*

The asterisk (*) is a wildcard character. You are asking to see records in which the Zip field contains a value beginning with "1" followed by any other characters.

11 Click the *Or* tab at the bottom of the window

You are presented with another blank table in which you can type *the other value* you are looking for. As you see in Figure DB2-23b,

FIGURE DB2-23 ■ USING FILTERS

(a) Searching for zips beginning with the number "1" . . .
(b) . . . or the number "6."

(a)

Customer List: Filter by Form

First	Address	City	State	Zip
				1*

Look for | Or

(b)

Customer List: Filter by Form

First	Address	City	State	Zip
				6*

Look for | Or | Or

DB

12 Place the text insertion point in the Zip column by clicking it

13 Type 6*

Again, by using the wildcard character, you are asking for values that begin with "6" followed by any other characters. To apply the filter,

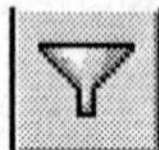

14 Click the *Apply Filter* button or *Filter, Apply Filter/Sort*

You should see a table containing those records beginning with "1" or "6". To remove the filter,

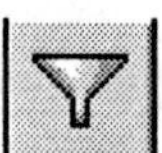

15 Click the *Apply Filter* button or *Records, Remove Filter/Sort*

Filters can be designed and applied to screen forms using the same techniques. Words or parts of words can also be used in a filter's criteria.

EDITING RECORDS

Once you position the pointer at a particular record, you can **edit** (modify) or view (simply look at) its data. This can be done with individual records, using the single-record format, or within the table format screen. The following exercises examine both techniques. To prepare,

STEPS

1 Launch Access and open the Customer database window

2 Open and display the CUSTOMER LIST table

3 Position the insertion point at the first record of the table

Figure DB2-24 contains a list of edits that you will make in the existing records. Use this figure as a guide in completing the exercises.

FIGURE DB2-24 ■ EDIT LIST

Last Name	Address	Paid
Burstein	100 N. 1st Street	100.00
Hill	1500 Michigan Avenue	456.78
Laudon	500 Fifth Avenue	0.00
Martin	50 Carmine Street	130.55
Parker	25 Cerillos Road	200.00
West	75 N. Wacker Drive	0.00
Williams	One Dryden Way	500.00

EDITING IN A RECORD FORM. The record form provides a full-screen editor that allows you to modify record contents. Once you locate a desired record, you can select the *AutoForm* button to switch to the record form edit screen.

STEPS

1 Click the *New Object* drop-down button, *AutoForm*, and then *Yes* (if needed)

Because the record pointer is positioned at the first record in the table (which has been sorted by name), the first customer in alphabetical order—Burstein—appears. You can now move freely to any field to enter *new* data or insert, delete, or type over *existing* data. The easiest ways to move from field to field are as follows:

- Press Tab to move right (or down).
- Press Shift + Tab to move left (or up).
- Click the desired field with the mouse.

Remember, if the entire field is highlighted, anything you type will replace the highlighted data. If you wish to insert or delete characters, press F2 to enter the edit mode.

The easiest ways to move from record to record are as follows:

- Click the scroll buttons at the bottom of the form.
- Press Ctrl + Pg Up to move to the previous record.
- Press Ctrl + Pg Dn to move to the next record.

2 Move the insertion point to the ADDRESS field

3 Type 100 N. 1st Street

4 Move to the PAID field

5 Type 100

6 Press Page Down to advance to the next record

Complete the following steps.

7 Enter ADDRESS and PAID data for Hill

8 Advance to the appropriate records, then enter ADDRESS and PAID data for Laudon, Martin, and Parker

Once the Parker data has been entered, exit from the screen form:

9 Click *View*, then click *Datasheet*

When the window containing the record form closes, the table form is visible again.

EDITING IN A TABLE FORM. Records can also be edited directly in the table screen. The following exercise completes the editing process for the last two records.

STEPS

1. **Move the insertion point to West's ADDRESS field**
2. **Type 75 N. Wacker Drive**

Because West has made no payment, you need not enter a value in the PAID field for West.

3. **Press the Down arrow key to move to the next record**
4. **Type One Dryden Way**
5. **Press ↵ five times to move to the Williams PAID field**
6. **Type 500**

To close the table form window,

7. **Click the *Close* button**

When Access asks you whether you want to save the form,

8. **Click *No***
9. **Close all windows in the Access work area**

LOCATING AND EDITING A RECORD. Assume that Rita West has moved. You can use any locating technique to position the pointer at her record and then edit it directly. (You'll try this one in Record Form mode.) For example,

STEPS

1. **Open the CUSTOMER LIST table**
2. **Click the *New Object* drop-down button and then *AutoForm***
3. **Position the text insertion point in the LAST field**

4. **Click *Edit, Find***  [Ctrl + F]

The *Find* dialog box appears. Using Figure DB2-25 as a model, complete the dialog box:

5. **Type West as the value, click the *Find First* button, and then click the *Close* button of the dialog box**

The West record appears.

6. **Move to the ADDRESS field**
7. **Type 908 N. Elm**

FIGURE DB2-25 ■ FINDING A RECORD IN A FORM

The West record has been found and can be edited in *Form* view.

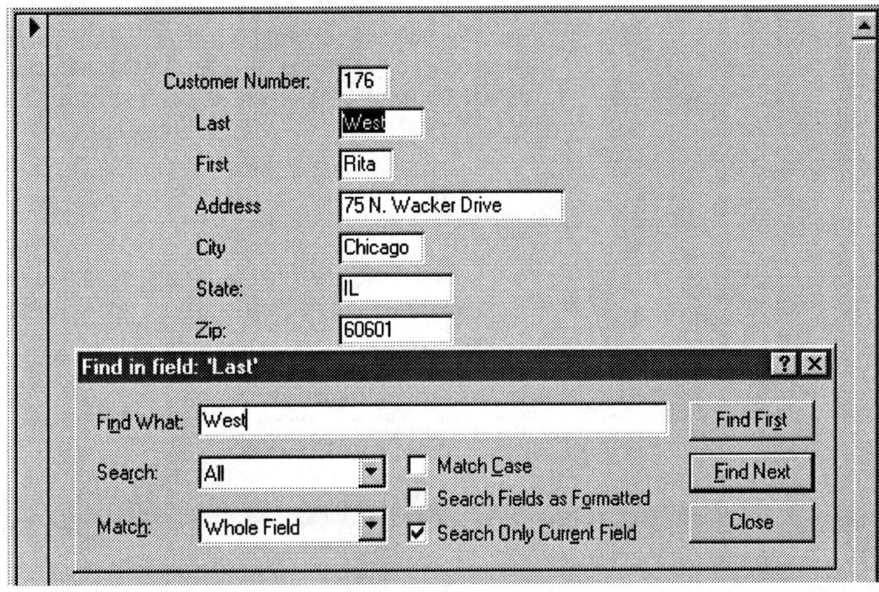

8 **Move to the CITY field and type Hinsdale**

9 **Move to the ZIP field**

10 **Type 60521**

The previous value of the ZIP field was "60601." Now it is "60521." Next,

11 **Click the *Close* button of the Autoform window and then *No***

12 **Close all windows in the Access work area**

CHECKPOINT

- ✓ Open the Library table in the Books database.
- ✓ Assume that you have renewed the books in Records 2 and 5 for an additional two weeks. Change the Due Date fields accordingly.
- ✓ Display the current record in a form.
- ✓ Scroll to Record #1. Change the due date in this record to show a one-week extension.
- ✓ Return to datasheet view and confirm that the change is visible.

CHANGING DATA WITH QUERIES

Editing is fine for individual record changes, but it can be tedious when performing the same update on many records. For example, perhaps you want to change all zip codes that start with 100 to 113, or add $20 to all AMOUNT fields. You can use an Update Query screen to alter data in specified fields in the table.

Warning: Altering data in a group of records is a potentially hazardous technique, for one mistake can inadvertently change *thousands* of records! It is advisable to create a backup (copy) of your table for safekeeping before attempting Update queries.

MODIFYING DATA IN ALL RECORDS.

This first exercise appends the characters "0000" to the end of each current zip code. But first, heeding the previous warning, make a backup copy of the CUSTOMER LIST table.

STEPS

1 Open the Customer database window

2 Click *Table,* if necessary, and select *Customer List*

3 Click *Edit, Copy* [Ctrl + C]

4 Click *Edit, Paste* [Ctrl + V]

When asked to name the new table,

5 Type Customer Backup and Click *OK*

Access has made a copy of CUSTOMER LIST so that if an error is made in the next procedure, you could copy from CUSTOMER BACKUP to CUSTOMER LIST and be back where you started from.

Next, it will be necessary to change the size of the ZIP field so it can hold the additional characters. We can also use this opportunity to delete the FORM field, which will not be used in future exercises.

6 Click *Customer List,* then click the *Design* button

The Table Design screen appears.

7 Move to the FORM field, and then click its row selector

The entire row becomes highlighted

8 Press Delete

The FORM field disappears from the table's design screen. Access warns you that data in that field will be lost. No data is present in that field anyway, so

9 Click *Yes*

10 Place the insertion point anywhere in the Zip row

The properties for the field appear at the bottom of the screen.

11 Place the insertion point in the Field Size property and change it to 10

Compare your screen to Figure DB2-26a, then save the changes you have made to the table's structure:

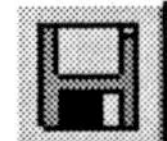

12 Click *File, Save* [Ctrl + S]

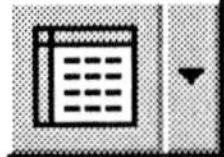

13 Click *View, Datasheet*

The table appears. Use Figure DB2-26b as a guide for the next part of this exercise.

14 Click the New Object drop-down button for its list

On the next dialog box,

15 Click *New Query,* then click *OK*

The Select Query Design screen appears. The type of query that changes the values in fields is the Update *query.*

FIGURE DB2-26 ■ USING A QUERY TO CHANGE FIELD VALUES

The size of the zip code field must be changed to accommodate the new data.

Customer List : Table

Field Name	Data Type	Description
Customer Number	Text	An identification code unique to this customer
Last	Text	Customer's last name
First	Text	Customer's first name
Address	Text	Customer's address
City	Text	Customer's city
State	Text	Customer's state
Zip	Text	Customer's five digit zip code
Amount	Currency	Amount owed by customer

Field Properties

General | Lookup

Field Size	10
Format	
Input Mask	
Caption	
Default Value	
Validation Rule	
Validation Text	
Required	No
Allow Zero Length	No
Indexed	No

The error message that appears when you enter a value prohibited by the validation rule. Press F1 for help on validation text.

DB

16 **Click *Query, Update***

17 **Drag the Zip field to the Field row in the first column**

In the Update To row,

18 **Type [Zip]+"-0000"**

The field name must be in square brackets. The literal string "-0000" contains the five characters that will be added to each zip code value. A **literal string** is a series of characters that always print or display without variation.

19 **Click *Query, Run***

Access opens a box informing you that seven records are about to be updated. This gives you a chance to abort the procedure in case you made a mistake.

20 **Click *Yes***

21 **Click *View, Datasheet***

Each zip code should have been changed so that the last five characters are "-0000". When you have finished viewing,

22 **Close all windows in the Access work area without saving**

REPLACING DATA IN SELECTED RECORDS

This exercise changes the data in CITY fields that read "New York" to "New York City." It does not change all records, only those that meet the stated condition.

STEPS

1 **Open the Customer database window and if desired, make a backup of CUSTOMER LIST**

2 **Open the CUSTOMER LIST**

3 **Open an Update Query window for the CUSTOMER LIST table (click the New Object drop-down button, *New Query, OK*, and then *Query, Update*)**

4 **Drag the CITY field to the Field row in the first column of the query**

5 **Place the text insertion point in the Update To row and type New York City**

6 **Place the text insertion point in the Criteria row and type New York**

This condition translates as "change the 'City' field for each record whose city is 'New York' to 'New York City'."

Tip: If you want to change *all* records, simply omit the search criteria as was done with zip codes before.

7 **Click *Query, Run***

The screen displays a message that two records will be changed.

8 **Click *Yes***

Verify that your changes are the expected ones, then

9 **Close all windows in the Access work area without saving**

USING A DIFFERENT SEARCH FIELD. Here is one more change using a separate search field to achieve the desired result. Assume you want to add $15 to the AMOUNT field of anyone who has not yet paid:

STEPS

1 **Open the Customer Database window and if desired, make a backup of CUSTOMER LIST**

2 **Open the CUSTOMER LIST**

Use Figure DB2-27 as an example for the following steps.

3 **Open an update query for the CUSTOMER LIST table**

4 **Drag "Amount" to the Field row in the first column of the query**

5 **Place the text insertion point in the Update To row of the first column and type [Amount]+15**

As written, this change will affect all records in the table. Since you do not want that to occur, you must add a search condition as follows:

6 **Drag "Paid" to the Field row in the second column of the query**

7 **Place the text insertion point in the Criteria row of the second column and type 0**

The complete query will now find all records whose PAID field is 0, and for those records only, add $15 to the AMOUNT field.

8 **Click *Query, Run***

The screen displays a message that two records will be changed, because two customers had Paid amounts of zero: Laudon and West.

FIGURE DB2-27 ■ ANOTHER UPDATE QUERY

An update query that adds a $15 penalty for nonpayment.

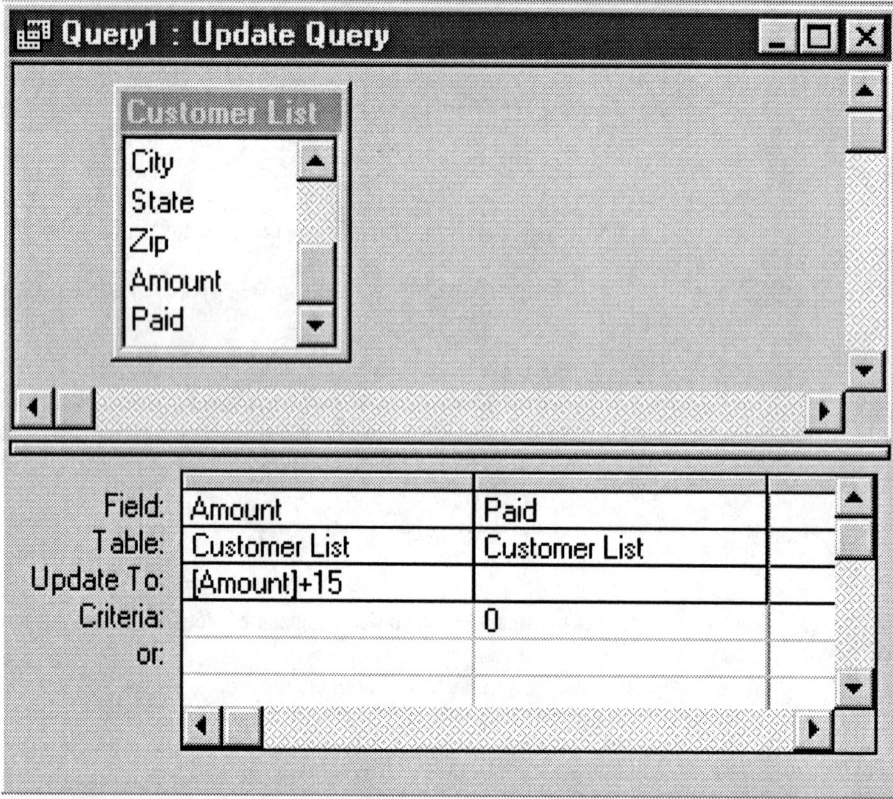

9 Click *Yes* and then close the Update Query window without saving

Verify that your changes are correct, then

10 Close all windows in the Access work area

There are thousands of ways to use Update Queries to modify current entries or change them entirely.

☑ CHECKPOINT

- ✓ In the DBTEST table, locate Record #2; then locate the record whose name is Smith.
- ✓ Find and then edit your record and add three points to Test1 and two points to Test2.
- ✓ Using CHANGETO, add five points to any score in Test1 that falls below 50.
- ✓ Modify the structure of DBTEST to add an EXAM_AVG field.
- ✓ Create a query that will calculate the average of all exams and store the results in the new field.

SUMMARY STATISTICS IN QUERIES

You can also use Query screens to generate summary statistics for an entire file (or selected records) using the Sum, Average, and Count commands. The following exercise demonstrates this application.

THE SUM COMMAND

The **Sum command** totals selected numeric fields in the table. As most other commands, the Sum command can be used with conditions to limit its scope. The following exercise presents three examples of the Sum command. Use Figure DB2-28a as a guide.

STEPS

1. **Open the *Customer* Database window and then the *Customer List***

2. **Open a New Query for the Customer table (click the *New Object* drop-down button, *New Query, OK)***

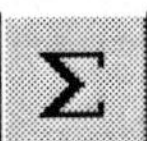

3. **Click the *Total* button on the toolbar**

4. **Drag "Amount" and "Paid" to the field row of the first two columns**

5. **Click the *Total* row of the Amount column, click the drop-down arrow, then select *Sum***

6. **Click the *Total* row of the Paid column, click the drop-down arrow, then select *Sum***

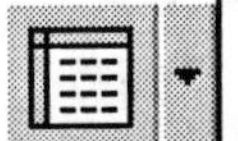

7. **Click *View, Datasheet***

Access displays the sums of the two fields. To return to the Query Design screen

8. **Click *View, Query Design***

Now, using Figure DB2-28b as a guide, add a feature that will total only those records with a zero in the PAID field.

9. **Type 0 in the Criteria row of the Paid column**

10. **Move to the Total row of the Paid column, click its drop-down button and then *Where* (use the scroll bar to locate the "Where" option if needed)**

The English translation of this query is "Sum the AMOUNT fields *where* Paid is zero."

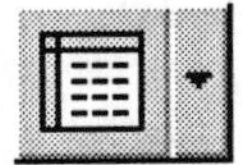

11. **Click *View, Datasheet***

This time, a total is shown in the AMOUNT field but only for those records whose PAID fields were equal to 0. Perform one more Select query using Sum (see Figure DB2-28c as a guide):

FIGURE DB2-28 ■ THE SUM COMMAND

(a) This select query sums values in the Amount and Paid fields.
(b) This query sums amount WHERE Paid = 0.

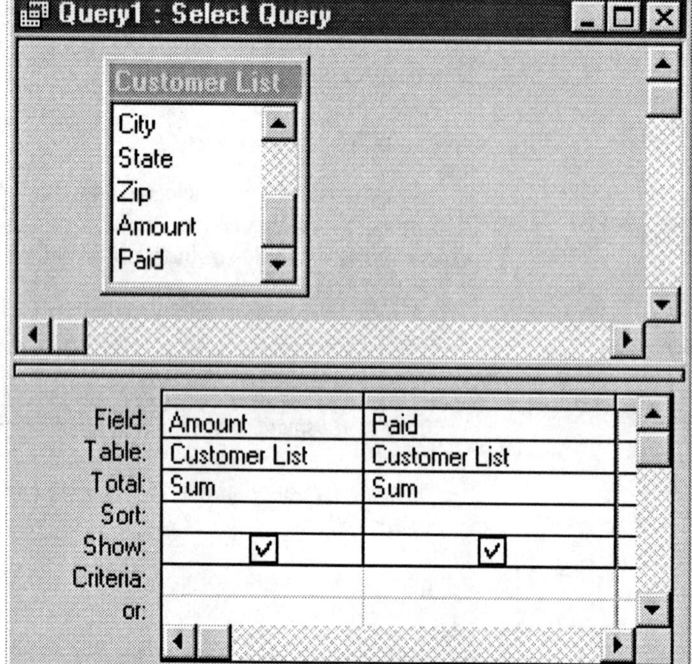

(a)

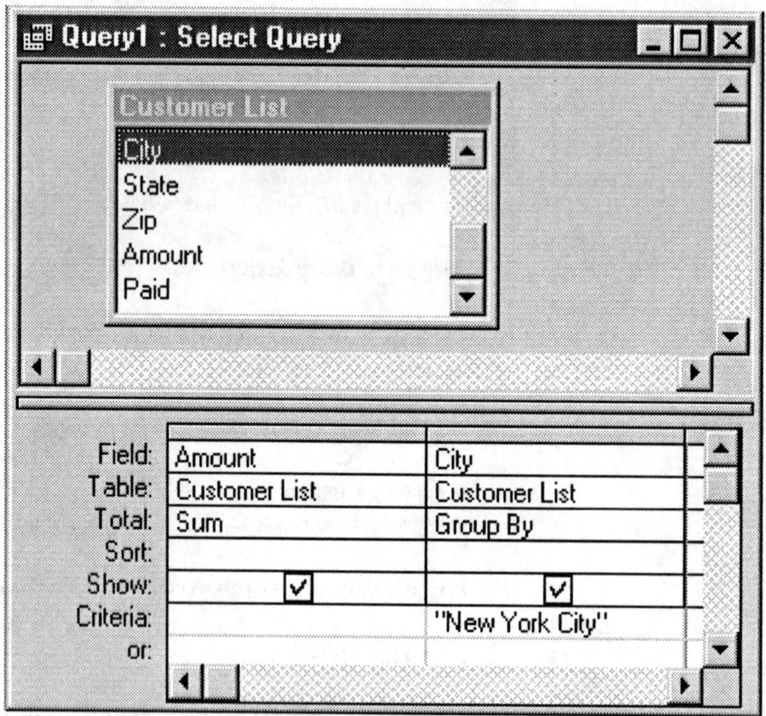

(b)

(continued)

FIGURE DB2-28 ■ *(continued)*

(c) This query sums amounts owed by New Yorkers.

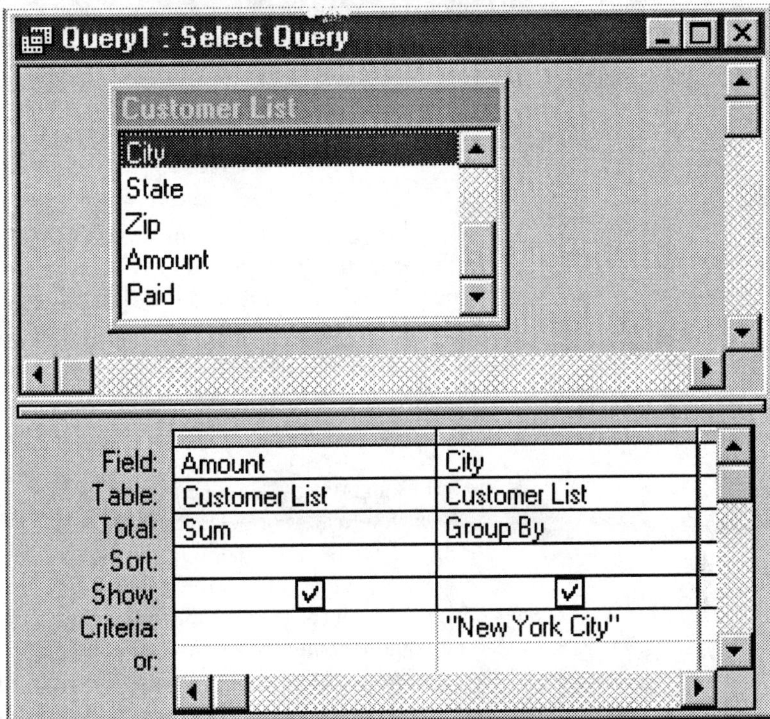

(c)

12 **Click *View, Query Design***

13 **Place the insertion point in the field row of the Paid column and backspace over "Paid," then type City**

14 **Select *Group By* in the Total row**

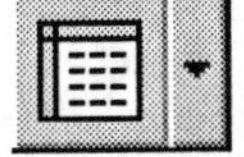

15 **Type New York City in the Criteria row**

16 **Click *View, Datasheet***

This query totals only those records whose CITY field value is "New York City."

17 **Close all windows in the Access work area without saving**

18 **Exit Access and shut down Windows if desired**

THE AVERAGE COMMAND

The **Average command** computes the arithmetic mean (average) of all numeric fields or expressions. It is invoked in a similar fashion to that of the Sum command but replaces Sum with Avg. Try some on your own.

THE COUNT COMMAND

The **Count command** tabulates the number of records that meet a stated condition. Like the Sum and Average commands, it can be used in the query form to tabulate any desired condition. For example, if you were to select *Count* in the STATE field, Access would count the number of records with entries (nonblank values) in the STATE field in the table. (All seven records have entries, so the resulting count would be seven in this case. However, if a customer's state had not been recorded, the count would be six.)

CHECKPOINT

- ✓ Using the DBTEST table, sum all test fields for all records.
- ✓ Average all test fields for all records.
- ✓ Count the number of records that have a zero for Exam1.
- ✓ Average records whose Test1 grade exceeds 80.
- ✓ Count records whose Test2 grade is less than or equal to 80.

SUMMARY

- The design process—invoked by the *Design* button or the *View, Design* command—allows you to alter or delete existing fields or add new fields to a table structure.
- Records can be arranged in other sequences with the *Sort Ascending* and *Sort Descending buttons.* This rearranges the records within the main table itself.
- A report form (or specification) is a formalized layout that identifies page options and column contents. When the command is issued to print the report, field masks in the form will be filled in with data from the active table and sent either to the screen or to the printer. Records appear in the table order and can be limited to those that match stated conditions using a query. Records can also be grouped and subtotaled by adding a group band to the design screen.
- Each column of data in a report form contains objects, which generate contents (field names or math expressions); literals (headings), which never vary in content; and properties, which determine width and format. Summary statistics can be added. The Report Design screen can be used to alter the contents of a report form after it has been created.
- A report form can be copied and modified to alter any of its contents—columns can be inserted, deleted, or changed.
- The Access record pointer can be positioned by scroll buttons, arrow keys, record number, or value at specific record locations.
- Once a record has been located, it can be edited with a full-screen record edit or in table form. The Update query can alter all records or only those that meet a stated condition. The filter process can be used to limit the display of records to those meeting specified conditions.
- The math operators Sum, Average, and Count can be used to find the total, mean, or tabulation of records that meet stated conditions.

KEY TERMS

Average command (DB141)
Band (DB95)
Banded report (DB95)
Count command (DB142)
Detail band (DB95)
Edit (DB130)
Group band (DB95)
Handles (DB100)

Landscape orientation (DB91)
Literal string (DB136)
Natural order (DB87)
Page Footer band (DB95)
Page Header band (DB95)
Portrait orientation (DB91)
Report Footer band (DB95)
Report form (DB87)
Report Header band (DB95)
Select (DB96)
Sort direction (DB122)
Sorting (DB83)
Sum command (DB139)
Tabular report (DB91)
Vertical report (DB91)

QUIZ

TRUE/FALSE

___ 1. Tables are designed and modified at the same screen.
___ 2. To insert a new field into a table structure, select *File* then *New.*
___ 3. The *Sort Ascending* button places Text fields in alphabetical order.
___ 4. The *Sort Descending* button places values in numerical order.
___ 5. A report form can be used with conditional expressions to limit records included in the report.
___ 6. Press Shift + Delete to remove a field while restructuring a table.
___ 7. The Detail band forms the body of the report.
___ 8. Group reports only show totals—no detail.
___ 9. The *Find* button is used to advance to a specified record number.
___ 10. A literal in a report specification is not replaced with data when the report is generated.

MULTIPLE CHOICE

___ 11. Which keystroke allows you to add a new field into a file structure?
a. Insert
b. Alt, N
c. Ctrl, Insert
d. Ctrl, N

___ 12. Which command allows records in a table to be shown in another sequence?
a. Locate
b. Place field
c. Arrange
d. Sort

___ 13. In which band of the design screen can you set titles that will appear on each page?
a. Page header
b. Report header
c. Table band
d. Group band

___ 14. How can the width of a column in a report be changed?
a. Select the *Width* button
b. Select Width on the *Properties* menu
c. Drag and drop the column margin
d. Delete and reinsert the column at the new width

___ 15. A word that appears at the top of a column as a title or heading is a
a. Content
b. Label
c. Literal
d. Sum

___ 16. Which command will search through records for a certain value in a specified field?
a. Sort
b. Count
c. Find
d. Seek

___ 17. Which command closes and saves changes in a table?
a. Ctrl + F4
b. File-Close
c. Double-clicking the *Control-Menu* box
d. All of the above

___ 18. Which of the following presents only one record at a time for editing?
a. Query
b. Table
c. Datasheet view
d. Form

___ 19. The contents of many records can be changed at one time using which of the following:
a. Reports
b. Queries
c. Forms
d. Properties

___ 20. When referred to in reports, field names are placed in which of the following?
a. {Curley brackets}
b. (Parentheses)
c. [Square brackets]
d. "Quotation marks"

MATCHING

Select the term that best matches each feature indicated on the Access desktop screen shown in the figure.

___ 21. Column selector
___ 22. Copy
___ 23. Create a new table
___ 24. Database window
___ 25. Paste
___ 26. *Print* button
___ 27. Query Design screen
___ 28. Row selector
___ 29. *Scroll* button
___ 30. Table names

FIGURE DB2-A ■ MATCHING EXERCISE

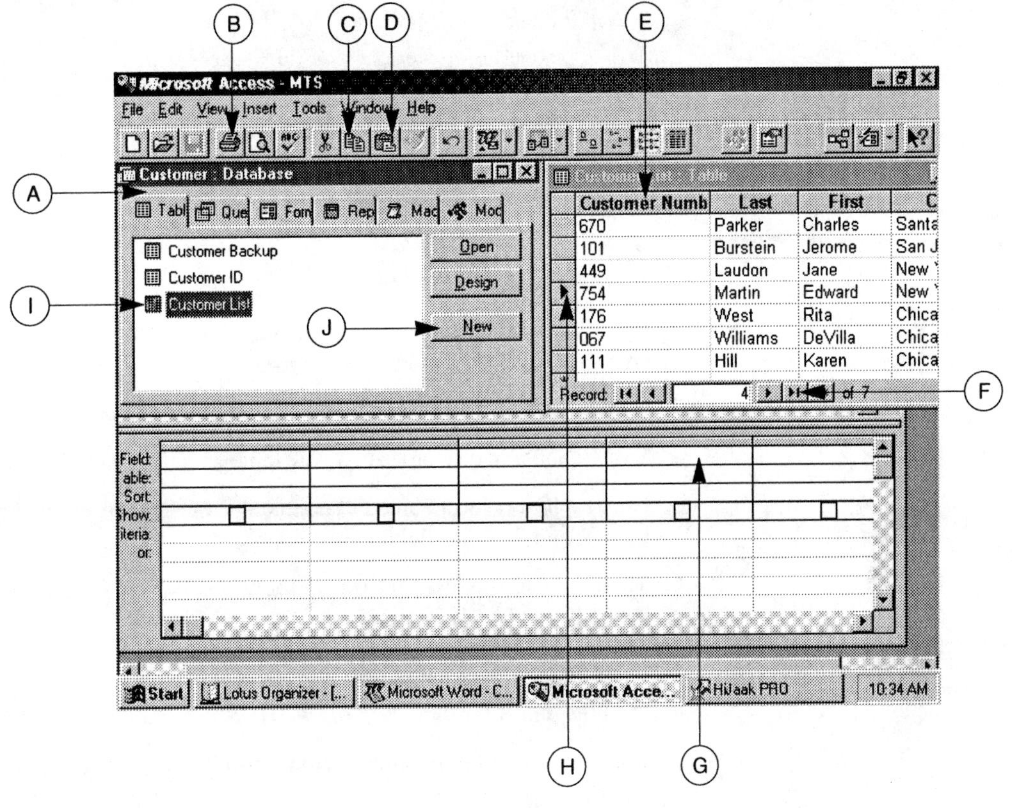

ANSWERS

True/False: 1. T; 2. F; 3. T; 4. T; 5. T; 6. F; 7. T; 8. F; 9. F; 10. T
Multiple Choice: 11. a; 12. d; 13. a; 14. c; 15. c; 16. c; 17. d; 18. d; 19. b; 20. c
Matching: 21. e; 22. c; 23. j; 24. a; 25. d; 26. b; 27. g; 28. h; 29. f; 30. i

EXERCISES

I. OPERATIONS

Provide the Access sequence of keystrokes or actions required to do each of the following operations. Assume that your data will be stored in the root directory of Drive A. Further assume that your data disk contains a table named ADDRESS, which has the following structure:

Field	Name	Data Type	Field Size
1	Lastname	Text	15
2	First	Text	12
3	Phone	Text	12
4	Street	Text	25
5	City	Text	20
6	State	Text	2
7	Zip	Text	5
8	Size	Number	

1. View the ADDRESS table.
2. Modify the table structure in ADDRESS to include a Text field named "Title," 4 characters in width, in Field 3 of the structure.
3. Change the CITY field to hold a maximum of 25 characters.
4. Sort the table in city order to a new table called ADDRESS2.
5. Create a report form named "Phonlist." Have the report display the LASTNAME, FIRST, and PHONE fields.
6. Modify the report to add a column (between the FIRST and PHONE fields) to show the SIZE field *without totals.*
7. Generate the report on the screen.
8. Print the report for those records whose phone number begins with a 718 area code.
9. Copy the report to "Phonlis2." Add a column for "State" at the right side. Print the report.
10. Reposition the record pointer at Record 6 using the Record text box at the bottom of the window.
11. Locate the record whose last name is Smith and then change the first name to Mary.
12. Add 10 to all values in the Size field.
13. Change the Size data values that are less than 500 to a new value of 0.
14. Place an asterisk after the CITY field values for those people whose state is New York.
15. Calculate the sum and average of the size field for the entire database file and then count the number of records whose size equals 0.

II. COMMANDS

Describe fully, using as few words as possible in each case, what command is initiated or what is accomplished in Access by pressing each series of keystrokes or actions given below. Assume that Access has already been invoked and that each exercise part is independent of any previous parts. If the series of commands is not complete, indicate what action should be taken to finalize this command. If there is more than one interpretation, select only one.

1. Clicking the *Design View* button
2. In the Table Design screen, pressing Insert
3. Right-clicking an object
4. Clicking *File, Save As*
5. Clicking the ellipsis (...) on a menu command
6. Clicking the *Sort Ascending* button
7. Clicking the *Print* button
8. Clicking *File, Open, Database*
9. Clicking the *Print Preview* button on the Report Design screen
10. Clicking *File, Save*
11. Clicking *File, Close*
12. Clicking the *Record* text box at the bottom of the window and then typing a desired record number
13. In a query screen, typing Sum in the Pay column and Santa Fe in the City column.
14. Typing New York in the Criteria row and in the State column of a Query screen.
15. Typing Pay*1.05 in the Update column of a Query screen.

III. APPLICATIONS

Perform the following operations using your computer system. You will need a system with Access on it. You will also need your data disk to store the results of this exercise. In a few words, explain how you accomplished each operation and describe its result. If you want to continue these exercises later, be sure to exit properly after each operation. Note that these exercises should be performed in sequence. Make sure you label each printed result with the exercise number, your name, and your class. To prepare, start Access.

APPLICATION 1: SCHOOL: NOTES ON HISTORY OF THE PC

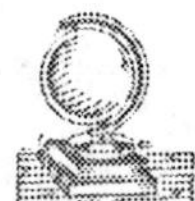

1. Create a table named SILICON with this structure:

Field Name	Field Type	Width
Name	Text	25
Company	Text	25
Product	Text	25
Comment	Text	75

2. Enter the following records and adjust column widths as needed:

Name	Company	Product	Comment
Gates, Bill	Microsoft	MS-DOS, Windows, Basic	Billionaire, founder of Microsoft
Kapor, Mitch	Lotus Development	Lotus 1-2-3	Created Lotus 1-2-3, took market from Visicalc
Jobs, Steve	Apple, NeXT	Apple computer	Guided Apple Computers in the early years and initiated the personal computer industry
Bricklin, Dan	Software Arts	Visicalc	Programmer who invented the first spreadsheet
Wozniak, Steve	Apple	Apple computer	Engineer who invented the Apple I and Apple II computers
Kildall, Gary	Digital Research	CP/M	Developer of the CP/M operating system
Fylstra, Dan	Personal Software	Visicalc	Publisher of Visicalc

3. Sort the table by name.
4. Print the contents in the new order.
5. Sort the table by company.
6. Print the contents in the new order.
7. Create a report called PCHIST. Include all of the fields as columns in your report in the order in which they appear in the file. Include two title lines in the Report Header band. Be sure that your name is included in the second title line.
8. Print the report in company order.
9. Print the report in product order.
10. Copy the report to PCHIST2.
11. Change the order of the columns in PCHIST2 so that Company is the first column, Name is second, Product is third, and Comment is fourth.
12. Print the report in product order.
13. Create a query that will find only those records whose Product value is "Apple computer."
14. Print and save the query as ANSWER.
15. Exit Access.

APPLICATION 2: SCHOOL: CREATING A DEGREE PROGRESS REPORT

1. Open the DEGREE table you created for Chapter 1.

2. Create a report named PROGRESS that contains all four fields as columns. Be sure the report has two title lines and that your name is included on the second line.
3. Sort the data into course order.
4. Print the report in the new order.
5. Copy the report to PROGRESS2 and then sort the data into grade order.
6. Print the report in the new order.
7. Modify the structure of the DEGREE table so that a new fifth field is added named POINTS, Type NUMBER. This field will hold the grade points that you are given for each grade.
8. Create a query that will replace items in the Points column with 4 for each A, 3 for each B, 2 for each C, 1 for each D, and 0 for each F. Run the query and verify the results.
9. Modify PROGRESS2 so that the columns are in this order: Grade, Points, Course, Number. Delete the Completed column from the report.
10. Save and then print PROGRESS2.
11. Sort the table into points order.
12. Print the report in the new order.
13. Exit Access.

APPLICATION 3: HOBBY: UPDATING THE VIDEO TABLE

1. Open the VIDEO table created in Chapter 1, and add these four records to the table:

Volume	Start	Subject	Type	Time
107	0000	WordPerfect	I	75
107	3,000	The Marx Brothers	0	125
101	1,125	The Boy and the Seals	C	45
101	2,050	Dear as Salt	C	50

2. Modify the table structure to add a TEXT type field of four characters named RATING directly after the SUBJECT field.
3. Copy the VIDEO table as VID_TYPE and then sort the table by type and subject.
4. Print this table's contents in this new order.
5. Create a report called VIDREP1. Include your name on the second line of the title that appears at the top of each page. Create columns that display all the fields in the structure, but no totals. Print the report in volume and start (counter) order.

6. Create a report to include only those subjects whose type is C and then print it. Create a second report for subjects whose time exceeds 60. Save and print it. (**Hint:** Create a query first.)

7. Replace all RATING data with "****" in the VIDEO table. Then replace the RATING data field with "**" only for those records with a volume of 106. Print the results.

8. Modify VIDREP1 to remove the Rating column and include another column with a heading of "Hours" that displays the result of dividing the TIME field by 60. Print the report.

9. Copy VIDREP1 to VIDREP2. Add summary statistics for the TIME and HOURS columns to show totals. Print the report.

10. Modify VIDREP2 to group data in the VOLUME field (create a group header and footer). Use "Volume Code" as your heading in the header. Add the subtotal of the Time and Hours columns for each volume in the footer. Print the results.

11. Copy VIDREP2 to VIDREP3. Modify VIDREP3 to remove the subtotals for the Hours column. Print the report.

12. Locate each of the following records and make the indicated edit to its data:

For:	Change:
101 (0650)	Start to 0750
104 (0000)	Time to 65
107 (3000)	Subject to Word and Time to 85

Sort the table in title order and then print and save it.

13. Use the update query to update the VIDEO table by reducing the TIME field by 5; then use another update query to set all RATING fields to a blank (" "). Print the updated VIDEO table.

14. Adjust the VIDREP1 report to include the sum and average of the TIME field and send the results to the printer.

15. Place a count statistic for the number of records in the VIDREP1 report.

16. Exit Access.

APPLICATION 4: HOBBY: UPDATE PERSONAL INVENTORY

1. Open the SOUNDS table created in Chapter 1, and add these four records to the table:

Rec	Item	Category	Year	New_Cost	Source
1	CD Tower Rack	Furn	1993	39.95	Furn-a-Mundo
2	Custom Woofer Covers	Acc	1994	28.85	Granny's Coverlets
3	Speaker Set	Elec	1993	249.99	Al's Stereos
4	Long Range Mike	Elec	1994	299.97	CIA Surplus Sale

2. Modify the table structure to add a CURRENCY type field named CURR_VALUE directly after the NEW_COST field. (**Hint:** Use the Advance Filter/Sort dialog box.)
3. Copy the SOUNDS table to a new table called VID_TYPE and then sort the table by category and item.
4. Print the new table.
5. Create a report called MINE. Include your name on the second line of the title that appears at the top of each page. (**Hint:** Use the Header band.) Create columns that display all the fields in the structure, but no totals. Print the report in item and category order.
6. Create and print a query with only those records whose category is Furn. Create and print a second report for subjects whose cost exceeds $100.
7. Replace all CURR_VALUE data with $0. (**Hint:** Use the Update query feature.)
8. Modify the MINE report to remove the NEW_COST column and include another column with a heading of "Value" that displays the result of dividing the NEW_COST field by 2. Resave and print the report.
9. Copy the MINE report to MINE2. Adjust the column widths as needed. Add summary statistics for the VALUE column to show totals. Save and print the results.
10. Modify the MINE2 report to group data in the CATEGORY field. (**Hint:** Create Header and Footer group bands.) Use the heading "Item Type." Add a subtotal of the VALUE column for each volume. Save and print the report.
11. Copy MINE2 to MINE3. Modify MINE3 to remove the subtotals for the VALUE column. Print the report.
12. Locate each of the following records and make the indicated edit to its data:

For:	Change:
Superwoofer	Current Value to $200
Stereo	Year to 1992
TV	Category to Junk

List the file in item order and then print it.

13. Use the Update query to update the table by increasing the CURR_VALUE field by 20.
14. Sum and average the COST and CURR_VALUE fields in the MINE report and send the results to the printer.
15. Count the number of records in the Category column of the MINE report and print the result.
16. Exit Access.

DB

APPLICATION 5: BUSINESS: ADJUSTED PAYROLL

1. Open the PAYROLL table created in Chapter 1, and add these four records to the table:

Name	Dept	Hours	Rate
Gold, Edward	SALES	52	11.25
Gold, Lesley	ACCTG	45	12.50
Green, Elissa	SALES	38	5.65
Silver, Andrea	PRSNL	38	5.50

2. Modify the table structure to add a CURRENCY field named BONUS directly after the DEPT field.
3. Copy the PAYROLL table to a new table called PAY_RATE and sort the table by the rate. Print the contents of the table.
4. Copy the PAYROLL table to a new table called PAYMENT and sort by department and name. Print the PAYMENT table contents in this order.
5. Create a report form named PAYREPT1. Include your name on the second line of the title that appears at the top of each page. Create columns that display each of the five fields in the structure, but no totals. Choose appropriate headings for each column. Print the report in alphabetical order by name.
6. Create a query to include only those employees in the sales department. Use this query to create a report called PAYREPT1. Create another query to include those employees whose hours exceed 40 and then a report from this query. Print each report.
7. Replace all BONUS data with $20. Then replace the BONUS data with $40 only for those employees in ACCTG. (**Hint:** Use the Update query feature.)
8. Modify the PAYREPT1 report to include a sixth column with a heading of "Gross" that displays the result of multiplying the HOURS field by the RATE field. Print the report.
9. Copy the report design to PAYREPT2. Add summary statistics for the Hours, Rate, Bonus, and Gross columns to show totals. Print the report.
10. Modify PAYREPT1 to group data in the DEPT field. Use "Department Code:" as your heading. Add a subtotal of the Hours and Gross columns for each department. Print the report.
11. Copy the report PAYREPT2 to PAYREPT3. Modify the report to remove the subtotals for the Hours column. Print the report.
12. Locate each of the following records and make the indicated edit to its data.

For:	Change:
Black	DEPT to ACCTG
Brown	HOURS to 41
Green	HOURS to 42 and RATE to $6.10

List the file in alphabetical order and print.

13. Use the Update query feature to update the database by reducing the HOURS field by 5 and then use another Update query to set all BONUS fields to 0.
14. Sum and average the HOURS field in the PAYREPT3 report and send the results to the printer.
15. Count the number of employees and print the result.

APPLICATION 6: BUSINESS: ADJUSTED SALES

1. Open the SALES table created in Chapter 1, and add these four records to the table:

Customer	Item	Quantity	Price
WIL-22	Computer, Laptop	1	800
WIL-11	Printer, Dot Matrix	1	125
BON-01	Printer, Dot Matrix	2	125
BON-01	Cable	2	35

2. Modify the table structure to add a currency field named DEDUCT directly after the PRICE field.
3. Copy the SALES table to SALPRICE. Sort the table by price and then print it.
4. Sort the SALES table by customer and item into the same table. Print the SALES table contents in this order.
5. Create a report called SALEREP1. Include your name on the second line of the Page Header that appears at the top of each page. Create columns that display each of the five fields in the table, but no totals. Choose appropriate headings for each column. Sort the report in alphabetical order by customer code. Print the report.
6. Create a query to include only those customers who ordered single quantities of any item (exclude for quantity > 1). Create a report from the query. Prepare a second query and report for those customers who ordered disks.
7. Replace all DEDUCT data with $10. Then replace the DEDUCT data field with $20 only for those customers whose item price exceeds $100.
8. Modify SALEREP1 to include a sixth column with the heading of "Total" that displays the result of subtracting the DEDUCT field from the PRICE field and then multiplying the result by the QUANTITY field. Print the report.
9. Copy the SALEREP1 report to SALEREP2. Change the report title to SALEREP2. Add summary statistics for the Quantity and Total columns to show totals. Print the report.
10. Modify SALEREP2 to group data in the CUSTOMER field. Use "Customer Code:" as your heading. Add a subtotal of the Quantity and Total columns for each customer. Print the report.

11. Copy SALEREP2 to SALEREP3. Change the report title to SALEREP3. Modify SALEREP3 to remove the subtotals for the Quantity column. Print the report.
12. Locate each of the following records and make the indicated edit to its data:

For:	Change:
MAR-75 (Screen)	Quantity to 2
PAR-15 (Trackball)	Price to 54.95
WIL-11 (Printer)	Item to Computer, Notebook

13. Use the Update query feature to update the database by reducing the PRICE field by 15 and then use another Update query to set all DEDUCT fields to 0.
14. Sum and average the PRICE field in the SALEREP1 report and send the results to the printer.
15. Count the number of customers int he SALEREP1 report and print the result.
16. Exit Access.

MASTERY CASES

The following mastery cases allow you to demonstrate how much you have learned about this software. Each case further extends a problem from Chapter 1 and can be solved using the skills you have learned in this chapter. If you do not have the referenced table, you will have to create it by following the instructions in Chapter 1. You are expected to design your response in ways that display your mastery of the software. You may have to restructure your table (add or adjust fields) to adequately respond to the case.

These mastery cases allow you to display your ability to

- Modify the file or table structure.
- Rearrange the table.
- Design and print a report.
- Edit records.
- Use summary statistics.

CASE 1. UPDATING YOUR DEGREE PROGRAM TABLE

You want to amend the table and data you created in the graduation progress table in Chapter 1. You want to indicate whether each course you took was required or an elective. You also want to add additional fields and data (such as quality points earned) that will let you calculate your grade point average using the accepted procedure of your school. After entering appropriate data for all courses, design and print a report that lists all courses in the order they were taken and calculates a cumulative grade point average.

CASE 2. UPDATING YOUR MUSIC COLLECTION TABLE

You have received an offer to program music shows for a local disc jockey and need to amend the table you created in the music catalog in Chapter 1. You want it to contain the play length (to the nearest minute) of each selection. After updating each record to reflect the new data, create and print your first "DJ" report that displays the most appropriate data about your collection in artist and title order.

CASE 3. UPDATING THE CLIENTELE TABLE

Your cosmetologist friend would like to be able to offer her clients a free manicure on their birthdays. Amend the table you created for her in Chapter 1 to accomplish this goal. After you update the records, create and print a report alphabetically by client's last name that will list each client's home phone and birthday.

3

TABLE MANAGEMENT, RELATIONAL DATABASES, GRAPHS, AND SHARING DATA

OUTLINE

OBJECTIVES

After completing this chapter, you will be able to do any of the following (based on your selection of modules):

1. Describe how to list tables and other files contained on a data disk.
2. Compare and contrast several file management commands to copy tables, records, and fields, as well as rename and erase tables.
3. Explain the techniques for creating, modifying, and printing labels.
4. Describe the procedures for creating and using customized screens.
5. Explain the steps necessary to use multiple tables in a relational database—creating master and detail forms by using one-to-many and many-to-one relationships.
6. Prepare line, bar, and pie graphs from table records.

7 List techniques for exporting data to and importing data from spreadsheet and word processing software.

8 Insert objects created by other applications into Access files, insert objects created by Access into data files created by other applications, and link (connect) Access data files to data files created by other applications.

OVERVIEW

This chapter presents additional topics of interest to the Access user. Each topic is presented as a separate module that can be studied independently of the others. Study the modules that are most useful to you. Module 1 presents table management techniques—various methods to list data disk contents, append records, and copy, rename, and erase Access objects. Module 2 explains the creation and use of printed labels—a procedure much like those for reports and record forms. Techniques for customizing data entry screens are presented in Module 3. Module 4 looks at true relational database techniques where separate tables are linked together to act as one large database. Module 5 introduces graphs in Access. Module 6 shows how to prepare data to be transferred between Access and other programs.

PREPARING FOR THIS CHAPTER

This text includes a separate data disk that contains files for use with this chapter. These files reduce the amount of basic keystroking you must do in each module. If you do not have this disk (or you want to practice), you can create the files as you need them.

COPYING THE DATABASE

The files must first be copied onto your data disk so they will be available for use. Check with your instructor or lab technician to see if the files are available, or follow the appropriate procedure below for your system. *Note:* Follow the appropriate instructions for copying with either one or two disk systems.

Because you are using Windows, you may prefer to copy the files to your data disk using Explorer. To run Explorer while Access (or from any other Windows application) is running,

STEPS

1 **Click the *Start* button on the taskbar**

2 **Point to *Programs*, then click *Windows Explorer***

You will see the Explorer window. Don't be concerned that you no longer see Access. It is still running in the background and you can return to Access by clicking the *Access* button on the taskbar.

As you see in Figure DB3-1, the table MAGIC has been selected.

2 **Click *Edit, Copy*** Ctrl + C

Access understands that your intention is to copy the table MAGIC, because that object was selected when you clicked the *Copy* button.

3 **Click *Edit, Paste*** Ctrl + V

This tells Access that you are ready to complete the copy process. A dialog box, similar to Figure DB3-2a, will give you some options. First, you must provide a name for the new object.

4 **Type Duplicate Copy of Magic as the name**

Then, you must tell Access whether you want to copy the table's structure only, copy the table's structure *and* data,or append the table's records to some other table.

5 **Click *Structure and Data*, then click *OK***

Access makes a duplicate copy of the table MAGIC, places it in the same database file (you will probably notice the disk drive light come on), and gives it the name you typed in. Your database window should display the new table's name along with the other table names.

Warning: This copy process has many uses, but it is *not* the best way to protect you from data loss. A true backup copy of your data is intended for use if the original is destroyed through human error, equipment failure, disaster (such as a fire or flood), or sabotage (disgruntled employees *have* deliberately destroyed data). If the MAGIC table were destroyed, the copy of MAGIC that you made in this exercise would probably be destroyed too, because it is in the same file and on the same disk. To protect your data with confidence, a verified backup copy must be made on a *different* disk—or on tape—and should ideally be *kept in a different location* than the original. (This may seem like a lot of trouble to go to, but it's a lot less trouble than retyping a few thousand inventory items!)

RE DB3-2 ■ COPYING AN OBJECT

ing the table's
and data.
ing structure only.

Paste Table As
Table Name:
Duplicate Copy of Magic
OK
Cancel
Paste Options
Structure Only
Structure and Data
Append Data to Existing Table

(a)

Paste Table As
Table Name:
Names
OK
Cancel
Paste Options
Structure Only
Structure and Data
Append Data to Existing Table

(b)

Tip: If you use Windows regularly, you should become familiar with Explorer. If you have not used Explorer before, consult your Microsoft Windows manual or *Mastering Today's Software: Windows 95* by Martin and Parker.

Place the Dryden data diskette in Drive A. If you have two floppy drives, place an empty, formatted diskette in Drive B.

Follow the instructions for your system.

SYSTEM WITH ONE FLOPPY DRIVE (A:)

3 **Insert the Dryden data disk in Drive A**

4 **Click the *Drive* C icon**

5 **Click *File, New, Folder***

6 **Type MAGIC and press ↵**

7 **Click the *3½ Floppy (A:)* icon**

8 **Double-click the *Access* folder**

9 **Click *Edit, Select All* to select all of the files in the folder**

10 **Drag and drop the selected files to the *Magic* folder in Drive C icon**

11 **Place your disk in Drive A**

12 **Click *View*, then click *Refresh***

13 **Click the Magic folder, then select all the files in it**

14 **Drag and drop the selected files to the *3½ Floppy (A:)* icon**

15 **Click the *Magic* folder in Drive C, then press Delete (if you want to delete the files from your hard drive)**

16 **Click Explorer's *Close* button and then launch *Microsoft Access***

SYSTEM WITH TWO FLOPPY DRIVES (A: AND B:)

3 **Insert the Dryden data disk in Drive A and your disk in Drive B**

4 **Click the *3½ Floppy (A:)* icon**

5 **Double-click the *Access* folder**

6 **Select all of the files in the directory (Select the first file, then shift-click the last file)**

7 **Drag and drop the files to the *3½ Floppy (B:)* icon**

8 **Click Explorer's *Close* button and then launch *Microsoft Access***

DB

If you have a single floppy system, your data files have been copied to the disk in Drive A. If you have a dual floppy system, your data files have been copied to the disk in Drive B.

MODULE 1: TABLE MANAGEMENT

File management is an important aspect of controlling data. Remember, all Access objects are contained within database files. These database files can be copied or erased using Windows Explorer. However, the objects within the database file—tables, queries, and so forth— can only be copied, erased, or modified from within Access.

Perhaps you need to review existing objects or copy them. You may also want to erase unneeded objects or change the name of an object. The following exercises examine ways to list table names, copy entire tables or selected records from one table to another, and erase or rename objects.

WORKING WITH FILES AND TABLES

At times, you will want to know what database files are available. Access will list for you the database files within each folder. Then, once you have selected a database file, its database window lists all the objects in the database—but you can only see objects of a particular type at any one time, such as only tables or only queries. The following exercise will help you to become more familiar with the database window.

WORKING WITH THE DATABASE WINDOW. Perform the following actions:

STEPS

1 If needed, press Esc to remove the Access dialog box and then click *File, Open Database*

> **Tip: The exercises in this chapter presume that your data files are contained in the disk in Drive A. If this is not the case, be sure to substitute the appropriate drive letter.**

The *Open Database Window* dialog box appears.

2 Click the *Look in* drop-down button for its list

3 Click *3½ Floppy (A:)*

You should now see the name of the file you want to open: MAGICAL

4 Click the database file MAGICAL, then click the *Open* button

If you receive a Convert/Open Database dialog box, do Steps 5 and 6; otherwise, go to Step 7.

5 Click the *Convert Database* option, *OK*

6 In the *Convert Database into* dialog box, type MAGIC and then click the *Save* button

7 If you do not receive a Convert/Open
MAGIC and then click the *Save* butto

This chapter uses the database MAGIC
The database window for the MAG
1. By clicking the various tabs on the data
you can display a list of all Access objec
each of the tabs in turn. Of course, in eve
names because there are no objects of tha

COPYING AN OBJECT. You might w
sons. For example, often you will want to c
similar to—but not exactly like—an existin
ify a copy of the existing object rather than c
may still want to preserve the original. The
and modify the copy, *leaving the original inta*
for, say, a very specialized list for a very spe
are asked to produce a list of 500 fictional nam
ing application. You know that you will never r
to devote a lot of time to designing a report o
full of real names. You could scramble the first
new names, but it would destroy the data in you
of the table, scramble the names *in the copy,* pr
the data in it is meaningless).
From the database window, it is easy to co
shows you how to make a copy of the MAGIC ta

STEPS

1 Click MAGIC

FIGURE DB3-1 ■ LISTING OBJECTS IN THE DATABASE

The Database window is your window on the objects in your database files.

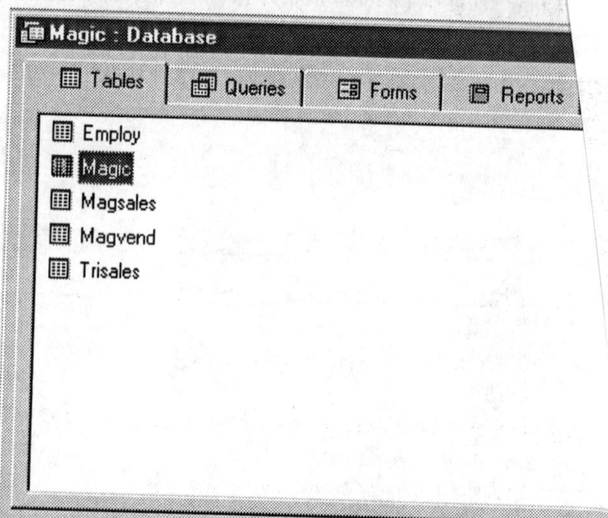

FIGU

(a) Cop
structur
(b) Cop

COPYING A TABLE STRUCTURE. The following exercise copies only the structure of the CUSTOMER LIST table to a new table called NAMES.

STEPS

1 **Open the Customer database window and click the table CUSTOMER LIST**

2 **Click *Edit, Copy*** Ctrl + C

3 **Click *Edit, Paste*** Ctrl + V

Once again, you will see the *Paste Table as* dialog box. Use Figure DB3-2b as your guide for the next step.

4 **Enter NAMES as the table name**

5 **Click *Structure Only* as the Paste option**

This indicates to Access that you want to copy the original table's structure but not the data (records).

6 **Click *OK***

To verify that the copy was properly made,

7 **Click NAMES and click the *Design* button**

You should see the same list of field names, types, and properties that you typed into CUSTOMER LIST. To close the table,

8 **Click the *Close* button**

9 **Close the Customer database window**

DB

COPYING SELECTED RECORDS. At times, you may not want to copy *all* records, only certain ones, into a new file. Perhaps you need to create a separate file of customers in Illinois or another of those who have not yet paid in full. You can accomplish this by creating a Make Table query. This exercise creates a new table called NAMES that contains only customers in New York City:

STEPS

1 **Open the Customer database window and then the CUSTOMER LIST table**

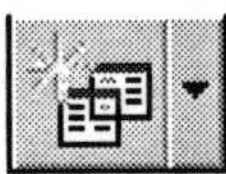

2 **Click the *New Object* drop-down button, then click *New Query, OK***

A Select query design screen appears.

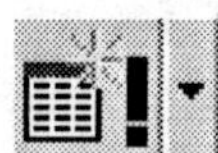

3 Click *Query, Make Table*

A dialog box appears asking for the name of the destination table. Using Figure DB3-3a as a guide,

4 Type Names as the table name, then click *OK*

It is possible to have the new table placed in another database file, but this table—being a list of customers—belongs in this database. It has no relationship to MAGIC, our only other database file. You should always try to keep *related* objects in the same database and resist inserting an unrelated object into a database file. Continue to design the query, referring to Figure DB3-3b.

5 Drag all field names to the Field row (Click *Customer Number,* press Shift + End and then drag the selection to the Field row)

> **Tip: To drag all field names in one mouse operation, click the first field name, shift-click the last field name, then drag all of them to the Field row of the first column.**

6 Tab (or Shift +Tab) to the City column

7 Move to the Criteria row and type New York City

FIGURE DB3-3 ■ COPYING SELECTED RECORDS TO A NEW TABLE

(a) The destination table name must be specified.
(b) This Make Query design screen will copy only "New York City" records to the destination table.
(c) Only the checked fields will be copied to the new table, NAMES.

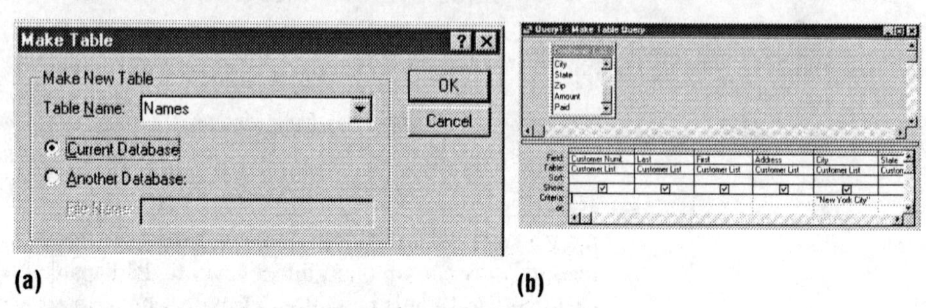

(a) (b)

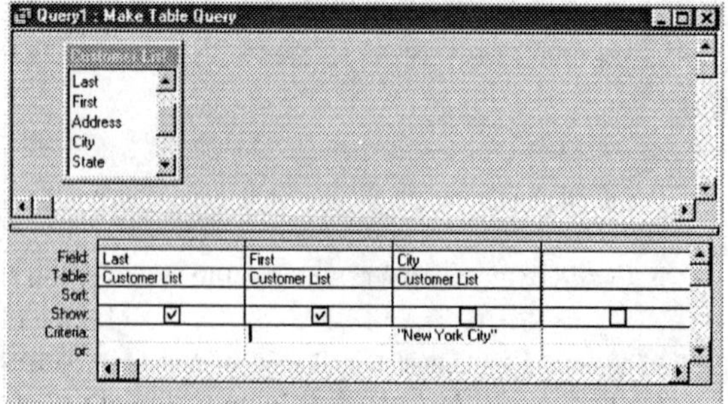

(c)

Tip: Any condition or combination of conditions can be used in the Query screen to limit the records that will be copied to the new table.

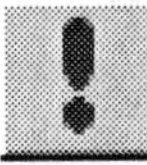

8 Click *Query, Run*

Access warns you that a table with the same name is about to be overwritten. This is, of course, the copy of CUSTOMER LIST's structure that you created in the last exercise. To approve the deletion of this table so the query can proceed,

9 Click *Yes*

In this example, only two records meet the stated condition. When Access asks you to confirm the addition of these two records to the table,

10 Click *Yes*

11 Close the Query window without saving the query

Next, verify that Access performed the query according to your expectations.

12 Click the *Database Window* button, if necessary

The database window should display the new table NAMES.

13 Display NAMES

It should contain only the Laudon and Martin records, who are the only two New York City customers. When you are finished,

14 Close all windows in the Access work area

COPYING SELECTED FIELDS. Not all fields need be copied into a new table. You may use the Make Table query to select fields, in addition to records, to appear in the destination table. Assume you wanted to create a new file with *only* first and last names (see Figure DB3-3c). You would follow the same procedure you used for copying selected records, but in Step 5 you would only drag the LAST, FIRST, and CITY fields to the Fields row of the Query design screen. The CITY field would not be copied to the destination table, but it would be used as criteria. Just be sure that the box in the Show row of the City column is not selected. The remaining steps are identical.

DB

ADDING RECORDS

Records can also be copied from one table to another simply by copying them to the Windows Clipboard and then pasting them into another table. The only restriction is that the fields in both the source table and the destination table must be of the same type and in the same order, because the paste procedure will place data from the first column of the source to the first column of the target, and so on. This exercise appends records of Illinois residents to the Customer Backup table, which you created in a previous exercise.

STEPS

1. **Open the CUSTOMER database window**

Now, copy the CUSTOMER LIST table to COPY OF CUSTOMER LIST.

2. **Click *CUSTOMER LIST***
3. **Click *Edit, Copy*** — Ctrl + C
4. **Click *Edit, Paste*** — Ctrl + V
5. **Open the CUSTOMER LIST table**

In the next step, you will select the records of those customers who live in Illinois. These records need to be grouped together so that you can select them in one mouse action.

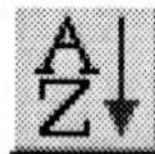

6. **Sort the table into State order (Reminder: Click the *State* column identifier, then click the *Sort Ascending* button)**

To select several records, the procedure is to click the row selector of the topmost record, then drag the highlight downward until all records have been highlighted. Use Figure DB3-4 as an example.

7. **Select the three Illinois records**

8. **Click *Edit, Copy*** — Ctrl + C

The records have been copied to the Windows 95 Clipboard. Next, display the destination table:

FIGURE DB 3-4 ■ ADDING RECORDS

Three records have been selected in Customer List to be cut and then pasted to another table.

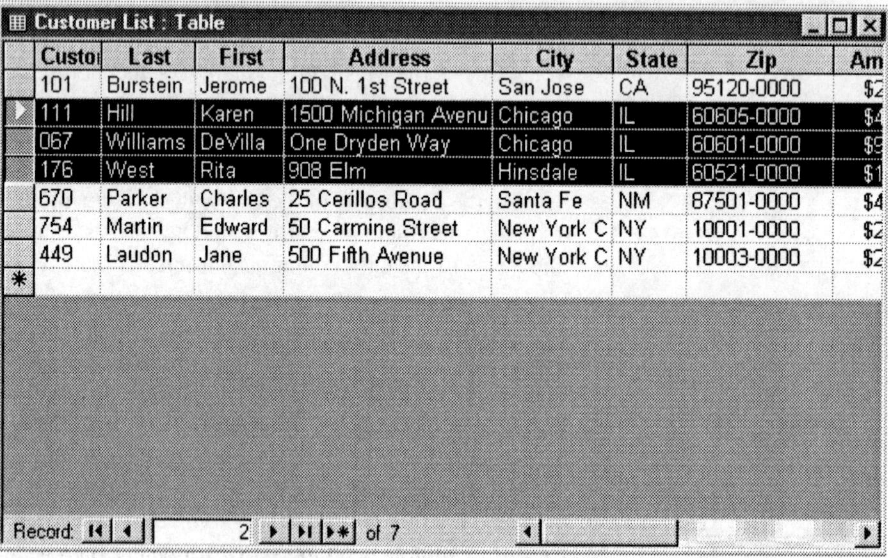

Customer List : Table

Custo	Last	First	Address	City	State	Zip	Am
101	Burstein	Jerome	100 N. 1st Street	San Jose	CA	95120-0000	$2
111	Hill	Karen	1500 Michigan Avenu	Chicago	IL	60605-0000	$4
067	Williams	DeVilla	One Dryden Way	Chicago	IL	60601-0000	$9
176	West	Rita	908 Elm	Hinsdale	IL	60521-0000	$1
670	Parker	Charles	25 Cerillos Road	Santa Fe	NM	87501-0000	$4
754	Martin	Edward	50 Carmine Street	New York C	NY	10001-0000	$2
449	Laudon	Jane	500 Fifth Avenue	New York C	NY	10003-0000	$2

Record: 2 of 7

9 Click the *Database Window* button

The database window is displayed.

10 Open the COPY OF CUSTOMER LIST table

If you have been following all the exercises in this book, you changed the width of the ZIP field since you created this copy. There will not be enough room for the wider zip codes unless you change the table's structure.

11 If needed, change the width of the ZIP field to 10, then return to datasheet view

12 Click *Edit*, then click *Paste Append*

Access will ask you to confirm the insertion of three records.

13 Click *Yes*

Your modified COPY OF CUSTOMER LIST table now contains ten records. When you are satisfied that the paste procedure was successful, you may as well remove the duplicate records:

14 Delete the records you just pasted using the procedure you learned in a previous exercise (select the 3 records, click *Edit, Delete Record, Yes*)

15 Close all windows in the Access work area without saving

RENAMING A TABLE

You can rename a table without affecting its contents. Renaming gives you the freedom to adjust names of files that already exit. This exercise changes the NAMES table to NAMES1.

STEPS

1 Open the Customer Database window

2 Click the NAMES table

3 Click *Edit*, then click *Rename*

4 Type NAMES1 then press ↵

The database window display should change to reflect the name change. You can use the same procedure to rename any object in an Access file.

DELETING A TABLE

At times you may want to remove, or delete, an object from the Database Window and the object's data from the database file.

DELETING OBJECTS IN THE DATABASE. For example, you may have designed a better report to use in place of an earlier report or you may have a sorted version of a table that you prefer to use in place of the unsorted version of the same data. You can delete a table —or any other object—by simply selecting the object name on the database window and pressing the Delete key. For example,

STEPS

1 **Display the Customer Database window**

2 **Click NAMES1**

3 **Press Delete**

Access will ask you to confirm the deletion:

4 **Click *Yes***

CHECKPOINT

- ✓ Display a list of all your reports in the CUSTOMER database.
- ✓ Display a list of all tables in the MAGIC database.
- ✓ Using DBTEST, copy only the table structure to DBTEST2.
- ✓ Copy only the names and TEST1 scores to DBTEST2
- ✓ Rename the DBTEST2 table to DBTEST3.
- ✓ Erase the DBTEST3 table.

MODULE 2: CREATING AND USING LABELS

Printing labels is an important activity for organizations that do a lot of mailing or shipping, and many Access users maintain mailing lists of employees, customers, subscribers, and so on. Labels can also be printed for inventory items in a warehouse or for file folders in a records department. To make the process of printing labels easier, Access includes a Label Wizard feature that walks you through the process of designing (in effect) a report that will print data on adhesive-backed, precut labels. Once printed in the appropriate positions, labels can then be removed and affixed to letters, packages, or files as needed. The following exercise demonstrates how to create and print data from the CUSTOMER LIST table on mailing labels. You need not have labels to perform the exercise. The data can be printed on regular paper as well.

CREATING LABELS

STEPS

1 **Open the CUSTOMER LIST table**

2 Click the *New Object* drop-down button, *New Report*

On the resulting *New Report* dialog box, shown in Figure DB3-5a, Access preselected the CUSTOMER LIST table because it was open. However, you could select another table at this point if desired.

3 Click *Label wizard*, then click *OK*

You will see the first in a series of *Label Wizard* dialog boxes that will walk you through the process of designing labels. The first step is to describe to Access all of the data you want printed on each line of the label. Typically, the data on any line of the label consists of the following:

- Field values from your data file
- Ordinary punctuation marks or spaces
- Abbreviations, words, or phrases (for example, "SSNO-" might precede the employee's Social Security number on a personnel file folder label)

If you examine Figure DB3-5b, you will see that the first *Label Wizard* dialog box displays a list of commercially available label types. If you intend to print on mailing labels, choose that type. If you are printing on plain paper,

4 Click *Avery number 5096*, then click the *Next >* button

Tip: If you are using a laser or ink jet printer, select *Sheet feed*. If you are using tractor feed paper in a dot matrix printer, select *Continuous*.

On the next dialog box, choose the *Font Name, Font Size,* and *Font Weight* that you prefer. The choices that are presented to you will depend on the printer you are using. In Figure DB3-5c, the choices you will see are Arial, 10 pt., medium weight. It is best not to select a font size larger than 10 point or the data may not fit on the label. Although you may choose any font, for this exercise,

5 Choose Arial, 10 pt., medium weight and then click *Next >*

As you see in Figure DB3-5d, Access provides you with a list of fields from CUSTOMER LIST and a rectangular area in which you can design the *prototype label.* You want to design a standard mailing label that will look like this:

ID# 754
Edward Martin
50 Carmine Street
New York, NY 10001-0000

The first line will contain the **literal string** ID#, a space and the customer number. The second line will contain the customer's first name, a space, and the customer's last name. The first line of the label facsimile is already selected. To begin,

6 Type ID# (Don't forget the trailing space)

FIGURE DB3-5 ■ DESIGNING MAILING LABELS

(a) First, select the Label Wizard.
(b) Choose the appropriate size.

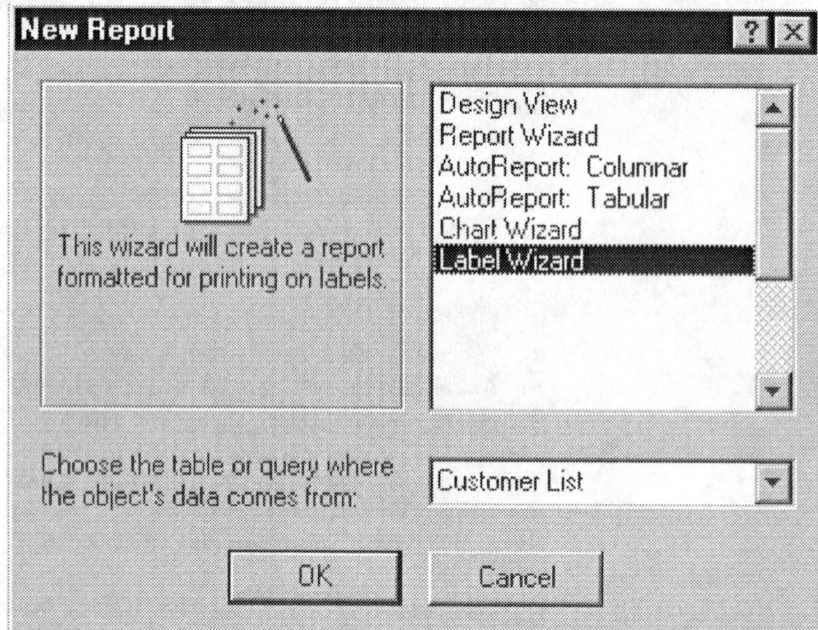

(a)

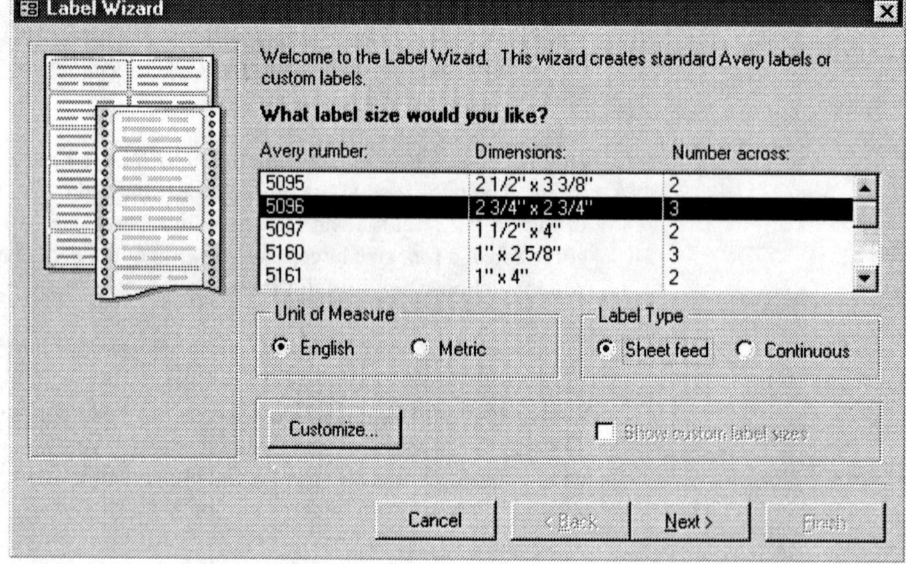

(b)

(continued)

This literal string will appear exactly as you typed it on every label. Next, insert the field CUSTOMER NUMBER.

7 Click CUSTOMER NUMBER in the Available fields list box, then click the > button

FIGURE DB3-5 ■ *(continued)*

(c) Choose the font and style you desire.
(d) Select the data that is to be printed on the label.

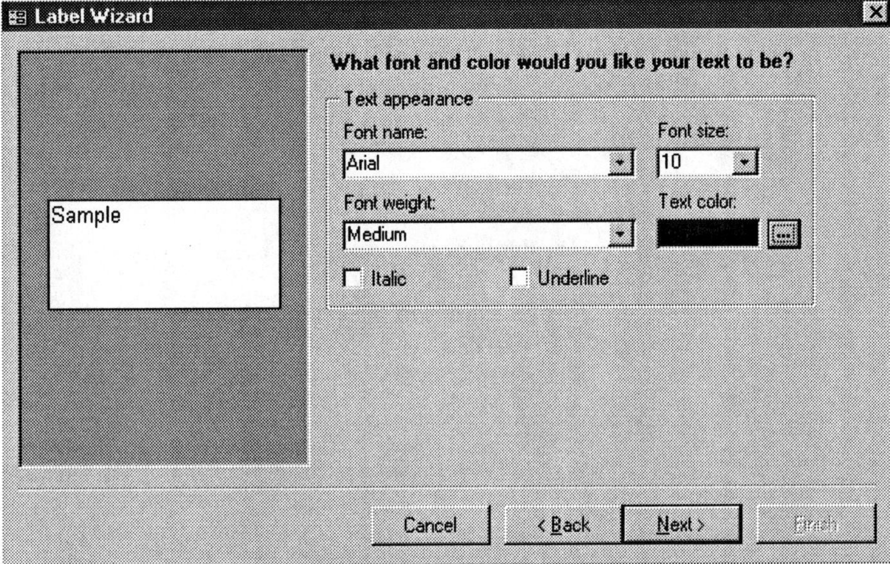

(c)

(d)

The field name should be inserted at the insertion point in curly braces as you see in the figure. You are ready to enter the next line on the Prototype label. To move the text insertion point down one line,

8 Press ↵

The second line of the prototype label is now selected.

DB

9 Click *FIRST*, then click the > button

You should see the field name FIRST appear on the facsimile of the label. Next, add a space and the last name:

10 Press Spacebar, click LAST, then click the > button

The address is next, but it belongs on another line, so:

11 Press ↵

The third line should now be selected on the label facsimile. Next,

12 Click ADDRESS, then click the > button

The ADDRESS field should appear on the second line.

> **Tip: If you make a mistake—like placing the ADDRESS field on the second line instead of the third line—you can remove an item from a line using the Delete and Backspace keys. You can move the text insertion point using the arrow keys or the mouse. To move to the fourth line,**

13 Press ↵

14 Click *CITY*, then click the > button

15 Press the Comma key , , then Spacebar

16 Click *STATE*, then click the > button

17 Press Spacebar twice

18 Click *ZIP*, then click the > button

Your screen should resemble Figure DB3-5d. Look over your design and make corrections as needed. Then,

19 Click the *Next* > button

Access opens a dialog box that asks in what order the labels are to be printed. The Post Office will give us a better rate on bulk mail if the envelopes are in zip code order.

20 Click *Zip* in the Available fields list box, then click the > button

Compare your screen to Figure DB3-6a, then

21 Click the *Next* > button

FIGURE DB3-6 ■ FINALIZING THE MAILING LABEL DESIGN PROCESS

(a) Select the field(s) by which the labels are to be sorted.
(b) The Label report needs a name, like any other Access object.

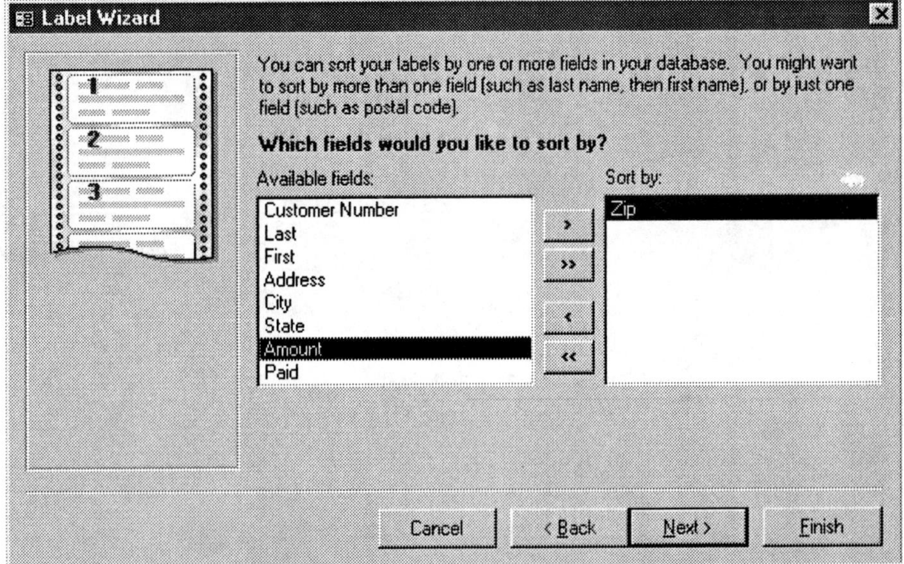

(a)

Label Wizard
What name would you like for your report?
Customer Labels by Zip Code
That's all the information the wizard needs to create your labels!
What do you want to do?
See the labels as they will look printed.
Modify the label design.
After it creates the label report, do you want the Wizard to display Help on working with labels?
Yes, help me work with labels.
Cancel
< Back
Next >
Finish

(b)

(continued)

On the final dialog box, Access asks if you want to provide a name for the label report object and if you want to see the labels as they will be printed. Using Figure DB3-6b as a guide,

22 **Type Customer Labels by Zip Code**

23 **Click the *See the labels as they will look printed* option, then click the *Finish* button**

FIGURE DB3-6 ■ *(continued)*

(c) The print preview of the labels.
(d) The design view of the label report.

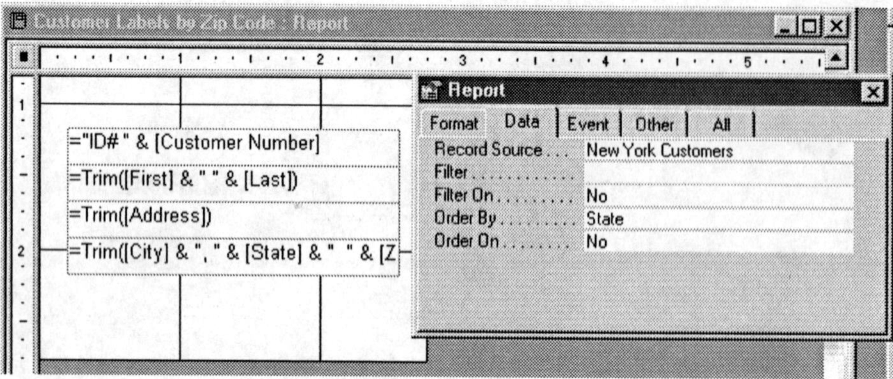

Depending on the speed of your processor and hard drive, Access may need a few seconds for processing. Then you will see an image of the first row of mailing labels on your screen similar to Figure DB3-6c. Note that the labels are sorted by zip code. Note also that the labels are three across, just as you selected. Use the scroll bars to verify that all seven labels were generated.

The Mailing Label wizard created a report that prints labels. This report can be modified in the same way that any other report can be modified. To see what objects were placed in the report,

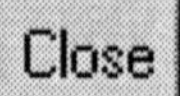

24 Click the *Close* toolbar button

CUSTOMER LABELS BY ZIP CODE was saved to the CUSTOMER database. It will appear on the Report Tab of the database window. Now, examine the screen.

Access displays the Design view of the label report form, as is shown in Figure DB3-6d. As you can see, it consists of a variety of objects that you could delete, edit, or move. The objects all have properties that can be altered. Of course, whether the Customer Labels report prints names in one, two, three, or more columns depends on the label product that you told Access you intended to use. Access stores the measurements of the most popular labels and uses them to design a report that will print properly on the label product you designate. If you purchase labels that are not on the list that comes with Access, you can enter the measurements of the new product.

After inspecting the report, print the labels:

25 Click *File, Print, OK*

26 Close all windows in the Access work area

If Access asks whether changes to the report should be saved,

27 **Click *Yes***

MODIFYING LABELS

Label forms are like any other report. They can be copied and modified for other uses. If you want to experiment with this on your own, use the procedures you learned to copy CUSTOMER LABELS BY ZIP CODE to PRACTICE LABELS, and then open the report for design. You will arrive at the Report Design screen, within which format parameters (object positions and properties) can be altered and saved.

PRINTING LABELS

Once a label form has been designed and saved as an object within the database, labels can be printed whenever desired. The steps are the same as those used to print any other report:

STEPS

1 **Open the CUSTOMER database window**

2 **Click the *Reports* tab, then *Customer Labels by Zip code* (or the name of the desired label form)**

3 **Click *File, Print, OK*** Ctrl + P , ↵

PRINTING LABELS FROM A QUERY. The source data for a label form can be changed so that the data is from a table other than the one for which the form was originally designed. Of course, the new table must have the field names and data types that the form expects. The following exercise prints labels from table created by a query.

STEPS

1 **If needed, open the CUSTOMER database window and then the Customer List table**

2 **Design a Select query that selects only those records for which the State value is NY**

3 **Save the query as New York Customers**

Remember, the query must include all of the fields that CUSTOMER LABELS BY ZIP CODE needs: CUSTOMER NUMBER, LAST, FIRST, ADDRESS, CITY, STATE, and ZIP. Other fields may or may not be included as you wish, since they will not be used in the process of printing the labels.

4 **Display the database window**

5 **Click the *Reports* tab, then click *CUSTOMER LABELS BY ZIP CODE***

6 Click the *Design* button

When the Label Form design screen appears,

7 Click *View, Properties*

A list of report properties appears.

8 Click the drop-down button next to Record Source, then click NEW YORK CUSTOMERS

9 Click the *Data* tab, move to the Order by row and type STATE

Compare what you have done with Figure DB3-6d. Then,

10 Click *File, Print, OK* Ctrl + P, ↵

When a report is attached to a query instead of a table, Access runs the query before printing the report. Any new customers from New York would be included in the print job. You should have two labels printed from your two New York state customers.

9 Close all windows in the Access work area without saving

CHECKPOINT

- ✓ Using DBTEST, create a two-line label form named DBTEST LABELS that will print the name on line 1, and the words "Test 1:" on line two followed by the Test1 grade. Select a label product that prints one across.
- ✓ Print DBTEST LABELS for the entire file; then print labels for those students whose Test1 grade exceeded 80.
- ✓ Modify the label form to include Test2 results on Line 3 labeled appropriately. Print the labels.
- ✓ Using the Label wizard, create another label form named DBTEST LABEL2 that uses a label product that prints three across. Instruct Access to sort the labels by Test2 score. Print all labels.
- ✓ Modify DBTEST LABEL2 so that Test1 is not printed. Move field and text objects so that the labels print neatly.

MODULE 3: CREATING CUSTOMIZED SCREENS

Using the *Autoform* feature (located on the New Object's drop-down list), Access will quickly create a Data Entry screen for any table. As you have seen, this Data Entry screen presents the field names at the left with highlighted entry areas to the right of each field. Although this screen is sufficient for most uses, you may want to design a screen that better suits your needs (or the needs of other users). You might want to rearrange the order of fields to match an input form, or use prompts that more clearly describe the data to be entered rather than the actual field names themselves. You may also want to title the screen, or add more fields to appear on one screen than the Access default screen allows.

DESIGNING A FORM

The Access Form Design screen allows you to specify a customized layout of your screen for data input, in much the same way you customized your report output. For example, Figure DB3-7a displays a customized screen for the CUSTOMER LIST table in Form view. Figure DB3-7b displays the same form in Design view. Although the fields are similar to the default entry screen, the layout and descriptions have been modified for better data entry. The first steps in designing this form are to open and size the Form Design screen:

FIGURE DB3-7 ■ DESIGNING A SCREEN FORM

(a) The data view of the screen form.
(b) The Form Design screen showing the completed form.

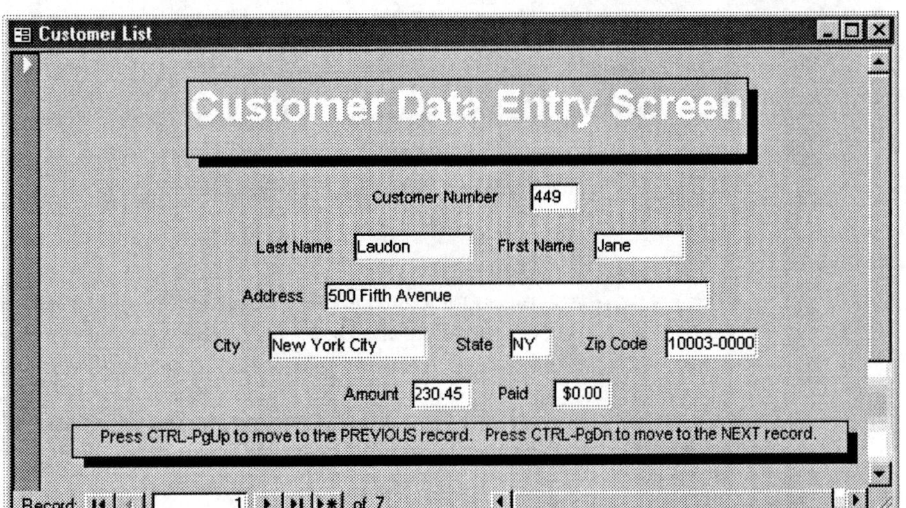

(a)

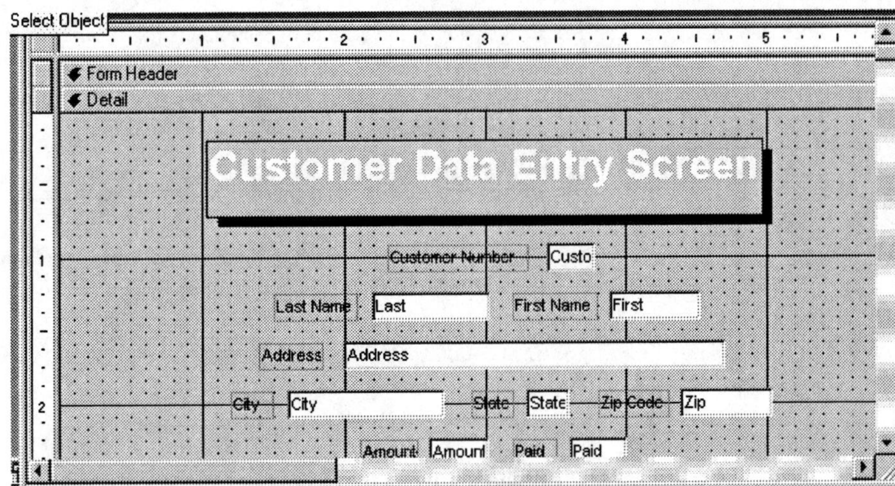

(b)

DB

STEPS

1. **Open the Customer Database window**
2. **Click the *Forms* tab, then click the *New* button**

On the resulting dialog box, indicate the table that this form is to be associated with:

3. **Click the *Choose the table or query. . .* drop-down button, click *Customer List,* click *Autoform: Columnar,* then click *OK***

Access will take a few moments to produce a standard screen form. Once this work has been finished, you can modify the form as you wish. When Access has displayed the finished form,

4. **Click *View, Form Design***
5. **Click the *Maximize* button of the *Form 1: Form* window** Alt + –, X
6. **Move the toolbox and Field List windows as needed**

THE FORM DESIGN SCREEN. Access is now displaying the same form in the Form Design screen. Like the Report Design screen, this screen is where you can insert text, field objects, and graphics.

STEPS

As you examine the Form1: Form window, notice that the Field objects currently occupy the left side of the Detail band, and the right side is empty. You will first resize the Field objects area using the horizontal and vertical rulers as a guide.

1. **Slowly point to the right vertical margin of the Detail band's Field objects area until your pointer changes to a cross with double-arrow heads on the horizontal line**
2. **Drag and drop the right margin to 6" on the horizontal ruler**
3. **Drag and drop the bottom margin about 1½" down (4" on the vertical ruler)**
4. **Select all the objects on the screen and drag them downward to a point below the 1" mark on the vertical ruler**
5. **Display the toolbox (click the *Toolbox* button on the toolbar)**
6. **Click the Label *button* on the toolbox and draw a rectangle that is 3/4" tall and stretches from 1" to 5" on the horizontal ruler**
7. **Type Customer Data Entry Screen and press ↵**

8. **Click *View, Properties***

The properties menu for the text object appears. Adjust the properties using Figure DB3-8a as a guide.

FIGURE DB3-8 ■ MODIFYING A FORM DESIGN

(a) Changing the properties of the text object.
(b) The object's appearance is different because of the changes in its properties.

(a)

Label: Label18

Format | Data | Event | Other | All

Caption	Customer Data Entry Screen
Visible	Yes
Display When	Always
Left	1"
Top	0.1667"
Width	4"
Height	0.5833"
Back Style	Normal
Back Color	12632256
Special Effect	Shadowed
Border Style	Solid
Border Color	0
Border Width	5 pt
Fore Color	16777215
Font Name	Arial
Font Size	20
Font Weight	Bold
Font Italic	No
Font Underline	No
Text Align	Center

(b)

(continued)

DB

9 **Click the *Format* tab and then set properties for the label object using Figure DB3-8a as a guide (Note that clicking a row's drop-down button or "..." button will display its options.)**

To verify that the object displays as you want it to,

10 **Close the Properties dialog box**

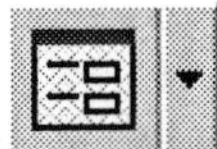

11 **Click the *View, Form* button**

After you have compared the results of your work with Figure DB3-8b,

12 **Click *View, Form Design***

FIGURE DB3-8 ■ *(continued)*

(c) Changing the properties of the label object.
(d) The resulting changes.

(c)

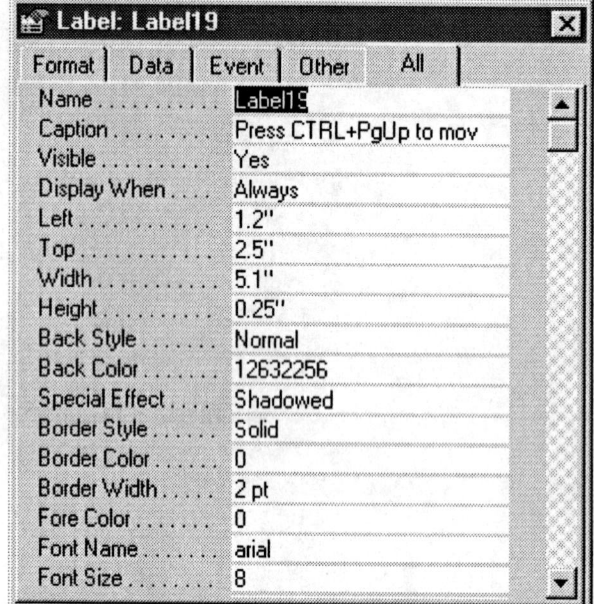

(d)

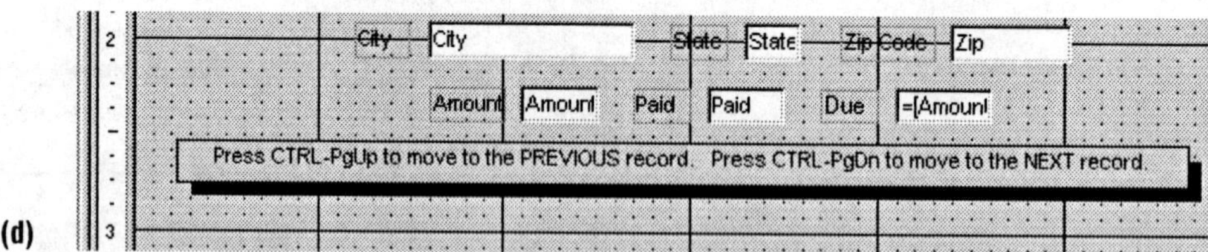

Now, change the Last, First, and Zip label objects to Last Name, First Name, and Zip Code and then move and resize all fields and related label objects as in Figure DB3-7b.

13 **Double-click the *Last* label object to place the insertion point there**

14 **Move the insertion point to the end of Last, press Spacebar, type Name and then press ↵**

15 **Repeat Steps 13 and 14 to change the label objects *First* to *First Name* and *Zip* to *Zip Code***

16 **Click the *Customer Number* label object and then shift-click the *Custo* field object to select them**

17 **Drag the selected objects to the position indicated in Figure DB3-7b and then release your mouse**

18 **Use the procedures in Steps 16 and 17 to move the other objects to the positions displayed in Figure DB3-7b**

19 **If needed, resize the objects by selecting them and then dragging one of their selection handles (small square boxes on the selection walls)**

Next, to create the label as indicated in Figure DB3-8d,

20 **Click the *Label* button on the toolbox and draw a label object that is 1/4" in height stretching across the lower portion of the form**

21 **In the new label object, type Press CTRL-PgUp to move to the PREVIOUS record. Press CTRL+PgDn to move to the NEXT record. and then press ↵**

22 **Click *View, Properties* for its dialog box**

23 **Adjust the properties for the label object (see Figure DB3-8c—your label number may differ)**

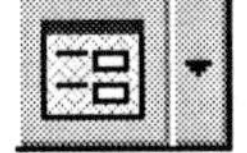

24 **Compare the appearance of the text box to Figure DB3-8d**

The objects associated with fields in the CUSTOMER LIST table can now be positioned as needed. There are several aspects of handling objects in the Form Design screen that you should practice until you are confident:

- *Selecting One Object.* An object can be selected by clicking it.
- *Selecting Multiple Objects.* Multiple objects can be selected by either shift-clicking each of them in turn or dragging the mouse along either the horizontal or vertical rulers. The mouse pointer will change to an arrow. Click and drag the arrow along the ruler and all objects located between the starting and stopping points of the procedure will be selected.
- *Appearance of Selected Objects.* When an object is selected, it becomes outlined and black rectangles, called *handles,* are associated with the boundaries of the object.
- *Resizing an Object.* Dragging and dropping a handle causes the boundary attached to the handle to be stretched in the direction that you are dragging.
- *Deleting a Selected Object.* Pressing the Delete key deletes all selected objects.
- *Moving a Selected Object.* If you place the mouse pointer on a boundary between handles, the pointer changes shape to that of a hand. When the mouse pointer assumes this shape, the entire object can be moved to another location on the Design screen using drag and drop.
- *Moving Multiple Selected Objects.* If several objects are selected, they can all be moved at once. Position the mouse on the boundary of one of the selected objects so that the pointer changes to a hand. Drag and drop all objects to the desired position.
- *Moving One Selected Object When Several Objects Are Selected.* Note that the upper-left handle of a selected object, called the **move handle,** is larger than the other handles. If you place the mouse pointer over the move handle, its shape changes to that of a hand with extended index finger. When the mouse pointer assumes this shape, you can drag and drop that object to another location on the Design screen. Other selected objects are not moved.
- *Handling Field Objects.* When placed on the Design screen, *field objects* are composed of two component objects: the field *name* and the field *value.* The field name is on the left. The field value is on the right.

Field name objects and field value objects are associated and can be moved together. However, by dragging and dropping the move handle, you can move one of the objects without moving the other.

Field name objects display the field name as a default value. However, clicking a selected field name object places a text insertion point inside the object. Existing text can be deleted. New text can be typed in. The object will grow to accommodate the new text.

Tip: The rules and procedures that apply to the Form Design screen apply equally to the Report Design screen.

25 Adjust the position of the objects, switching between Form view and Design view as needed

SAVING THE SCREEN FORMAT

Be sure to save the form to the CUSTOMER database. While in Design view,

STEPS

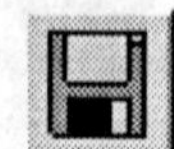

1 Click *File, Save* **Ctrl + S**

A dialog box will ask you to name the object.

2 Type Customer Form 1 and click *OK*

3 Close the Form window

MODIFYING A SCREEN FORMAT

Like report and label formats, screen formats can be modified as needed. The following exercise demonstrates the modification procedure by adding frames around a few Data fields for emphasis and creating a calculated field. Figure DB3-9a shows the finished form that is your goal for this exercise.

STEPS

1 Open the CUSTOMER database

2 Click the *Form* tab, then click *Customer Form 1*

3 Click the *Design* button

The Form Design *screen* reappears. At this point, you could execute any of the following choices:

- Exit the screen without making changes by closing the window.
- Insert and reposition objects by dragging and dropping them to new locations.
- Add or erase descriptive text or table fields.
- Enhance the screen with frames.
- Create calculated fields.

The first choice requires no further explanation. You may want to explore the next two possibilities on your own at a future date—the process of modifying a form is just like designing it. This exercise examines the final choices—enhancing the screen and creating calculated fields.

7 If you do not receive a Convert/Open Database dialog box, click *File, Save As/Export,* type MAGIC and then click the *Save* button to resave the database as MAGIC

This chapter uses the database MAGIC in many of the exercises.

The database window for the MAGIC database appears, as you see in Figure DB3-1. By clicking the various tabs on the database window (table, query, form, and so forth), you can display a list of all Access objects of a particular type. Experiment by clicking each of the tabs in turn. Of course, in every case except *Table,* there will be no object names because there are no objects of that particular type in the database.

COPYING AN OBJECT. You might want to make a copy of an object for many reasons. For example, often you will want to create an object (like a report or form) that is similar to—but not exactly like—an existing object. It may be easier and faster to modify a copy of the existing object rather than create a new one from scratch. However, you may still want to preserve the original. The solution is to create a copy of the object and modify the copy, *leaving the original intact.* Occasionally a one-time need will arise for, say, a very specialized list for a very special purpose. Suppose, for example, you are asked to produce a list of 500 fictional names that will be used for some sort of training application. You know that you will never need this list again, so you have no reason to devote a lot of time to designing a report or typing in 500 names. You have tables full of real names. You could scramble the first names and last names, creating a list of new names, but it would destroy the data in your table. The solution is to create a copy of the table, scramble the names *in the copy,* print the list, then *erase the copy* (since the data in it is meaningless).

From the database window, it is easy to copy an object. The following exercise shows you how to make a copy of the MAGIC table.

STEPS

1 Click MAGIC

FIGURE DB3-1 ■ LISTING OBJECTS IN THE DATABASE

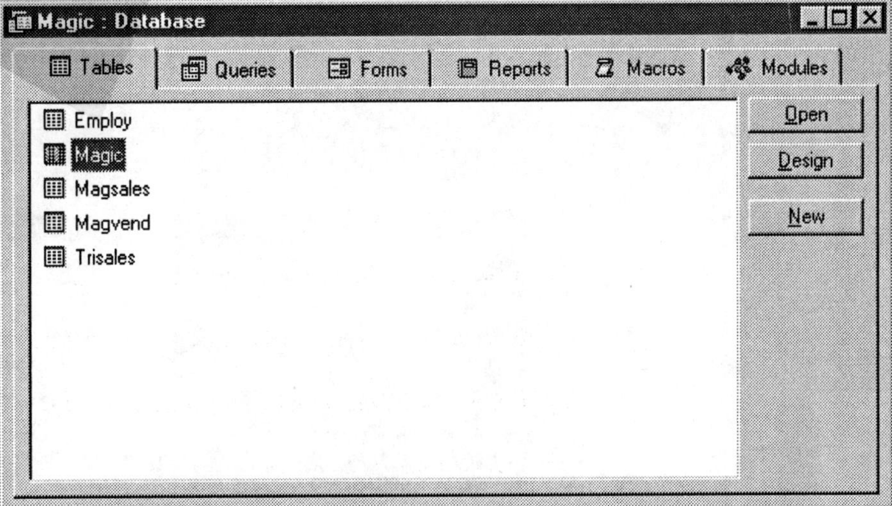

The Database window is your window on the objects in your database files.

DB

As you see in Figure DB3-1, the table MAGIC has been selected.

2 Click *Edit, Copy* **Ctrl + C**

Access understands that your intention is to copy the table MAGIC, because that object was selected when you clicked the *Copy* button.

3 Click *Edit, Paste* **Ctrl + V**

This tells Access that you are ready to complete the copy process. A dialog box, similar to Figure DB3-2a, will give you some options. First, you must provide a name for the new object.

4 Type Duplicate Copy of Magic as the name

Then, you must tell Access whether you want to copy the table's structure only, copy the table's structure *and* data,or append the table's records to some other table.

5 Click *Structure and Data*, then click *OK*

Access makes a duplicate copy of the table MAGIC, places it in the same database file (you will probably notice the disk drive light come on), and gives it the name you typed in. Your database window should display the new table's name along with the other table names.

Warning: This copy process has many uses, but it is *not* the best way to protect you from data loss. A true backup copy of your data is intended for use if the original is destroyed through human error, equipment failure, disaster (such as a fire or flood), or sabotage (disgruntled employees *have* deliberately destroyed data). If the MAGIC table were destroyed, the copy of MAGIC that you made in this exercise would probably be destroyed too, because it is in the same file and on the same disk. To protect your data with confidence, a verified backup copy must be made on a *different* disk—or on tape—and should ideally be *kept in a different location* than the original. (This may seem like a lot of trouble to go to, but it's a lot less trouble than retyping a few thousand inventory items!)

FIGURE DB3-2 ■ COPYING AN OBJECT

(a) Copying the table's structure and data.
(b) Copying structure only.

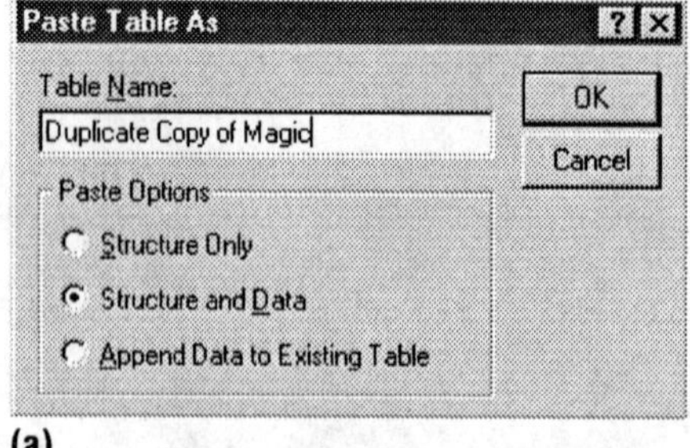

If you have a single floppy system, your data files have been copied to the disk in Drive A. If you have a dual floppy system, your data files have been copied to the disk in Drive B.

MODULE 1: TABLE MANAGEMENT

File management is an important aspect of controlling data. Remember, all Access objects are contained within database files. These database files can be copied or erased using Windows Explorer. However, the objects within the database file—tables, queries, and so forth— can only be copied, erased, or modified from within Access.

Perhaps you need to review existing objects or copy them. You may also want to erase unneeded objects or change the name of an object. The following exercises examine ways to list table names, copy entire tables or selected records from one table to another, and erase or rename objects.

WORKING WITH FILES AND TABLES

At times, you will want to know what database files are available. Access will list for you the database files within each folder. Then, once you have selected a database file, its database window lists all the objects in the database—but you can only see objects of a particular type at any one time, such as only tables or only queries. The following exercise will help you to become more familiar with the database window.

WORKING WITH THE DATABASE WINDOW. Perform the following actions:

STEPS

1 If needed, press Esc to remove the Access dialog box and then click *File, Open Database*

> **Tip: The exercises in this chapter presume that your data files are contained in the disk in Drive A. If this is not the case, be sure to substitute the appropriate drive letter.**

The *Open Database Window* dialog box appears.

2 Click the *Look in* drop-down button for its list

3 Click *3½ Floppy (A:)*

You should now see the name of the file you want to open: MAGICAL

4 Click the database file MAGICAL, then click the *Open* button

If you receive a Convert/Open Database dialog box, do Steps 5 and 6; otherwise, go to Step 7.

5 Click the *Convert Database* option, *OK*

6 In the *Convert Database into* dialog box, type MAGIC and then click the *Save* button

Tip: If you use Windows regularly, you should become familiar with Explorer. If you have not used Explorer before, consult your Microsoft Windows manual or *Mastering Today's Software: Windows 95* by Martin and Parker.

Place the Dryden data diskette in Drive A. If you have two floppy drives, place an empty, formatted diskette in Drive B.

Follow the instructions for your system.

SYSTEM WITH ONE FLOPPY DRIVE (A:)

3. **Insert the Dryden data disk in Drive A**
4. **Click the *Drive* C icon**
5. **Click *File*, *New*, *Folder***
6. **Type MAGIC and press ↵**
7. **Click the *3½ Floppy (A:)* icon**
8. **Double-click the *Access* folder**
9. **Click *Edit*, *Select All* to select all of the files in the folder**
10. **Drag and drop the selected files to the *Magic* folder in Drive C icon**
11. **Place your disk in Drive A**
12. **Click *View*, then click *Refresh***
13. **Click the Magic folder, then select all the files in it**
14. **Drag and drop the selected files to the *3½ Floppy (A:)* icon**
15. **Click the *Magic* folder in Drive C, then press Delete (if you want to delete the files from your hard drive)**
16. **Click Explorer's *Close* button and then launch *Microsoft Access***

SYSTEM WITH TWO FLOPPY DRIVES (A: AND B:)

3. **Insert the Dryden data disk in Drive A and your disk in Drive B**
4. **Click the *3½ Floppy (A:)* icon**
5. **Double-click the *Access* folder**
6. **Select all of the files in the directory (Select the first file, then shift-click the last file)**
7. **Drag and drop the files to the *3½ Floppy (B:)* icon**
8. **Click Explorer's *Close* button and then launch *Microsoft Access***

FIGURE DB3-9 ■ FURTHER MODIFICATIONS TO THE FORM'S DESIGN

(a) Draw a rectangle around Customer Number, Last Name, and First Name.
(b) Adjust the properties associated with the rectangle.
(c) Create a calculated field.

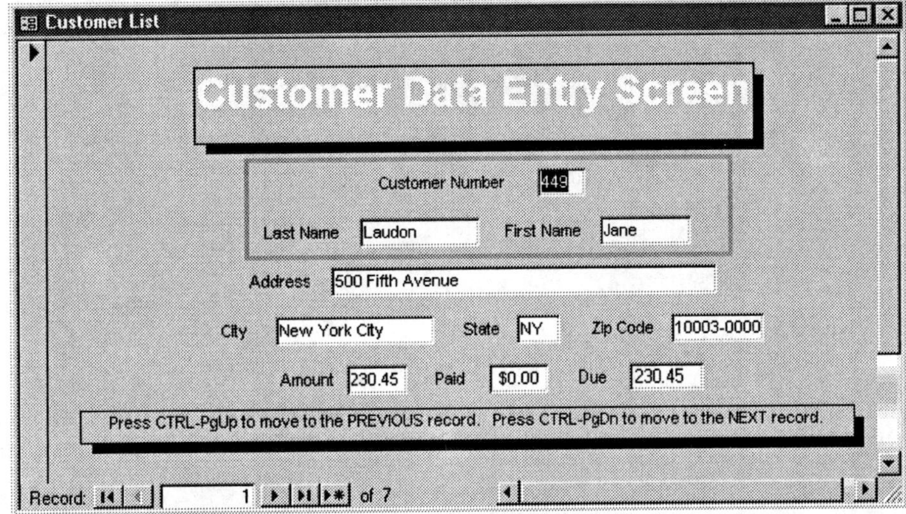

(a)

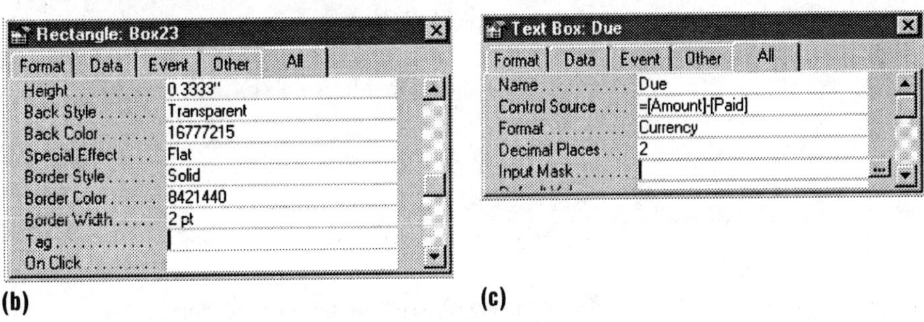

(b) (c)

CREATING FRAMES. Frames are **borders** that surround portions of a screen to separate its components or provide emphasis. They can be composed of lines of varying styles and thicknesses. This exercise creates frames around two portions of the form. The first frame will surround the customer number and name.

STEPS

1 If needed, open the toolbox

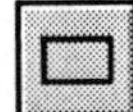

2 Click the *Rectangle* button on the toolbox (bottom right)

3 Draw a rectangle around the CUSTOMER NUMBER, LAST, and FIRST fields like the one seen in Figure DB3-9a (point to the position of the top left corner of the rectangle and drag diagonally southwest to the position of the bottom right corner)

Do not be concerned if the rectangle covers the objects inside it. This property can be easily adjusted. Using Figure DB3-9b as a guide and with the new rectangle still selected,

4 Display the *Properties* dialog box, then adjust the properties of the rectangle

Set the rectangle's properties as follows:

Back Style	Transparent
Back Color	White (or your preference) (use the "..." button)
Special Effect	Flat (or your preference)
Border Style	Solid (or your preference)
Border Color	Dark Gray (or your preference)
Border Width	2 pt (or your preference)

5 Close the *Properties* dialog box

6 Click *View, Form*

Examine your results and compare them to the figure. To return to Design view,

7 Click *View, Form Design*

8 Close all windows in the Access work area, resaving the changes under *Customer Form 1*

CREATING A CALCULATED FIELD. Screens can also be designed to display calculated fields. A **calculated field** manipulates data from other table fields to display results that are not normally contained within the table. You might perform math on field values or constants, compare dates, or combine text material. This exercise creates a calculated field that displays the amount owed by customers (by subtracting the PAID field from the AMOUNT field).

First, of course, CUSTOMER FORM 1 must be opened for design, if necessary.

STEPS

1 Open the CUSTOMER database window

2 Click the *Forms* tab, then click *Customer Form 1*

3 Click the *Design* button

Customer Form 1 should appear in the design mode. Next, to add the "Due" objects as in Figure DG3-9,

4 Select the AMOUNT and PAID objects and then drag and drop them to the left as in the figure

5 If needed, open the toolbox

6 Click the *Text Box* button on the toolbox

7 Point to the right of the PAID field, where the top left corner of the new object will appear, and click

This object has, as yet, no connection to any data in any table and is hence referred to as *unbound*. Begin by altering the label that appears with the object:

8 Click the new label object twice (do not double-click) to place a text insertion point there, delete any text, and type Due

9 Reposition and resize the objects as needed and then deselect the objects

10 Select the unbound object, then display the *Properties* dialog box

Next, Figure DB3-9c shows how to change the properties of the unbound object so that it performs a calculation.

11 Change the Name property to Due

12 Change the Control Source property to =[Amount] – [Paid]

Note that the equal sign (=) begins the formula and that [field] names are in square brackets. Next, Access needs to know what kind of number is being calculated.

13 Change the Format property to Currency

14 Change the Decimal Places property to 2 and then close the dialog box

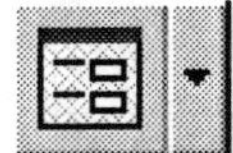

15 Click *View, Form*

Compare your results to Figure DB3-9. The next step will be to put a frame around the three numeric fields to set them off from the rest of the data on the form.

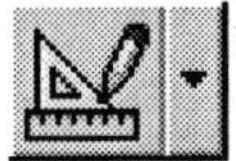

16 Click the *View, Form Design* button

17 Open the toolbox, if necessary

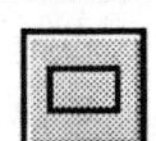

18 Click the *rectangle* button on the toolbox and draw another rectangle on the Form Design screen around the *Amount, Paid,* and *Due* objects as in Figure DB3-10

19 With the rectangle object selected, click *View, Properties*

Make the rectangle's properties correspond to those shown below:

20 Change the Back Style property to Transparent

21 Change the Special Effect property to Flat

22 Change the Border Style property to Solid

23 Change the Border Width to 2 pt and then close the dialog box

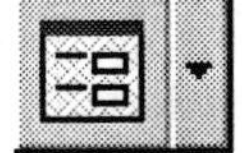

24 Click *View, Form*

Compare your results with the figure. As you can see, a screen form can be continually modified to enhance user satisfaction, improve the accuracy of data entry, or reflect changing needs.

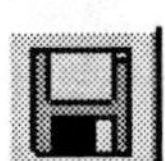

25 Save your changes and close all windows in the Access work area

USING THE SCREEN FORM

Screen formats can be selected for use from the database window. The following exercise demonstrates how to use your newly designed format to view, enter, and edit data in the table.

VIEWING DATA. Viewing data through a screen format is a simple process.

STEPS

1 **Open the CUSTOMER database**

2 **Click the *Forms* tab**

3 **Select *Customer Form 1*, then click the *Open* button**

The first record of the table is displayed in the form you have designed as you see in Figure DB3-10a. The screen format alters the way the table's data are presented. Note that the calculated field automatically displays a value that is not normally contained in the table's data.

You can now scroll through the records by using the scroll buttons Access provides at the bottom of your form. Using the scroll buttons,

4 **Advance to the last record** Ctrl + End

5 **Return to the first record** Ctrl + Home

6 **Advance to Record 2** Ctrl + PgDn

> **Tip: To advance to a particular record, place the text insertion point in the record number window at the bottom of the form, delete the value, type in a new value, and press ↵.**

From the screen form, you can toggle back and forth from Form view to Datasheet view and back again using buttons on the toolbar.

7 **Click *View, Datasheet***

To return to the screen form,

8 **Click *View, Form***

DATA ENTRY. To see the effect of the new screen format, try the following data entry exercise:

STEPS

1 **Open Customer Form 1, if necessary**

FIGURE DB3-10 ■ ENTERING NEW RECORDS ON A SCREEN FORM

(a) A blank form is ready for data.
(b) The completed form.
(c) Zip code changes to be entered.

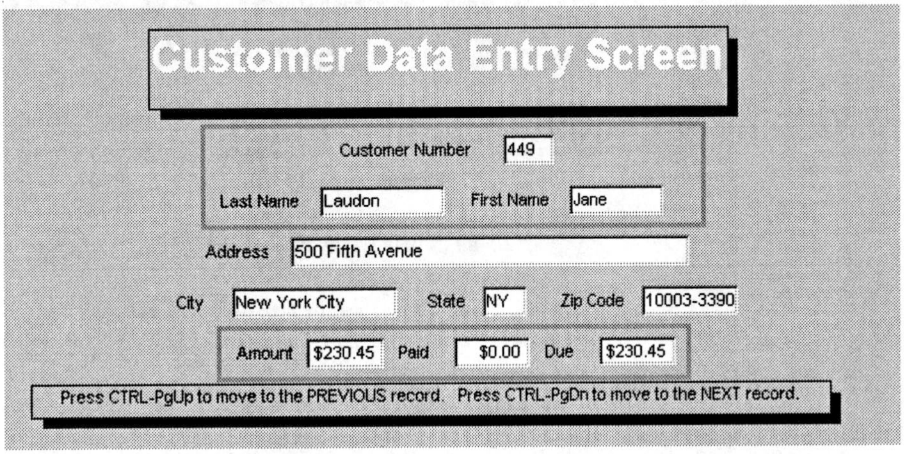

Customer Data Entry Screen

Customer Number 449
Last Name Laudon First Name Jane
Address 500 Fifth Avenue
City New York City State NY Zip Code 10003-3390
Amount $230.45 Paid $0.00 Due $230.45
Press CTRL-PgUp to move to the PREVIOUS record. Press CTRL-PgDn to move to the NEXT record.

(a)

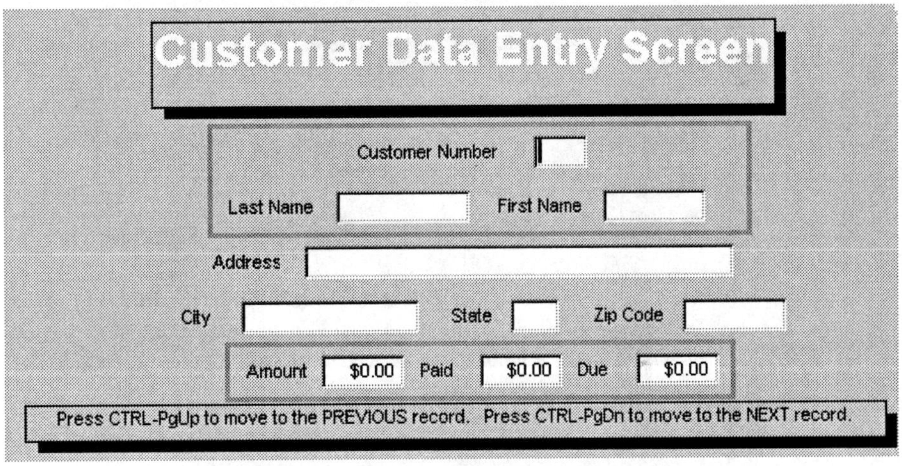

Customer Data Entry Screen

Customer Number
Last Name First Name
Address
City State Zip Code
Amount $0.00 Paid $0.00 Due $0.00
Press CTRL-PgUp to move to the PREVIOUS record. Press CTRL-PgDn to move to the NEXT record.

(b)

Last	First	Zip
Burstein	Jerome	95120-1234
Hill	Karen	60605-0078
Laudon	Jane	10003-3390
Laudon	Kenneth	10003-1101
Martin	Edward	10001-2220
Parker	Charles	87501-9283
West	Rita	60521-1666
Williams	DeVilla	60601-5577

(c)

2 Click the *New Record* button at the bottom of the window

> **Tip: Another *New Record* button appears to the right of the scroll buttons at the bottom of the form. Use either one.**

Access advances immediately to the blank record at the bottom of the table as shown in Figure DB3-10b. The text insertion point is waiting in the first field—CUSTOMER NUMBER—for you to begin filling in this record. Enter these data:

3 Enter the ID number as 450

Press **Enter** or **Tab** to advance to the next field. **Shift**, **Tab** moves the text insertion point to the previous field.

4 Type Laudon for the last name and Kenneth for the first name

5 Type the address as 501 Fifth Avenue

6 Type the city and state as New York City and NY

7 Type the zip code as 10003-0000

8 Type the amount owed as 455.62

9 Type the amount paid as 400.00, then press Tab

Note that the Due amount is calculated automatically by the formula you entered in a previous exercise. As the Due amount is calculated, it cannot be edited. That is, you cannot change or type over the figure Access calculated.

10 Click the *Next Record* button at the bottom of the form **Ctrl + PgDn**

Access advances to the blank record that is found at the bottom of every table so the entry process can continue. Instead of entering a new record,

11 Close all windows in the Access work area

EDITING. The format screen can also be used when you edit records. This exercise will change the zip codes for all your records to those listed in Figure DB3-10c. To make this easier, first sort the CUSTOMER LIST table into alphabetical order:

STEPS

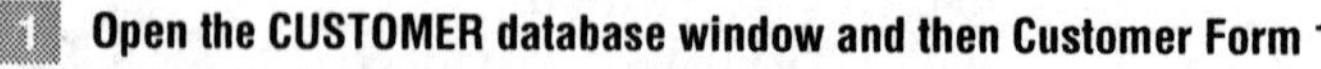

1 Open the CUSTOMER database window and then Customer Form 1

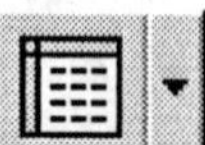

2 Switch to *Datasheet* view

3 Select the *Last Name* and *First Name* field columns

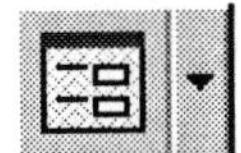

4 Click *Records, Sort, Ascending*

Access sorts the records in ascending order by last name, because that was the left-most highlighted column. Whenever records had the same value in the LAST field (like Laudon), Access sorted those records by the FIRST field, because it was the next highlighted column.

5 Switch to *Form* view

6 Tab to the ZIP CODE field

7 Type the zip code for Burstein: 95120-1234

8 Click the *Next Record* scroll button at the bottom of the form Ctrl + PgDn

Access advances to Hill's record, because it is the next one in alphabetical order by last name. The ZIP CODE field is highlighted because Access keeps the insertion point in the same field when you scroll from record to record.

9 Enter the remaining zip codes using this process and the data in Figure DB3-10

10 Close all windows in the Access work area

CHECKPOINT

- ✓ Create a customized screen for DBTEST named Form 1. Have it display the NAME field at the left and TEST1 and TEST2 fields at the right of the screen.
- ✓ Modify the screen to draw a 3 pt. frame around the NAME field.
- ✓ Using the screen, add two more names and sets of test scores to the DBTEST table
- ✓ Put a calculated field—AVERAGE—on the form that averages exam scores.
- ✓ Place a frame around the average.

MODULE 4: RELATIONAL DATABASES—USING MULTIPLE TABLES

Until now, you have used Access as a file management system—that is, using only one table at a time. However, Access is a true relational database. This means that you can work with more than one table at a time, sharing data as if the files were part of one large table.

At times, you will want to use data from more than one table to create lists or reports, or you may even want to develop editing screens that display data from a number of sources. Access will do this for you by creating separate forms for each table and then linking the tables together using a common data field.

For clarity, the form for the main table you are using will be called the **master form**, whereas each form to which it refers will be called a **detail form**. The Access program can *embed* (place) detail forms in the master form. There is one basic rule for linking tables:

- One field must be common to both the master table and the detail (linked) table—it must have the same data type and size in both tables. This field serves as the connection between two separate tables.

The following exercises demonstrate two types of links that are available in Access: a *one-to-many* link and a *many-to-one link.* (Although Access can also create one-to-one and many-to-many links, they are not discussed here.) The exercises use two tables that should be available on your data disk: MAGIC and MAGVEND. You should find them in a database named MAGICAL.

Access will develop forms for the MAGIC and MAGVEND tables, and then it will embed one in the other, thus linking data from the two tables. Figures DB3-11a–d show the structure and data for these two tables. MAGIC contains a sample product list for a small mail-order business; MAGVEND contains detailed listings for suppliers. Note that the VENDOR code field is identical in both, making it the common field that will link the two tables. If you do not have these tables on your disk (or if you want to practice), create them now using the data contained in the figures.

CREATING A ONE-TO-MANY LINK

In a **one-to-many link**, each master record is linked to a group of detail records. In this exercise, a MAGIC table detail form (products) will be embedded into a master MAGVEND table form (vendor), so that the screen will show all the products associated with a given vendor. The procedure is going to be performed mostly by the Access wizard feature. You will then smooth out a couple of rough edges using techniques you have already learned in working with the Report Design screen. The final product is shown in Figure DB3-12. Take a minute to examine this form. Note that it displays the MAGIC R US record from the MAGVEND table. Beneath that record is a list of all the products that our store purchases from that vendor. One field is common to both tables: The VENDOR field. This is the field on which the two tables are linked in this report.

Note also that there are two sets of scroll buttons. One set permits you to scroll through the MAGVEND (vendor) table and the other lets you scroll through the MAGIC (product) table. In the following exercise, you will create this form.

STEPS

1 Open the MAGIC database window

You will see a list of tables. MAGIC and MAGVEND are two of the tables on the list. You may wish to display them and compare them to the figures so you can become familiar with their contents and structure. To begin the work of creating the form itself,

FIGURE DB3-11 ■ MAGIC AND MAGVEND TABLES

(a) Magic's records.
(b) The structure of Magic.

(a)

ID	ITEM	COST	PRICE	VENDOR	STOCK
B68	BALLOONS	$6.80	$9.95	TRI	8
C45	CARD ON CEILING	$4.50	$6.95	TRI	8
E11	CHANGING PICTURE	$1.10	$1.95	TMH	22
E68	CHINESE STICKS	$16.80	$24.95	MRU	13
M98	CIGAR THRU QUARTER	$19.80	$29.95	TMH	38
E60	CLOSEUP PAD	$6.00	$8.95	TMH	28
E67	COLOR CHANGING CAR	$0.90	$0.95	TRI	8
E30	INCREDIBLE PEN	$13.00	$18.95	TMH	36
E49	LOLLIPOP TRICK	$0.90	$0.95	TRI	8
D72	MAGIC DICE	$7.20	$10.95	TMH	28
E41	MULTIPLYING RABBITS	$4.10	$5.95	TRI	10
E68	NOISE BOX	$16.80	$24.95	TMH	36
E25	PAPER HAT TEAR	$2.50	$3.95	MRU	13
C17	PLAYING CARDS	$1.70	$2.95	TRI	7
R44	RAINBOW ROPES	$14.40	$21.95	MRU	13
R16	ROPE TO SILK	$21.60	$31.95	MRU	14
E29	SLIP OFF SPOTS	$2.90	$3.95	MRU	13
S34	SPONGE BALLS 1"	$0.90	$1.20	TMH	18
S13	SPONGE BALLS 2"	$1.30	$1.95	TMH	22
C12	THREE CARD ROUTINE	$1.20	$1.95	TRI	9
E26	TOP HAT	$12.60	$18.95	MRU	13
M50	VANISHING QUARTER	$5.00	$7.95	TRI	9
E81	WATCH WINDER	$8.10	$11.95	MRU	15
E34	WISH BOTTLE	$3.40	$4.95	TRI	9
E22	ZIPPER BANANA	$2.20	$2.95	MRU	15

(b)

MAGIC : Table

Field Name	Data Type	Description
ID	Text	Item identification number
ITEM	Text	Item name
COST	Currency	Cost per unit
PRICE	Currency	Sales price per unit
VENDOR	Text	Vendor selling item
STOCK	Number	Count of item/units on hand

Field Properties

(continued)

2 Click the *Forms* tab, then click the *New* button

The *New Form* dialog box asks you for a table name. The master table in this exercise will be MAGVEND, which contains a list of the three vendors that sell merchandise to our retail store.

3 Click *Form Wizards*, click the *Choose the table or query ...* drop-down button, click *MAGVEND*, and then click *OK*

FIGURE DB3-11 ■ *(continued)*

(c) The structure of Magvend.
(d) Magvend's records.

(c)

VENDOR	COMPANY	ADDRESS	CITY	STATE	ZIP
TRI	TRICKS, INC.	9876 Wand Way	Denver	CO	80110
TMH	THE MAGIC HOUSE	75 Rabbit Hutch	Hollywood	CA	90021
MRU	MAGIC R US	1735 Showbiz Street	Brooklyn	NY	11201

(d)

MAGVEND : Table

Field Name	Data Type	Description
VENDOR	Text	Vendor identification code
COMPANY	Text	Vendor name
ADDRESS	Text	Vendor address
CITY	Text	Vendor city
STATE	Text	Vendor state
ZIP	Text	Vendor zip code

On the first *Form Wizards* dialog box, shown in Figure DB3-13a, you must indicate which fields you want displayed on the form. Select all of them:

4 Click the >> button to select all fields and then click the *Next* > button

The next dialog box (see Figure DB3-13b) asks which type of layout is preferred. In this case, Columnar is the closest to our end product:

5 Click the *Columnar* option, then click the *Next* > button

FIGURE DB3-12 ■ A FORM USING A ONE-TO-MANY LINK

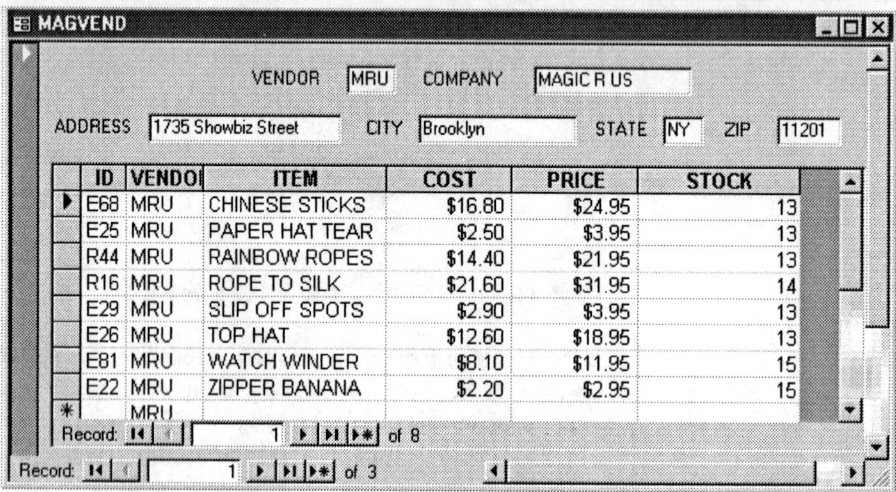
MAGVEND

VENDOR MRU COMPANY MAGIC R US

ADDRESS 1735 Showbiz Street CITY Brooklyn STATE NY ZIP 11201

ID	VENDOR	ITEM	COST	PRICE	STOCK
E68	MRU	CHINESE STICKS	$16.80	$24.95	13
E25	MRU	PAPER HAT TEAR	$2.50	$3.95	13
R44	MRU	RAINBOW ROPES	$14.40	$21.95	13
R16	MRU	ROPE TO SILK	$21.60	$31.95	14
E29	MRU	SLIP OFF SPOTS	$2.90	$3.95	13
E26	MRU	TOP HAT	$12.60	$18.95	13
E81	MRU	WATCH WINDER	$8.10	$11.95	15
E22	MRU	ZIPPER BANANA	$2.20	$2.95	15
	MRU				

Record: 1 of 8

Record: 1 of 3

FIGURE DB3-13 ■ CREATING A FORM USING A ONE-TO-MANY LINK

(a) Select the fields you want on the form.
(b) Choose the layout you desire.

Form Wizard

Welcome to the Microsoft Access Form Wizard.
Which fields do you want on your form?
You can choose from more than one table or query.

Tables/Queries:
Table: MAGVEND

Available Fields:

Selected Fields:
VENDOR
COMPANY
ADDRESS
CITY
STATE
ZIP

Cancel < Back Next > Finish

(a)

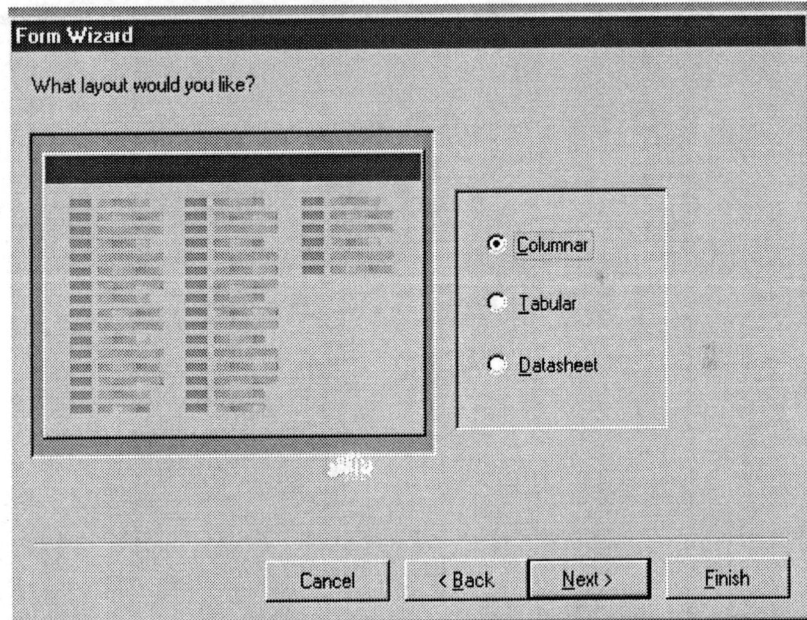

(b)

(continued)

The next dialog box (Figure DB3-13c) asks you to designate a style. You can select the style you want, but the figures in this book used *Standard.*

6 Click *Standard*, then click the *Next* > button

DB

FIGURE DB3-13 ■ *(continued)*

(c) Choose the style you prefer.
(d) Enter the report's title.

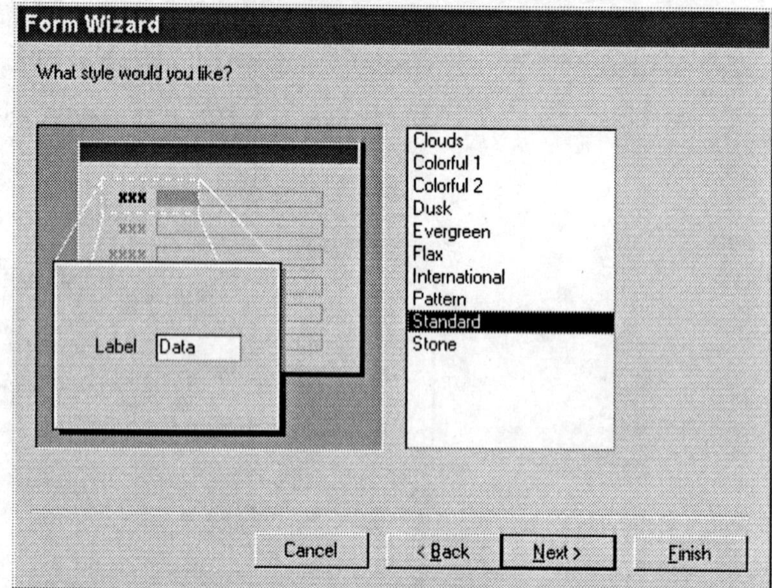

(c)

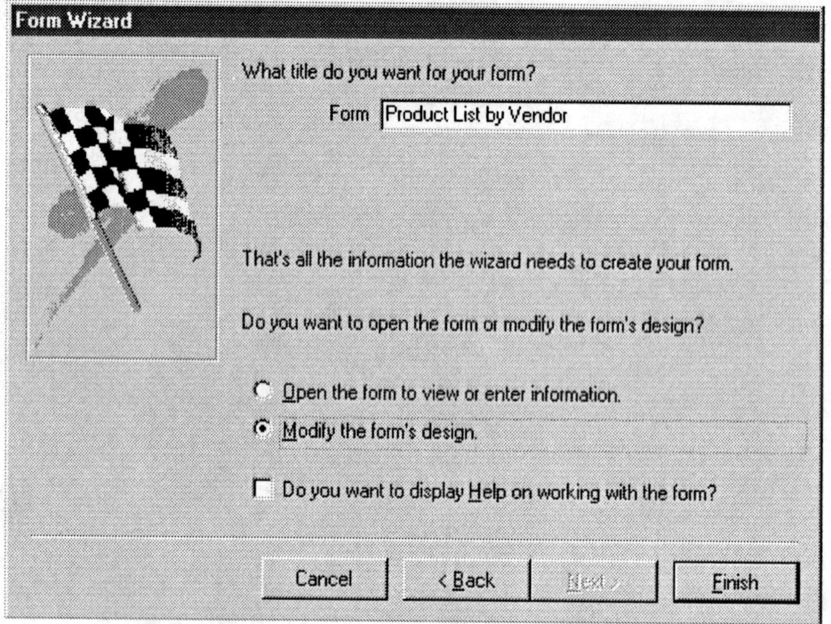

(d)

Next, indicate the title for the report (see Figure DB3-13d):

7 Type Product List by Vendor , click the *Modify the form's design* option, then click the *Finish* button

Access will use the information you have provided on these dialog boxes to create the form. Access displays the form in Design view (see Figure DB3-14a). You could have designed this form without the Access Form wizard, but this saved several minutes work. Now, some modifications need to be made. Using Figure DB3-14b as a guide:

8 Drag the right margin of the objects area in the Detail band rightward to 6" (use the horizontal ruler as a guide)

9 Rearrange and resize the field objects as shown in Figure DB3-14b (Remember, first select each object, drag it to move, or drag a selection handle to resize)

The fields from MAGVEND are now clustered toward the top of the form. Next, fields from the detail table—MAGIC—will be placed in the lower portion of the form.

10 Display the toolbox, if necessary

To perform the next steps, the Developer Tools feature must be installed on your system. Check with your instructor. Next, using Figure DB3-12 as a guide,

11 Click the *Subform/Subreport* button on the toolbox, then draw a rectangle to contain the subform table as in Figure DB3-12

FIGURE DB3-14 ■ MODIFYING THE FORM

(a) This is the form as designed by the Access Wizard.
(b) Rearrange the objects on the form so that they look like this.

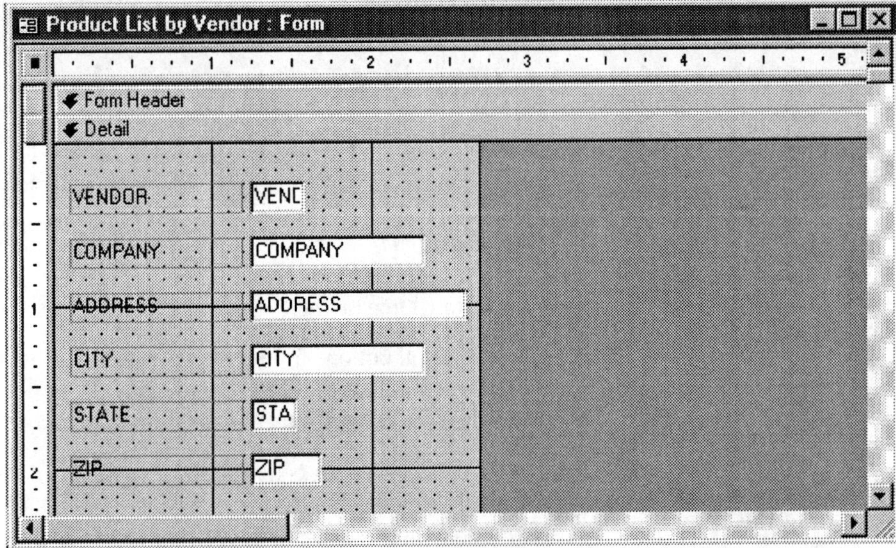

(a)

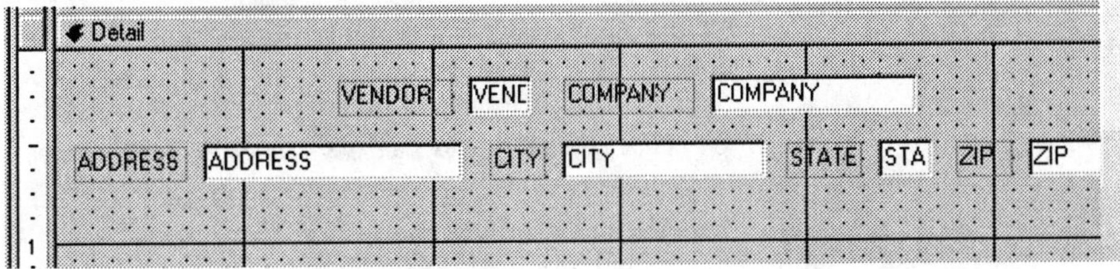

(b)

DB

Tip: The subform rectangle can easily be repositioned or resized, so do not be concerned if you don't position it perfectly the first time.

Not only does this procedure result in the position of the subform being indicated, but it activates the Access Subform/Subreport wizard. You will see a series of dialog boxes on which you can record your preferences for the subform.

The first dialog box (see Figure DB3-15a) asks whether you want to use an existing form or whether a new one has to be designed from a table or query.

12 Click the *Table/Query* option, then click the *Next >* button

As you see in Figure DB3-15b, Access wants to know which table and which fields from the table are desired.

13 Click the Tables and Queries drop-down button, click MAGIC as the table, select the fields in the order shown in Figure DB3-15b, and then click the *Next >* button

Next, Access searches through the fields of the two tables (MAGVEND and MAGIC) for possible links (fields of the same type and width). As you see in Figure DB3-15c, Access found only one: VENDOR. Because this field is present in both tables, it is the field we will use to link the data.

14 Click *Show MAGIC for each record in MAGVEND using VENDOR*, then click the *Next >* button

Finally, Access needs a name for the subform. As shown in figure DB3-15d

15 Type MAGIC Subform1, then click the *Finish* button

The Subform/Subreport wizard inserts the subform into the rectangle you drew and displays the final product in Design view. Verify that your work is comparable to Figure DB3-12.

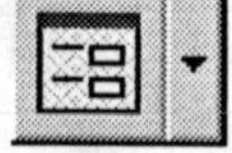

16 Click *View, Form*

Note the following features:

- A set of scroll buttons for the master table
- A set of scroll buttons for the detail table
- A vertical scroll bar for the detail table

Recognize that the vendor code for all the products corresponds with that of the Vendor. Normally, you would not need to have the VENDOR field displayed in the subform, but it was done in this exercise so you can verify with your own eyes that the two files are linked on this field. If you use the scroll buttons to change vendors, all of the detail records change to correspond to that vendor. First, save the form and then take some time to explore its features.

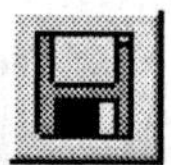

17 Click *File*, click *Save As/Export*, name the form Vendor Product List, then click *OK*

This form would be more useful if as much of the detail table as possible could be seen.

18 Alternate between Design view and Form view, resizing and moving objects as needed

FIGURE DB3-15 ■ THE SUBFORM/SUBREPORT WIZARD

(a) Indicate to Access that you intend to create a new subform.
(b) Select the fields to be on the subform.

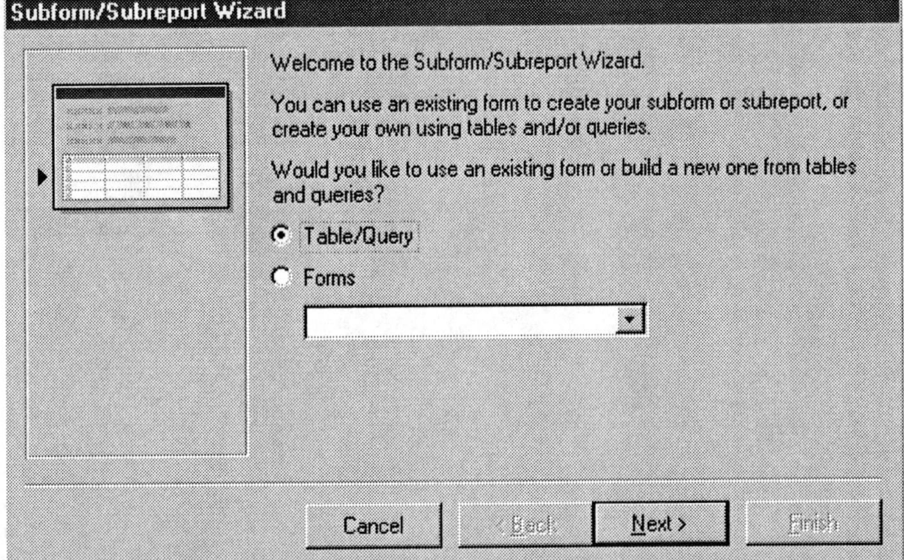

(a)

Subform/Subreport Wizard
Which fields would you like to include on the subform or subreport?
You can choose fields from more than one table and/or query.
Tables and Queries
Table: MAGIC
Available Fields
Selected Fields
ID
VENDOR
ITEM
COST
PRICE
STOCK
Cancel
< Back
Next >
Finish

(b)

(continued)

DB

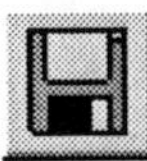

19 Save any changes to the form and close all windows in the Access work area

USING THE LINKED TABLES. Once a subform is embedded in the master form and tables are linked through a common field—whether you designed the form or the

FIGURE DB3-15 ■ *(continued)*

(c) Define the link between the two tables.
(d) Finally, name the subform.

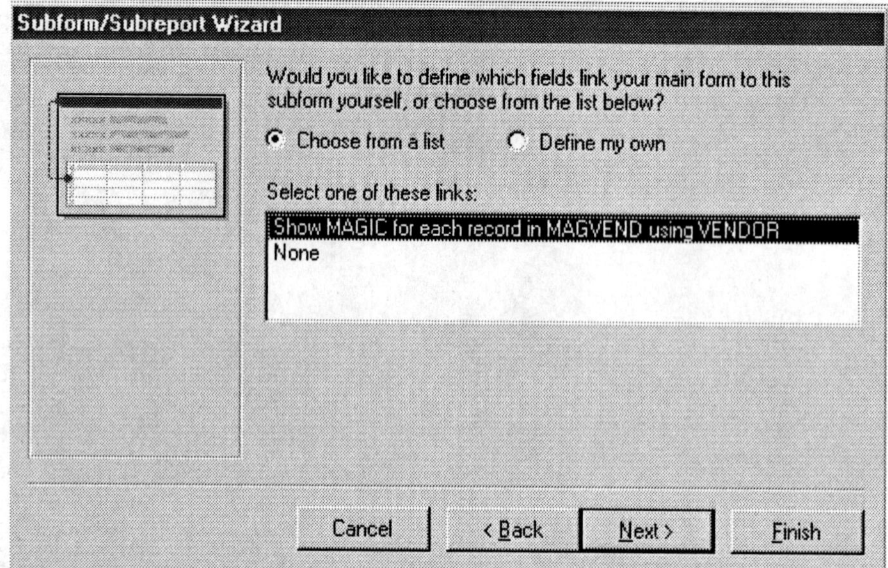

(c)

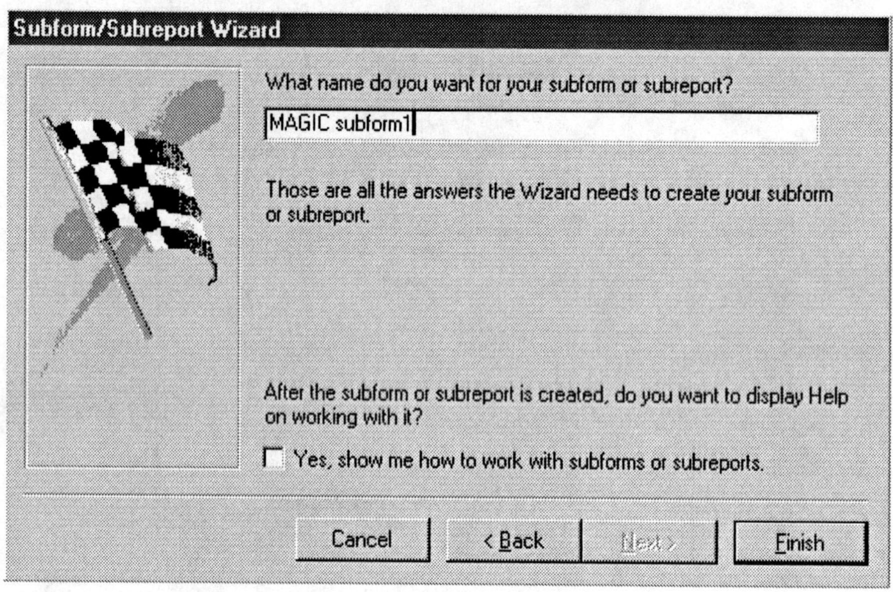

(d)

Form wizard did—you need only view the completed master form to display the desired fields. The following exercise demonstrates the uses of the one-to-many link.

STEPS

1 **Open the MAGIC database and then the form Vendor Product List**

The form displays the first vendor in the MAGVEND table with an embedded detail list of products in the MAGIC table that relate to this vendor. Values in either table can be edited directly in this form. New records may be appended and existing records can be deleted. Column widths can be adjusted. One problem with this form is that part of the product names have been truncated. However, if column widths are adjusted, then this problem can be offset without having to change the design of the subform.

2 **Adjust the column widths so the product names are completely visible**

3 **Close all windows in the Access work area**

CREATING A MANY-TO-ONE LINK

In a **many-to-one link,** each record within a group of master records is linked to one detail record. In this exercise, a MAGVEND table detail form (vendor) will be embedded into a master MAGIC table form (product), so that the screen will show the specific vendor information associated with each product. The procedure is mostly the inversion of the process of designing the previous report. The final product of this exercise is shown in Figure DB3-16.

In this case, however, you are first going to design the detail form. Then you will design the master form. Finally, you will insert the detail form in the master form. Naturally, we will get Access Wizards to do most of the work for us.

STEPS

1 **Open the MAGIC database window, if necessary**

FIGURE DB3-16 ■ THE FINAL PRODUCT

This form displays data from two tables.

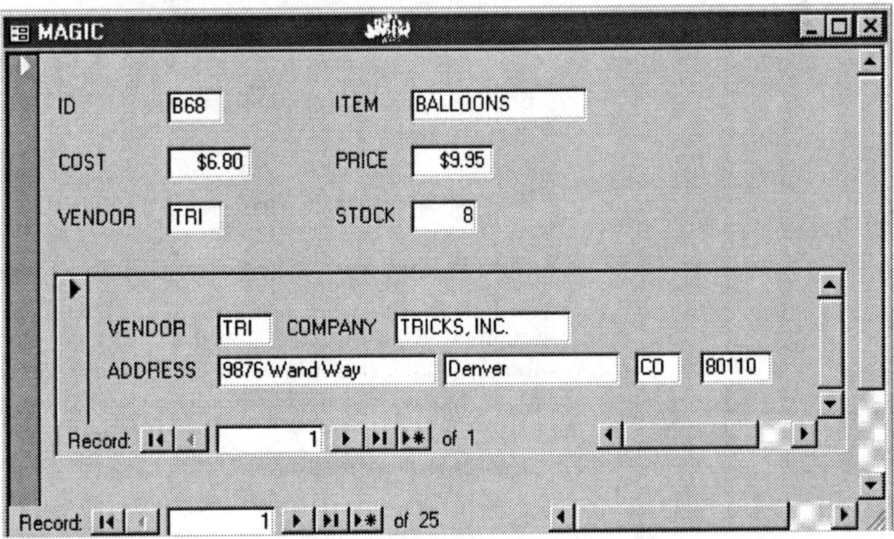

DB

2 **Select the *Tables* tab, then click MAGVEND**

3 **Click the *New Object's* drop-down button, and then *Autoform***

Access will create a simple form using all the fields in MAGVEND. When the form has been created,

4 **Click *View, Form Design View***

5 **Drag the right margin of the objects area to the 6" horizontal position (use the horizontal ruler as a guide)**

6 **Select only the City, State, and Zip label objects (do not select the related field objects) and then press Delete to remove them**

7 **Rearrange and resize the objects and then the band's height to resemble Figure DB3-17a**

Next, to save the form as MAGVEND Subform1 and close its window:

8 **Click the Form window's *Close* button, *Yes*, type MAGVEND Subform1 , and then click *OK***

The subform is now ready to be inserted in the master form. To create a master form:

9 **If needed, open the MAGIC database window**

10 **Click the *Tables* tab, then click MAGIC**

11 **Click the *New Object's* drop-down button and then *Autoform***

Access will create a simple form using all the fields in MAGIC. When the form has been created,

12 **Click *View, Form Design***

13 **Drag the right margin of the objects area to the 6" horizontal position (use the horizontal ruler as a guide)**

14 **Rearrange and resize the objects and then the band height to resemble Figure DB3-17b**

15 **Click *File, Save*, type Magic Product Information , and then click *OK***

Now, both forms have been designed. It is time to insert the detail form (MAGVEND Subform1) into the master form (Magic Product Information). At this point, you should see Magic Product Information on your screen in Design view.

16 **Open the toolbox, if necessary**

17 **Click the *Subform/Subreport* button on the toolbox and draw a rectangle filling the bottom half of the form to contain the subform as in Figure DB3-16**

FIGURE DB3-17 ■ CREATING A MANY-TO-ONE LINK

(a) Rearrange .the objects placed on the form by the Access Wizard.
(b) Rearrange these objects as well.
(c) Indicate that you want to insert the subform you just created.

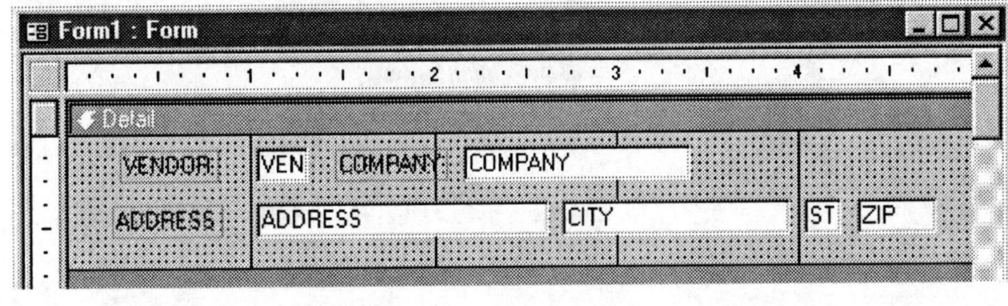

(a)

(b)

(c)

Access again activates the Subform/Subreport wizard. Again, you will see a series of dialog boxes, but in this case, the subform already exists. Using Figure DB3-17c as a guide,

18 Click the drop-down button, click MAGVEND Subform1, then click the *Next* > button

In the next dialog box, Access recognizes that VENDOR is the only possible link between these two tables. The dialog box should display "Show MAGVEND for each record in MAGIC using VENDOR." All you have to do is

DB

19 Click the *Next* > button

Finally, Access asks what name should be assigned to the subform. The default name is fine, so

20 Click the *Finish* button

At this point, Access displays the finished product in Design view.

21 Select the object label MAGVEND Subform1 and on the top left of the Subform field object, press Delete

22 Alternate between Design view and Form view, making adjustments as necessary to agree with Figure DB3-16

When you are finished, take some time to look at the form in Form view. Note again that the vendor code for the product corresponds with that of the vendor. If you use the scroll buttons to change products, the detail record changes to correspond to that product. Save the form and then take some time to explore its features.

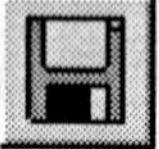

23 Click *File*, *Save* Ctrl + S

24 Close all windows in the Access work area

UNLINKING TABLES

Tables are linked only when you use a form or report that has been designed using a many-to-one or one-to-many relationship. Tables can be used separately by selecting other forms or using no forms at all. You need not worry about unlinking tables.

CHECKPOINT

- ✓ Create a table called DBNAME that includes a NAME field and an ID field (Social Security number). Type in the names from DBTEST into this table and then create ID numbers for each student.
- ✓ Create a master form called DBLINK that will link the DBNAME and DBTEST files together using NAME as the relational **key field.** The form should display "NAME," "ID," "TEST1," and "TEST2" on one screen.
- ✓ Print the form.
- ✓ Modify the form so that records on the subform are locked.
- ✓ Move the subform to another part of the screen and print the form.

MODULE 5: CREATING BASIC GRAPHS

Most people understand information faster when it is presented as a **graph** — a pictorial representation of data. The graph features in Access allow you to quickly develop a basic graph from table data. The following exercises demonstrate how to generate, view, and print graphs.

FIGURE DB3-18 ■ CREATING GRAPHS

This is the graph you will create.

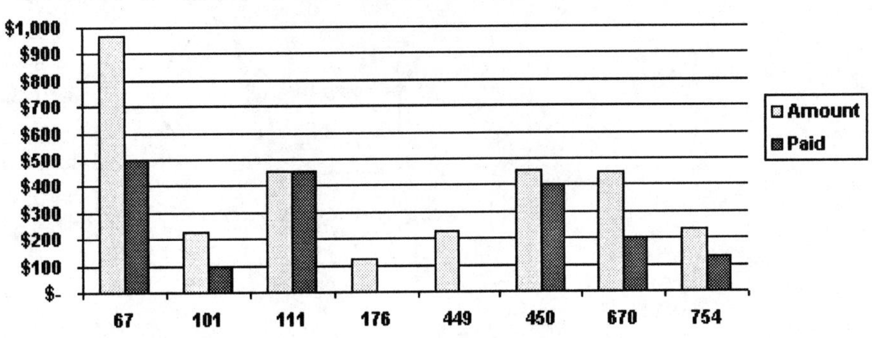

CREATING THE GRAPH

The following exercises create the column graph shown in Figure DB3-18. Graphs appear on Access forms and reports. You will follow two basic steps to create a graph:

- Activate the Chart wizard and provide answers to a series of dialog boxes about the data to be graphed and the kind of graph you want.
- Make modifications to the graph by running Microsoft *Graph* — a graphic application shared by several Microsoft products, including Access.

A **column graph** displays numeric data as a set of evenly spaced vertical bars whose relative heights indicate values in the range being graphed.

Tip: In Access, a *column graph* is a graph that displays vertical bars. A *bar graph* displays bars horizontally.

STEPS

1. **Launch Access**

2. **Open the CUSTOMER database window**

3. **Click the *Form* tab on the database window, then click the *New* button**

On the *New Form* dialog box (see Figure DB3-19),

4. **Click *Chart Wizard,* click the *Choose the table or query...* drop-down button, click *CUSTOMER LIST*, then click *OK***

You now see the first in a series of four dialog boxes that will help you construct a chart. These dialog boxes are reproduced in Figures DB3-20a through DB3-20d. Use these figures to guide you in the completion of these dialogs.

DB

FIGURE DB3-19 ■ STARTING THE CHART WIZARD

The Chart Wizard is initiated from the *New Form* dialog box.

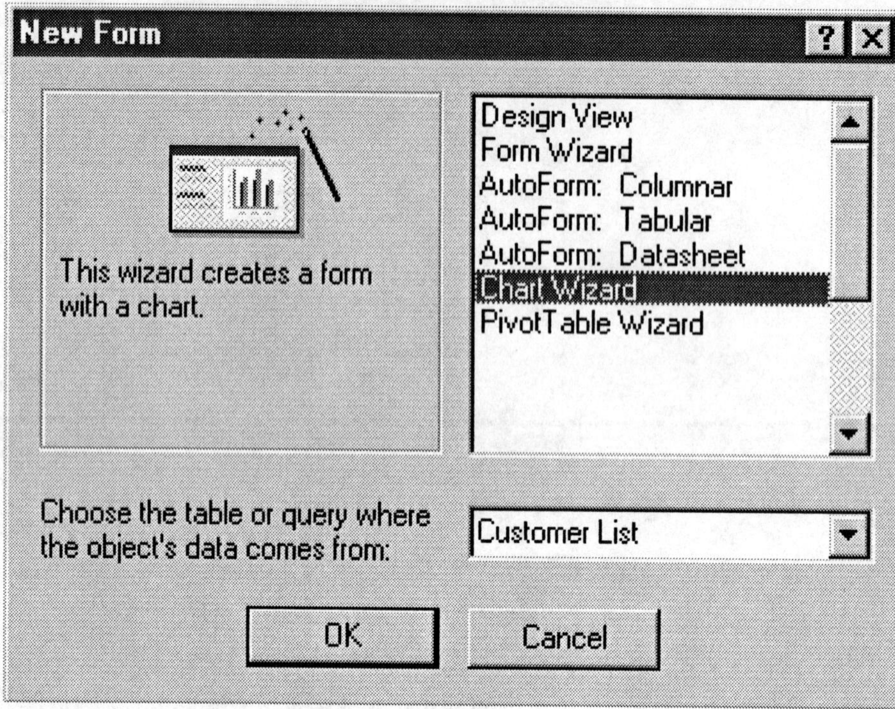

5 **Select the fields CUSTOMER NUMBER, AMOUNT, and PAID as in Figure DB3-20a, then click the *Next* > button**

6 **Click *Column Chart,* then click the *Next* > button as in Figure DB3-20b**

7 **Verify that the three selected fields are in the position shown in Figure DB3-20c**

If the fields are not in the position corresponding to the figure, then drag and drop the appropriate field button to the proper location.

8 **Click the *Preview Chart* button on the dialog box to verify that the chart is approximately correct, then click the *Close* button**

9 **Click the *Next* > button**

As you see in Figure DB3-20d,

10 **Type Customer Account Information as the chart title, then click the *Finish* button**

Access will need a moment for calculations, then the graph will appear. The graph will probably need some additional attention, though your results may vary depending on the default settings that you or your system's manager have provided. Any changes that need to be made must be done from the Design screen, so

FIGURE DB3-20 ■ USING THE CHART WIZARD

(a) Select the fields containing the data you wish to graph.
(b) Select *Column Chart* as the chart type.

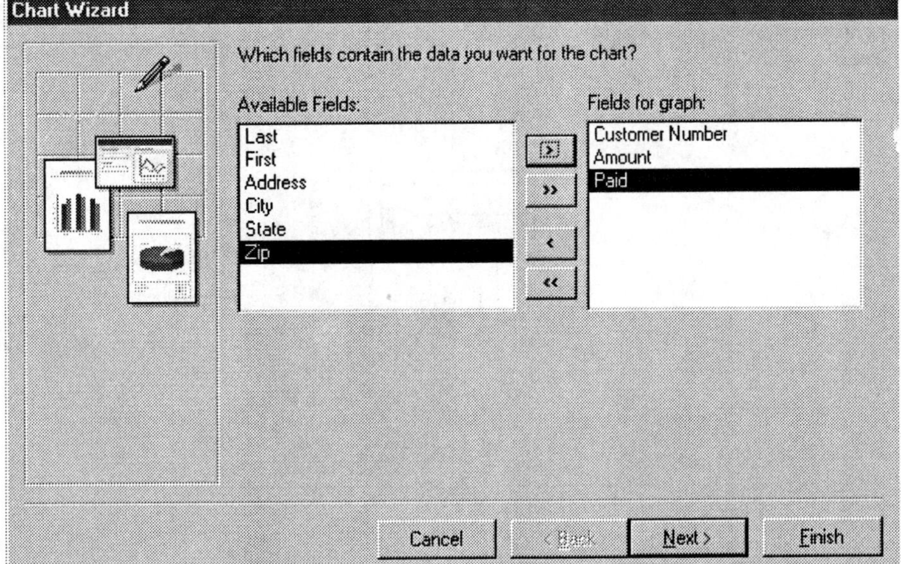

(a)

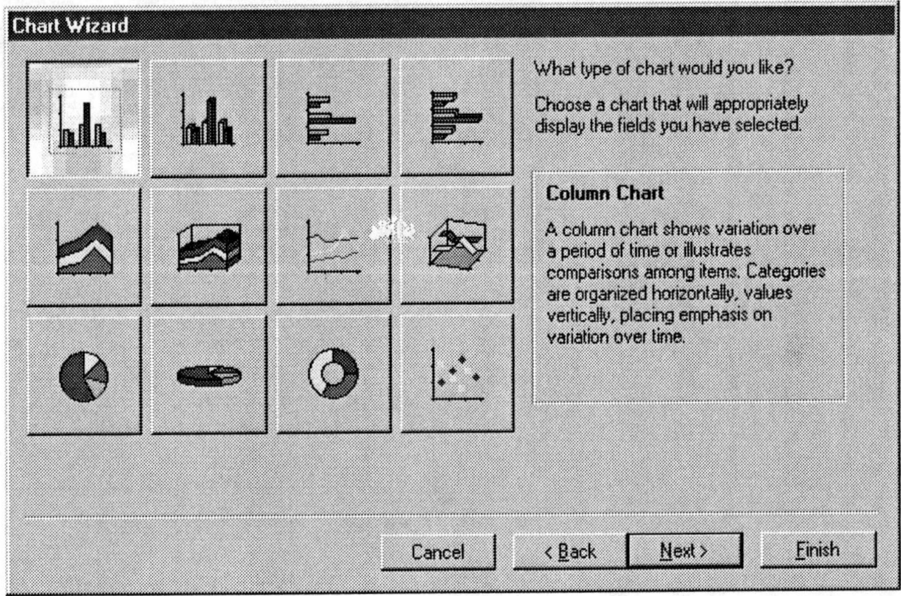

(b)

(continued)

11 Click *View, Form Design*

Your graph will need more room than is available now. Only the detail (gray) area can contain objects, so

12 Drag and drop the right drop-down button of the Detail area to the right and down so that it is approximately 6" wide by 4" high

DB

FIGURE DB3-20 ■ *(continued)*

(c) Indicate how you want the data laid out.
(d) Give the chart a title.

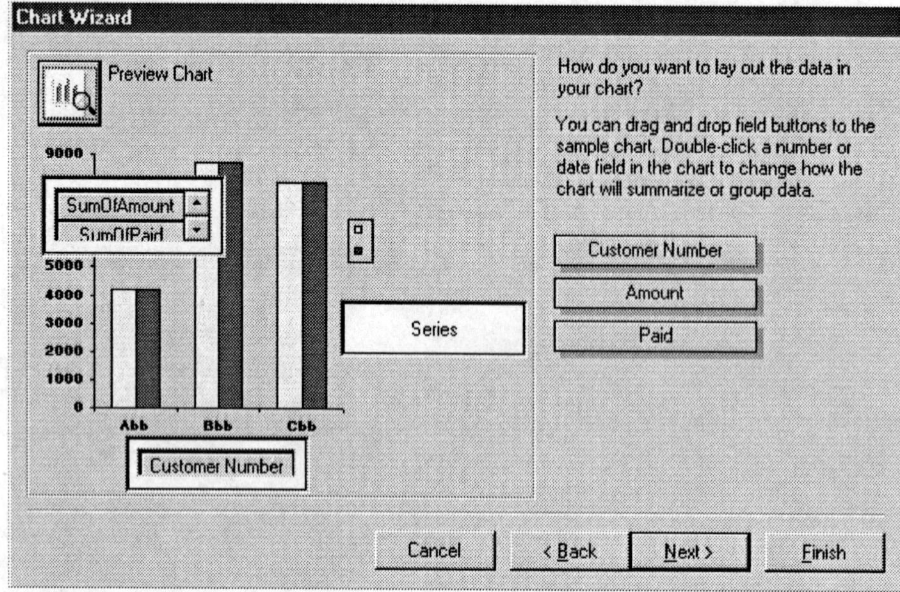

(c)

Chart Wizard

What title do you want for the chart?

Customer Account Information

Do you want the chart to display a legend?

Yes, display a legend.

No, don't display a legend.

After the wizard finishes creating your graph, what do you want to do?

Open the form with the graph displayed on it.

Modify the design of the form or the graph.

Display help showing me how to work with my chart.

Cancel | < Back | Next > | Finish

(d)

13 Select the graph object and drag its handles rightward and downward so that it fills a space approximately 4" wide by 2" high

If this graph suited your needs, you could simply print it as is or save it for later use. However, more often than not, you will need to adjust the graph properties and options to generate a more appropriate graph. Check the appearance of your graph by alternating between Form view and Design view until you are satisfied with its dimensions. Then,

14 **Click the *Close* button, saving the form as Customer Account Column Chart**

Tip: The process for inserting a graph on a report is identical to that of placing it on a form. If your intent is to see the graph on your monitor, place it on a form. If your purpose is to print it, insert the graph on a report.

MODIFYING THE GRAPH

If, after designing the graph, you decide that you want to modify it, Access offers numerous tools for doing so. However, you should be aware that working with graphs is a little different than working with other kinds of objects in Access. The reason is that your graph was not actually created by Access. It was created by another program called Microsoft Graph, which is shared by Access, Microsoft Word, Microsoft Excel (in some versions), and some other Microsoft applications. The purposes for this design, of course, are efficiency and standardization across various Microsoft applications. The downside of this design is that you have one extra program to learn.

At times, when you are modifying a graph in Access, you will notice that the screen suddenly has a different look and that the title bar now states that Microsoft Graph is the current application. A thorough examination of the capabilities of Graph is beyond the scope of this book. Fortunately, for most graphs that you will design, the procedures and customs you have already learned will suffice, and you have the Graph Help screens to guide you. Finally, you can be guided by an old proverb in the computer business: "If all else fails, read the manual."

The following exercise explores some of the ways you can modify a graph in Access. To begin,

STEPS

1 **Open the Customer List database window**

2 **Display the Customer Account Column Chart form in design view**

You already know that the graph object can be moved and resized. Experiment now with changing the type of graph. Access offers 12 kinds of graphs, which are summarized in Figure DB3-21 (also refer back to Figure DB3-20b for a glimpse at each graph type). To activate Microsoft Graph,

3 **Double-click the graph object**

Notice that the title bar, menu, and toolbar changed when Graph became active (see Figure DB3-20a). To see a menu of graph types,

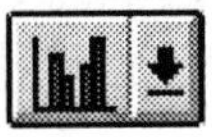

4 **Click *Format*, *Chart Type*, *3-D*, the *Column Chart* button, and then *OK***

Tip: The *chart type* tool bar button is a stack of buttons with a drop-down button. Like other stacked lists, click the drop-down button, then select from the list of choices. The most recent choice remains at the top of the stack.

DB

FIGURE DB3-21 ■ GRAPH TYPES AVAILABLE IN MICROSOFT ACCESS

	Graph Type	Display	Emphasis
1	Area Chart	Like a line chart, but fills in the areas between line with patterns or colors	Emphasizes amount of change over time
2	Bar	Horizontal bars represent values at a given moment in time; stacked-bar subtype places bars end to end, representing subtotals contributing toward a total	Facilitates comparisons of values. Stacked bar subtype emphasizes grand total rather than subtotal
3	Column	Similar to bar type, except that bars are vertical	Facilitates comparison of values
4	Doughnut	Similar to a pie chart, except that it shows values in more than one series in concentric circles around a "doughnut hole"	Round display of more than one series of values
5	Line Chart	Presents each series as a line	Emphasizes rate of change over time
6	Pie	Displays each value as a slice cut from a circle; can only show one series of values	Shows the relationship of parts to a whole; usually, emphasizes one part by exploding that slice out of the pie
7	XY (scatter)	Displays each observation as a dot on the screen or page	Used mostly in scientific applications
8	3D Area Chart	A three-dimensional area chart	Emphasizes amount of change over time
9	3D Bar	A three-dimensional version of the bar chart	Facilitates comparison of values
10	3D Column	A three-dimensional version of the column chart	Facilitates comparison of values
11	3D Line Chart	Like a line chart, but it displays lines as three-dimensional ribbons	Emphasizes rate of change over time
12	3D Pie	A three-dimensional pie chart	Seen on edge, gives additional emphasis to the foremost slice

The 3D-column graph is displayed. If this is exactly what you want, you can now leave Graph. To return to Access,

5 Click *File*, then click *Exit and return to the Customer Account Column Chart*

Graph transfers the modified graph over to Access and terminates. To see the resulting graph as shown in Figure DB3-22a,

FIGURE DB3-22 ■ GRAPH TYPES OFFERED BY ACCESS

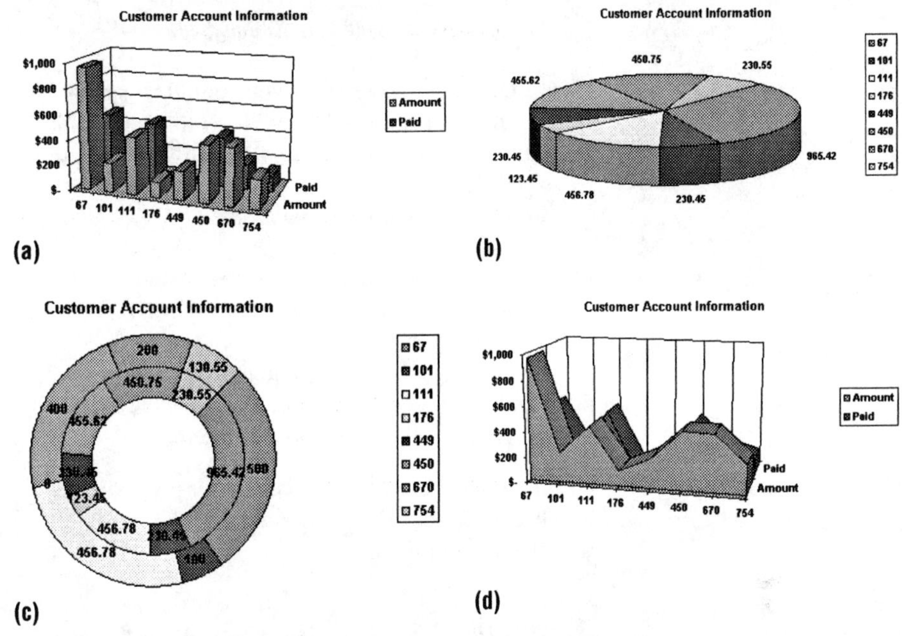

(a) The 3D Column Graph.
(b) The 3D Pie Chart.
(c) The Doughnut Chart.
(d) The 3D Area Chart.

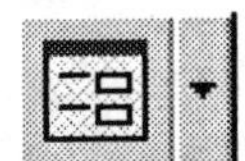

6 Click *View, Form*

To summarize, the process for changing graph type is as follows:

- Open the form containing the graph object in Design view.
- Double-click the graph object to launch Microsoft Graph.
- Click the drop-down button next to the *Graph Type* button, then select the desired type.
- Exit Graph.
- Click the *Form View* button.

> **Tip: When you have returned to Access, you can save the modified form under a different name if you don't wish to lose the existing form.**

Using these techniques, change the graph of this data to the following formats.

7 Change the chart to a *3D Pie* and remain in Microsoft Graph

To place amounts next to each slice of the pie,

8 Right-click the graph, then click *Insert Data Labels* on the resulting menu

9 Click *Show Value* on the resulting dialog box, then click *OK*

As you see in Figure DB3-22b, the graph is attractive, but it only shows one series: AMOUNT. This can be corrected—though not very satisfactorily—by using the doughnut type of graph:

10 Change the chart type to a *2D Doughnut*

Figure DB3-22c shows what you should be seeing on your screen. It does show both series, but it does not readily lend itself to interpretation. In fact, it would be easier to just look at the numbers. Try an area chart like the one in Figure DB3-22d. This time,

11 Change the chart type to a *3D Area*

This graph makes the amount we are owed look very large in proportion to payments we have received, especially since AMOUNT is the first series and is placed in front of PAID, eclipsing it.

Often, graphs are not just neutral data displays. In most cases, you want to make a point with your graph as well as to display the data in an easy-to-understand fashion. Select the graph type that does the following:

- Accurately displays the data in fair proportions
- Is easy for the viewer to interpret
- Makes your point

12 Click *File, Exit & Return to Customer Account Column...*

13 Save the form containing your final choice under an appropriate name

14 Close all windows in the Access work area

MODIFYING OTHER GRAPH SETTINGS

Your graph can be modified in two environments: Access and Graph.

In Access, when viewing the graph on a form or report in Design view, you can use all the techniques you have used before on other Access objects to change the size and position of the object. You can display the properties menu for the object and change the border, background color, and so forth as you have done before.

In Graph, you have much more control over the chart. You can add grid lines, change colors, annotate the graph with text boxes, change the orientation of 3D graphs, insert drawings, and so on. It will require a little exploration on your part to master those features of Graph that are important to your applications. Use the Help screens.

PRINTING A GRAPH

Graphs can be printed as easily as they are viewed. Because graphs are contained in forms or reports, they are printed when the form or report is printed. To print the graph you just created:

STEPS

1 Display the Customer List database window

2 **Click the *Forms* tab**

3 **Click *Customer Account Column Chart* (or your own selection)**

4 **Click *File, Print, OK*** Ctrl + P , ↵

CHECKPOINT

- ✓ Using DBTEST, create a standard stacked column graph that presents all test scores for students in the table.
- ✓ Change the graph to regular (not stacked) bar format. Print it.
- ✓ Change the graph to a 3D-area chart. Change the graph object properties so that it is framed. Print it.
- ✓ Using DBTEST, create a standard stacked column graph that presents average test scores for students in the table.
- ✓ Make the dimensions of the graph as large as possible. Print it.

MODULE 6: SHARING DATA AMONG APPLICATIONS

Like most software packages, Access saves data in its own unique format, adding special symbols to ensure proper formatting. At times, however, you may want to move data from Access to another software package. For example, an Access table might require the more sophisticated math manipulations offered in a spreadsheet, or you may want to combine table data with a word processed letter or report. Conversely, you may want to move data already prepared in another program into Access. Unfortunately, the special symbols and file format native to Access prevent its data from being used by other programs. However, it does provide ways to translate data into other formats.

EXPORTING AND IMPORTING

To ease the data transfer problem, many software packages (including Access) offer export and *import* commands. **Exporting** saves data in another format; **importing** *retrieves* data that has been saved in another format.

DB

DIRECT CONVERSION. The easiest way to share data is to copy them into a form that another program can readily understand. For example,you can convert an Access table directly into an Excel or Lotus spreadsheet or vice versa. You may have to make slight adjustments to the converted file, but these are usually minimal. Typically, direct conversions are offered for the most popular software packages. Below are the formats that Access will import:

- Text (delimited and fixed width)
- Microsoft Excel
- Lotus 1-2-3
- Paradox
- Microsoft FoxPro

- dBase III, IV, and V
- ODBC Databases

Data that is stored in one of these formats can be read (imported) by Access and converted to an Access table.

Data that is in an Access table can be saved (exported) to files that are in the following formats and can be read, loaded, retrieved, or opened by programs that use these formats.

- Text (delimited and fixed width)
- Microsoft Excel
- Lotus 1-2-3
- Paradox
- Microsoft FoxPro
- dBase III, IV, and V
- ODBC Databases
- Rich Text Format (RTF)
- MS Word Merge

ASCII—A COMMON DENOMINATOR. When direct conversion to a particular software package is not available, an ASCII conversion option may still allow data to be transferred. **ASCII** (pronounced "ask-key") stands for American Standard Code for Information Interchange. It is one of a few standard formats adopted by the computer industry for representing typed characters. ASCII eliminates the special symbols unique to each software package, providing a common style for sharing data or communicating data over phone lines. Of course, you may lose some of the special formatting included within the data, and you may have to make some adjustments before you can use the converted data in the new software application.

One of the text conversion options mentioned above permits Access to read and write text (ASCII) files. This capability is particularly useful when you need to move data to or from a mainframe.

THE WINDOWS CLIPBOARD. All Windows applications adhere to similar standards so that resources—like printing—can be shared. As you know, in most Windows applications that allow the user to create data files, data can be selected and then cut or copied to the Clipboard. The data that was most recently cut or copied remains in the Clipboard until you exit Windows or perform another cut or copy operation. Even if you close the application from which the data was copied or switch to another application, the data remains in the Clipboard. The contents of the Clipboard can then be pasted to another part of the same file or to a different file altogether. It is possible to copy data from an Access table to the Clipboard and then paste it into a file created by another Windows application.

EXPORTING DATA FROM ACCESS

In the following exercises, you will use Access to export the data in the CUSTOMER table into forms that can be used by Microsoft Excel and Word (it is assumed here that you are likely be using products that are companions to Access in the Microsoft Office suite product. To begin,

STEPS

1 **Open the Customer database Window**

EXPORTING TO EXCEL. First, you'll convert your table into an Excel spreadsheet.

Tip: If you don't use Excel, substitute the spreadsheet product of your choice in this exercise.

STEPS

1 **Open the CUSTOMER LIST table**

2 **Click *File*, then click *Save As/Export***

The dialog box that opens allows you to choose whether the data is to be saved to another object in the current database or to an external file.

3 **Click *To an external file or database,* then click *OK* for the *Save Table* dialog box**

4 **Click the *Save as type* drop-down button, and then *Microsoft Excel 5-7***

The dialog box (see Figure DB3-23a) you see next permits you to select the destination file type and filename. Access assumes that the CUSTOMER LIST table is the data source because it was selected when the process was begun. Access provides CUSTOMER LIST.XLS as the filename. Be sure the new file will be saved to the desired disk and folder.

5 **Click the *Export* button**

Although you cannot see it directly, Access has created a spreadsheet file named CUSTOMER LIST.XLS that can be read directly by Excel. When Excel has opened the spreadsheet, the file will appear as in Figure DB3-23b. Note that the column headings match the appropriate fields, as does the formatting. (The column widths were adjusted in the figure.)

Now, to view the CUSTOMER LIST Excel workbook as in Figure DB3-23b:

6 **Launch Microsoft Exce**

Tip: You can use the same procedure to create a Lotus or Quattro spreadsheet by selecting the appropriate product name in Step 2.

7 **Click File, Open**

8 **Click the *Look in* drop-down button and then *3½ Floppy (A:)* to set the default drive**

9 **Click the *CUSTOMER LIST* icon, and then the *Open* button**

FIGURE DB3-23 ■ EXPORTING DATA TO EXCEL

(a) Enter the spreadsheet filename on this dialog box.
(b) Access has exported this data to an Excel file.

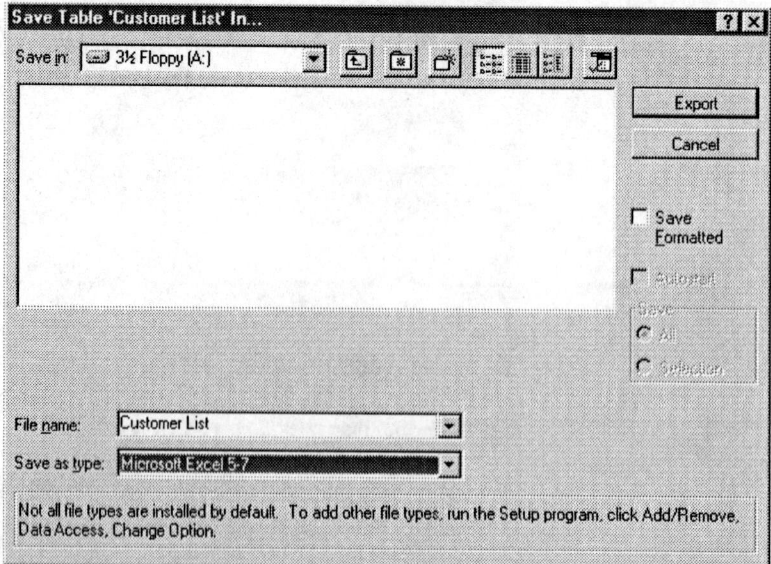

(a)

Microsoft Excel - Customer List.xls

File Edit View Insert Format Tools Data Window Help

Arial 10 | A1 | Customer Number

	A	B	C	D	E	F	G	H	
1	Customer	Last	First	Address	City	State	Zip	Amount	Pa
2	670	Parker	Charles	25 Cerillos Road	Santa Fe	NM	87501-9283	$450.75	$
3	101	Burstein	Jerome	100 N. 1st Street	San Jose	CA	95120-1234	$230.45	$
4	449	Laudon	Jane	500 Fifth Avenue	New York	NY	10003-3390	$230.45	
5	754	Martin	Edward	50 Carmine Street	New York	NY	10001-2220	$230.55	$
6	176	West	Rita	908 Elm	Hinsdale	IL	60521-1666	$123.45	
7	067	Williams	DeVilla	One Dryden Way	Chicago	IL	60601-5577	$965.42	$
8	111	Hill	Karen	1500 Michigan Avenue	Chicago	IL	60605-0078	$456.78	$
9	450	Laudon	Kenneth	501 Fifth Avenue	New York	NY	10003-1101	$455.62	$

Customer_List

Ready Sum=0 NUM

(b)

10 **Compare the workbook to Figure DB3-23b**

11 **Click *File*, *Exit* to exit Excel**

EXPORTING TO A DELIMITED ASCII FILE. Exchanging data between Access and a word processing program (such as Microsoft Word) is usually done through use of a *delimited* ASCII file. In a **delimited file**, each field value is delimited (separated) by a comma. Also, trailing blanks are removed from character data, which are then enclosed within quotation marks. This format can be read by many word processing programs for merging with form letters. Also, some accounting programs can read delimited ASCII files. To convert the CUSTOMER LIST table to a delimited ASCII file,

STEPS

1 If needed, open the CUSTOMER database window and click the CUSTOMER LIST table

2 Click *File, Save As/Export*, the *To an External File or Database* option, and then *OK*

On the following dialog box,

3 Click the *Save as type* drop-down button, click *Text Files* as the file type, and then click the *Export* button

On the next dialog box, Access will ask you whether you want a delimited or fixed width text file.

4 Click the *Delimited* option, click the *Finish* button, and then *OK*

Access creates the file and copies your data. When retrieved in a word processing program or text editor, the file will appear as in Figure DB3-24.

IMPORTING DATA INTO ACCESS

In the following exercises, you will use the Access menu to import data from spreadsheet and delimited ASCII files into Access tables.

FIGURE DB3-24 ■ EXPORTING TO A DELIMITED TEXT FILE

Access has exported this data to a text file.

DB

STEPS

1 Open or switch to the CUSTOMER database window, if necessary

IMPORTING FROM EXCEL. You can now convert an Excel spreadsheet into an Access table. You will use the spreadsheet file you just created (CUSTOMER LIST.XLS) for this purpose.

STEPS

1 Click *File*, then click *Get external data*, and then *Import*

On the following dialog box,

2 Click the *File of type* drop-down button, and then *Microsoft Excel* as the file type

3 Click CUSTOMER LIST and click the *Import* button

On the next dialog box, you will be given some options that are not important for our current purpose. Accept all defaults.

4 Click the *Next* > button

On the following dialog box,

5 Click the *First Row contains Column Headings* checkbox, then click the *Finish* button and then *OK*

You will see that Access has created a table called CUSTOMER_LIST.

6 Open CUSTOMER_LIST

As you can see, the Excel data was successfully imported.

7 Close the CUSTOMER_LIST table and then delete it

IMPORTING A DELIMITED ASCII FILE. To import the delimited text file you created in the exporting exercises:

STEPS

1 Click *File*, then click *Get external data*, and then *Import*

On the following dialog box,

2 Click the *File of type* drop-down button, and then *Text Files*

3 Click CUSTOMER LIST and click the *Import* button

On the following dialog box,

4 Click the *Delimited* option, then click the *Next* > button

On the following dialog box,

5 Click the *Next* > button

On the following dialog box indicate that you do not want to import the data into an existing table:

6 Click the *In a New Table* option, then click the *Next* > button

The next two dialog boxes provide choices that are not important. Accept the defaults in each case.

7 Click the *Next* > button in the succeeding two dialog boxes

Finally, you will have the opportunity to provide the name for a table to contain the data:

8 Type Imported Text Data as the table name, click the *Finish* button, and then *OK*

9 Open the IMPORTED TEXT DATA table

As you can see, Access has imported the data, but the field names are not the same, because no field names were in the text file. Access named the fields Field1, Field2 , and so on. To make this table more usable, you would have to change the field names in the table design screen, but that would be easily done. The data is the same, but some of the field widths are not the same. When a delimited text file is imported, Access bases field size on the widest field value in each column.

10 Close all windows in the Access work area and then exit Access

OBJECT LINKING AND EMBEDDING (OLE)

Object linking and embedding (OLE) is a phrase that generally refers to the transfer of data from a file created by one application into a file created by another application. Specifically, it refers to a published standard that is adhered to by software authors.

For example, you might want to include a table from Access in a Microsoft Word document or you might want to insert a graphic image onto an Access form. **Linking** means that the current version of data from the source file is inserted in the target file each time it is opened. **Embedding** means that data from the source file is inserted into the target file once and is not updated if the source file changes.

Many Windows 95 applications make it easy to link or embed data into their files. Usually, products produced by the same software publisher are designed to work together and to exchange data easily.

Some applications are published in groups and are called software suites. Suites typically contain a word processor, a spreadsheet, a database manager, and other applications. Lotus Development Corporation produces the word processor AmiPro, the spreadsheet Lotus 1-2-3, and the database manager Approach. Microsoft produces Word, Excel, and Access.

Even applications that are produced by different publishers can exchange data due to the standardization imposed by the operating system (Windows 95) and the awareness of software publishers that their customers expect these features to be built into their products.

Because Access is a Microsoft product, this text assumes that the other Microsoft products are available to you. If this is not the case, you can probably still perform the following exercises in linking and embedding using your own word processor and spreadsheet. However, the application that produces the document in which the data is to be embedded or linked will have different methods of performing these tasks, and you will have to consult the appropriate Help screens or documentation.

INSERTING DATA FROM ACCESS INTO OTHER OFFICE APPLICATIONS

In this exercise, the results of the query you designed to select only customers with AMOUNT values greater than $400 will be inserted into a Word document. Look at Figure DB3-25. It is a memo from a person in accounts receivable to the sales manager providing the list of customers. Since you have already created the query in Access, all you have to do is insert it into the Word document.

STEPS

1 Launch MS Word

2 Type the Sentence document as shown in Figure DB3-25 and then press ↵ twice

When you have reached the point at which the CUSTOMER data is to be inserted,

3 Click *Insert*, then click *Database*

Word opens a dialog box like the one shown in Figure DB3-26a.

4 Click the *Get Data* button

FIGURE DB3-25 ■ INSERTING OBJECTS INTO FILES CREATED BY OTHER APPLICATIONS

An Access query has been inserted into this Word document.

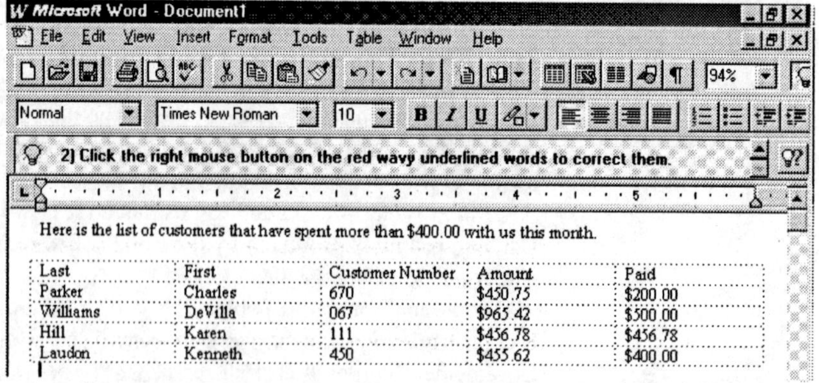

Last	First	Customer Number	Amount	Paid
Parker	Charles	670	$450.75	$200.00
Williams	DeVilla	067	$965.42	$500.00
Hill	Karen	111	$456.78	$456.78
Laudon	Kenneth	450	$455.62	$400.00

FIGURE DB3-26 ■ INSERTING AN ACCESS OBJECT INTO A WORD FILE

(a) First, indicate the source of the data.
(b) Next, open the data source.

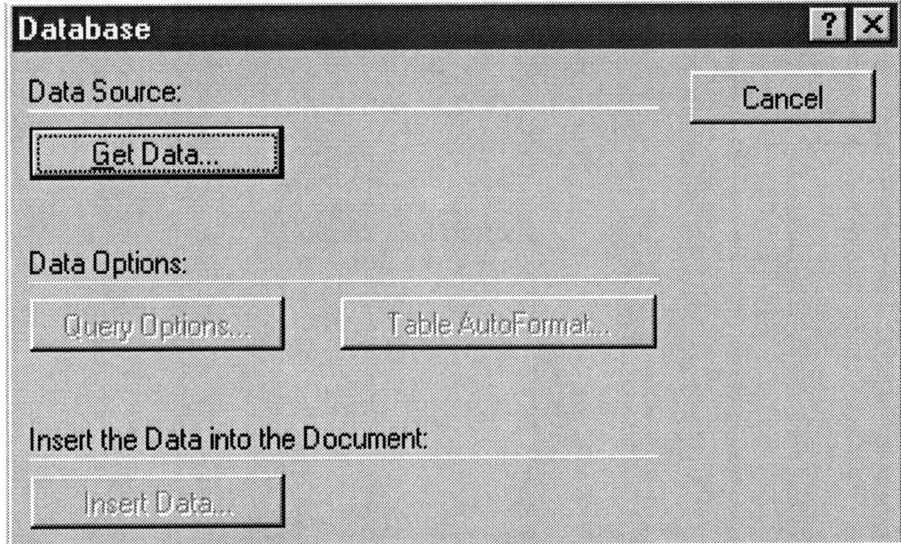

(a)

Open Data Source
Look in: 3½ Floppy (A:)
CUSTOMER
MAGIC
Magical
Open
Cancel
Advanced...
Select Method
Find files that match these criteria:
File name:
Text or property:
Find Now
Files of type: MS Access Databases
Last modified: any time
New Search
3 file(s) found.

(b)

(continued)

On the next dialog box, identify the Access database file CUSTOMER. Be sure to select the drive and folder appropriate for you. Use Figure DB3-26b as a guide:

5 Click the *Look in* drop-down button, *3½ Floppy (A:)*, *File of type* drop-down button, and *Microsoft Access Databases*

6 Click CUSTOMER, then click the *Open* button

Figure DB3-26c guides you through the next step.

DB

FIGURE DB3-26 ■ *(continued)*

(c) Then, select the query you designed.
(d) Finally, indicate that all records should be inserted.

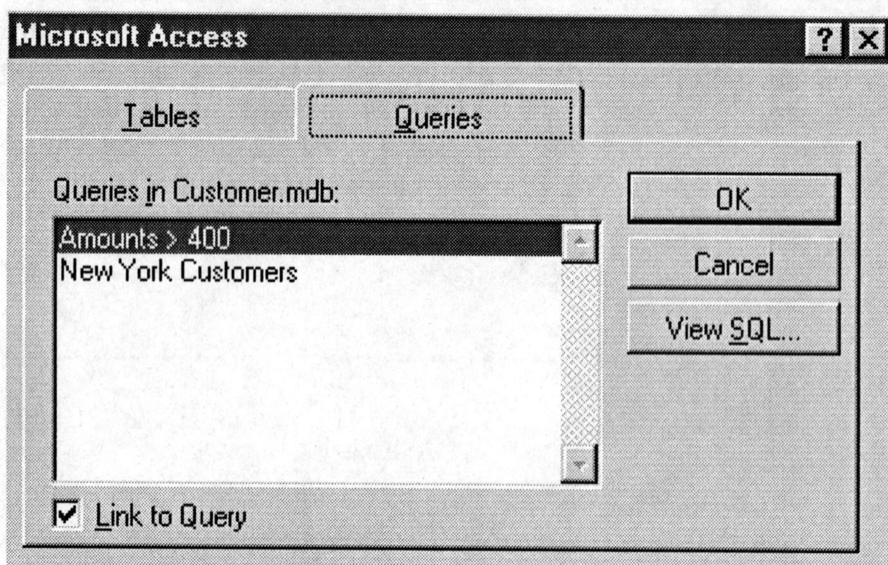

(c)

Insert Data
Insert Records
All
From:
To:
OK
Cancel
Insert Data as Field

(d)

6 **Click the *Queries* tab, click *Amounts > 400*, then click *OK***

At this point, a dialog begins between Word and Access. It may take a few moments before Access hands the data over to Word. As you see in Figure DB3-26d, you are next asked whether you intend to insert all records or just specific records.

7 **Click the *Insert Data* button, click *All*, then click *OK***

Word places the records in a table at the position of the text insertion point in your document. you can now save, edit, or print the document with the Access data in it.

8 **Exit Microsoft Word without saving**

FIGURE DB3-27 ■ CREATING A LOGO

This logo is a Paint file that was embedded in an Access form.

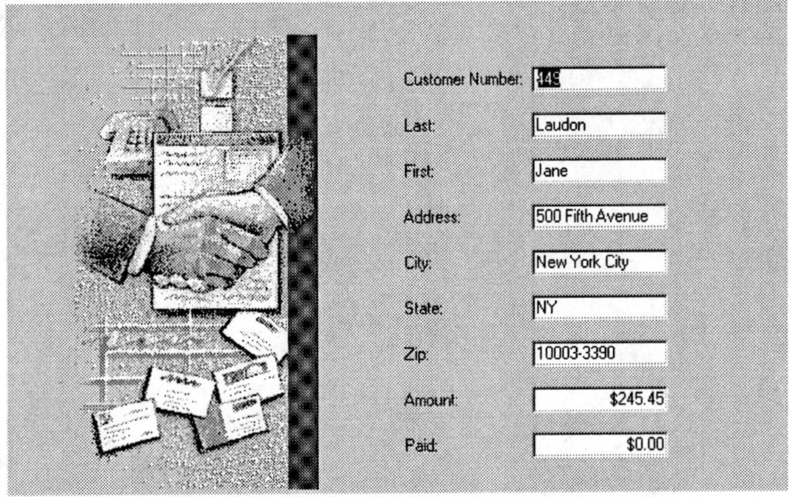

INSERTING GRAPHIC DATA INTO AN ACCESS FORM

In the next exercise, you will insert a bitmap image into an Access form (see Figure DB3-27). Bitmap images are gaphic images that may be created using Microsoft Paint, Microsoft PowerPoint, or other graphics programs. A bitmap file is identified with the DOS file extension ".BMP."

The following exercise inserts the bitmap image CONTRACT from Access's bitmap subfolder DWIZ into an Access form as in Figure DB3-27. These procedures can be used to insert bitmap images contained in any folder.

STEPS

1. **Launch Access, and open the CUSTOMER database window**
2. **Click the *Form* tab and then the *New* button for its dialog box**
3. **Click *Design View*, the *Choose the table or query...* drop-down button, *Customer List*, and then *OK***
4. **Drag the bottom right corner of the objects grid area to resize it to 6" wide by 4" high**
5. **Click the *Image* button on the toolbox (sixth button down on right side), point to 1/4" position from the top and left margins in the Detail band, and click (this will be the position of the top left corner of the image)**

An Insert Picture dialog box should now appear. This dialog box is similar to the Open dialog box and can be used to open a graphics file from any folder. Note that Access also allows you to insert a variety of graphics files in addition to bitmap files. To change the default folder to Dbwiz and select the *Contacts* file icon as in Figure DB3-28b:

DB

FIGURE DB3-28 ■ INSERTING A GRAPHIC FILE INTO AN ACCESS FORM

(a) First, create the form.
(b) Then, insert the file contents.

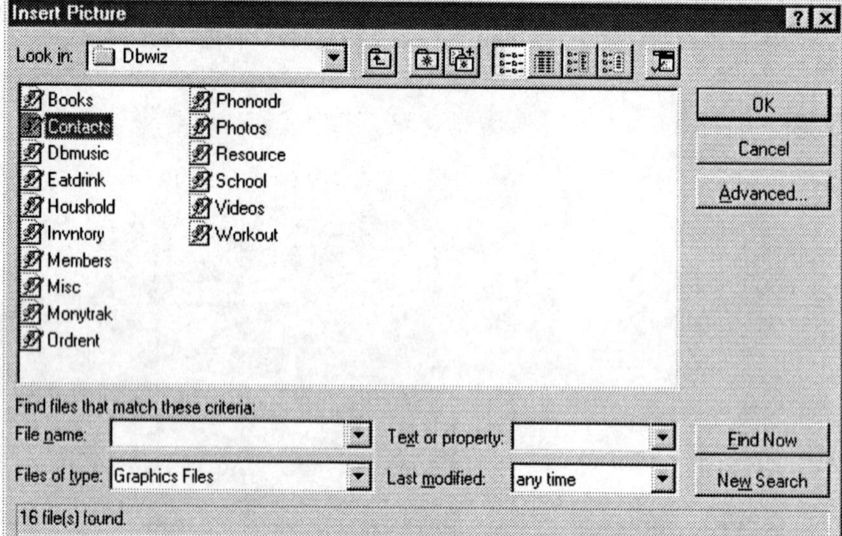

(a)

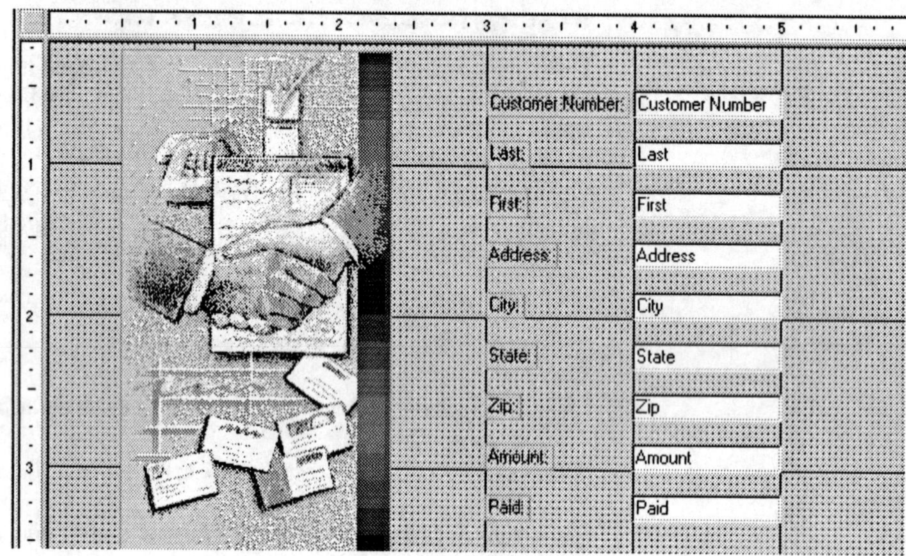

(b)

6 Click the *Look in* drop-down button, then the *C:* drive icon

At this point, you may open a folder on your hard disk that contains your desired bitmap file. For this exercise,

7 Double-click the *Access* folder icon in the list box, the *Bitmap* folder icon, the *Dbwiz* folder icons, and then the *Contacts* file icon

Your Insert Picture dialog box should resemble figure DB3-28b.

8 **Click *OK* to insert the graphic file**

9 **If needed, resize and move the image to resemble Figure DB3-28a**

10 **Using Figure DB3-28b as a guide, drag and drop the fields from the Field List window into the Design view window and then resize and move them to resemble the figure**

11 **Click *View, Form* and compare your form to Figure DB3-27**

12 **Close all windows in the Access work area and save the form as Customer Graphic Form**

13 **Exit Access and shut down Windows**

CHECKPOINT

- ✓ Export the data in the MAGIC table into a Quattro spreadsheet file named MAGIC.
- ✓ Export the data in the MAGIC table into a delimited file named MAGIC2.TXT.
- ✓ Import the MAGIC.WQ1 spreadsheet into a new table.
- ✓ Export the data in MAGVEND to an Excel spreadsheet file named MAGEXCEL.
- ✓ Import MAGEXCEL into an Access table and view the results.

SUMMARY

- File management is an important part of data control. It includes commands and procedures to list files and objects, copy objects, rename objects, and delete objects.
- Records can be copied from one table to another using cut and paste.
- Label forms can be designed using the Label wizard. The resulting report can be modified like any other report.
- Customized screen forms can be created using the Form wizard. These screens can be used for editing, viewing, and adding records. The screen form can be opened from the database window.
- A calculated field manipulates data from other table fields to display a value not normally contained within the data.
- The relational database feature of Access allows tables to be linked together through master and detail forms. A common data field is used as the link.
- Multiple table use requires that a few conditions be met: one field of the same type and size must be common to both tables.
- In a one-to-many link, a master record is linked to a group of detail records; in a many-to-one link, a group of master records is linked to one detail record.
- A graph is a pictorial representation of data. Basic Access graphs include column, bar, line, area, pie, and doughnut graphs. Three-dimensional versions of column, bar, line, area, and pie graphs are included.
- Exporting copies data in a format that can be read by another software product. Importing retrieves data that has been created in another format. ASCII is a standard text format that provides a common style for sharing data among software applications.
- Object linking and embedding (OLE) permits data created by one application to be inserted into a document created by another application.

KEY TERMS

Shown in parentheses are the page numbers on which key terms are boldfaced.

ASCII (DB212)
Border (DB183)
Calculated field (DB184)
Delimited file (DB215)
Detail form (DB189)
Embedding (DB217)
Exporting(DB211)
Graph (DB202)
Importing (DB211)
Key field (DB202)
Linking (DB217)
Literal string (DB169)
Many-to-one link (DB199)
Master form (DB189)
Move handle (DB181)
One-to-many link (DB190)

QUIZ

TRUE/FALSE

___ 1. The database window displays only tables.
___ 2. Reports are kept in separate files and are not part of the database file.
___ 3. The Empty command removes all records from a table.
___ 4. In screen design, an object can be selected by pressing the middle mouse button.
___ 5. In screen design, an object's properties menu can be displayed by pressing the middle mouse button.
___ 6. In screen design, the arrow keys can be used to move a selected object to a new location.
___ 7. In screen design, the mouse can be used to move a selected object to a new location.
___ 8. Calculated fields must be included in the table structure in order to be used in a screen or a report.
___ 9. The common field that links tables must have the same name in both table structures.
___ 10. The common field that links tables must be of the same type in both table structures.

MULTIPLE CHOICE

___ 11. Screen forms can be used to ______ records.
a. Add
b. Edit
c. View
d. All of the above

___ 12. To copy all records in which the AGE field exceeds 20 to a table called BACKUP, you should do which of the following?
a. Copy the table to BACKUP and query the new table.
b. Create a query called BACKUP where Age > 20
c. Create a Make Table Query for Age > 20
d. Delete from the BACKUP table all records for which Age > 20

___ 13. A box drawn around an object in a report or form is a _______.
a. container
b. boundary
c. outline
d. frame

___ 14. Which menu command would be used to begin the design of a new report?
  a. *File, New-Report*
  b. *File, Open-Report*
  c. *Report file,Open*
  d. None of the above

___ 15. Which of the following is *Not* a property of a text object?
  a. Color
  b. Frame
  c. Font
  d. All of the above

___ 16. A master record that is linked to one group of detail records creates a _______ link.
  a. one-to-many
  b. many-to-one
  c. one-to-group
  d. one-to-one

___ 17. Which of these statements about linked tables is true?
  a. One field must be common to both tables
  b. Detail records must be uniquely identified.
  c. The master table must contain no records
  d. The detail table must contain more records than the master table.

___ 18. Which graph type can only display one series?
  a. Radar
  b. Area
  c. Pie
  d. Doughnut

___ 19. Which graph type is useful for displaying trends over time?
  a. Bar
  b. Pie
  c. Line
  d. Stacked bar

___ 20. Which command saves data in another software package's format?
  a. Copy
  b. Save
  c. Import
  d. Export

MATCHING

Select the term that corresponds to the feature indicated on the Design screen reproduced in the figure.

___ 21. Border
___ 22. Detail band
___ 23. Graph button
___ 24. Field value object
___ 25. Properties dialog box
___ 26. Field list
___ 27. Selected object
___ 28. Literal string
___ 29. Used to insert literal string
___ 30. Used to insert calculated field

FIGURE DB3-A ■ MATCHING EXERCISE

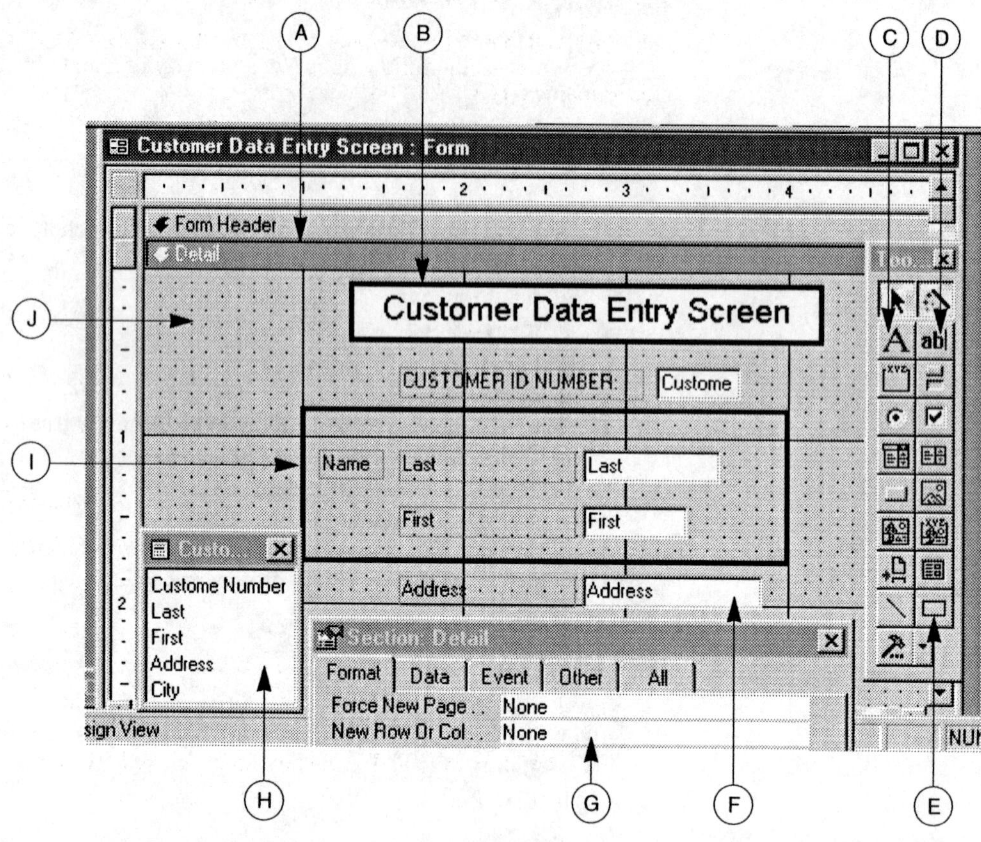

ANSWERS

True/False: 1. F; 2. F; 3. F; 4. F; 5. F; 6. F; 7. T; 8. F; 9. F; 10. T
Multiple Choice: 11. d; 12. c; 13. c; 14. d; 15. d; 16. a; 17. b; 18. c; 19. c; 20. d
Matching: 21. i; 22. j; 23. e; 24. f; 25. g; 26. h; 27. a; 28. b; 29. d; 30. c

EXERCISES

I. OPERATIONS

Provide the Access sequence of procedures or actions required to do each of the following operations. For each operation, assume that Access has been installed on Drive C and a data disk is in Drive A. Assume that the database named STOCK is present on Drive A and that it contains tables named STOCK1, STOCK2, STOCK5, and PARTS. STOCK1 contains text fields named ITEM and CATALOG, a currency field named COST, and a numeric field QUANT. A text file named STOCK5.TXT is also on the data disk.

1. Display a list of all database files on Drive A.
2. Display a list of all tables in STOCK.
3. Copy the STOCK1 table to STOCK3.
4. Add to STOCK3 those records in STOCK1 whose QUANT is greater than 99.
5. Rename STOCK2 as STOCK4.
6. Create a label form for STOCK1 that lists ITEM and CATALOG on the first line separated by a dash, QUANT on the second line, and COST on the third line of the label.
7. Create a customized screen that displays all four STOCK1 fields near the center of the screen.
8. View a STOCK1 record using the screen created in Exercise 7.
9. Create a screen form for STOCK1 using the autoform procedure.
10. Modify the screen created in Exercise 9 by repositioning its data fields one inch to the right and adding a 3-point. border around them.
11. Create a form that links the STOCK1 and STOCK4 tables by a common ITEM field using STOCK4 as the detail file. Use any appropriate data fields.
12. Create a column graph displaying COST and QUANT fields for each item in the stock table.
13. Modify the graph created in Exercise 12 to a bar graph and print it.
14. Import the ASCII delimited file named STOCK5.
15. Export STOCK1 to an Excel spreadsheet named STOCK6.

II. COMMANDS

Describe fully the procedure that is initiated or what is accomplished by executing the following menu commands or procedures. Access should be running. Each part of the exercise is independent of all other parts. If the series of commands is not complete, indicate what must be done to complete the process that the series initiates.

1. Opening the database window
2. Clicking the *Form* tab on the database window
3. Clicking the *Table* tab on the database window
4. Clicking the *Copy* button when a table name is selected on the database window
5. Pressing the Delete key when an object is selected on the Report or Form design screens
6. Pressing the Delete key when a table name is selected on the database window
7. Opening a form in the Design view
8. Opening a form in the Form view

9. Selecting the *Border* option on an object's properties menu
10. Selecting the *Font* option on an object's properties menu
11. Selecting the *Alignment* option on an object's properties menu
12. Selecting the *Graph* button on the toolbox
13. Clicking *File, Export,* then the file type delimited text
14. Clicking *File, Export,* then the file type Quattro
15. Clicking *File, Import,* then the file type delimited text

III. APPLICATIONS

Perform the following operations. You will need Access and a data disk. In a few words, tell how you accomplished each operation and describe its result. If you want to continue these exercises later, be sure to exit properly after each operation. Note that these exercises should be performed in sequence. Make sure you label each printed result with the exercise number, your name, and your class. To prepare, launch Access.

APPLICATION 1: LIBRARY BOOKS

1. Create a table named BOOKS with the following structure:

Field Name	Field Type	Width
Classcode	Text	5
Title	Text	25
Author	Text	15
Due_Date	Date	

2. Add the following records to BOOKS and adjust column widths as needed:

Classcode	Title	Author	Due_Date
Eng	Eyeless in Gaza	Huxley	10/24/95
CIS	Mgmt. of Info. Systems	Gray	10/24/95
Eng	Brave New World	Huxley	11/6/95
CIS	Human Use of Human Beings	Wiener	11/1/95
CIS	Systems Analysis	von Bertalanffy	11/1/95
Sci	Pyramid of Power	Mumford	10/31/95

3. Create a table named CLASSES with the following structure and adjust column widths as needed:

Field Name	Field Type	Width
Classcode	Text	5
Course	Text	25
Number	Text	15
Instructor	Text	15

4. Add the following records to CLASSES:

Classcode	Course	Number	Instructor
Eng	English	3345	Smith
CIS	Information Systems	3298	de la Torre
Sci	History of Science	3412	Ng

5. Create a label report named BOOKLBL1 so that your library books can be labeled with their due dates and the classcode for which they are being used (using, of course, specially designed removable library book labels). Print a set of labels. (Use Avery 5160 labels.)
6. Copy BOOKLBL1 to BOOKLBL2.
7. Modify BOOKLBL2 so that the due date is framed. Save your changes.
8. Print a set of modified labels.
9. Copy BOOKLBL2 to BOOKLBL3. Modify BOOKLBL3 so that the class code is printed in bold style.
10. Print a set of labels using BOOKLBL3.
11. Design a data entry form named BKCOUR1 that will display the classcode, instructor, and a list of all library books you are reading for that course. The book information should include title, author, and due date. Display and print a record.
12. Copy BKCOUR1 to BKCOUR2. Modify BKCOUR2 so that course and number are printed, too.
13. Print the screen.
14. Copy BKCOUR2 to BKCOUR3. Modify BKCOUR3 so that the due date is displayed first, then title, and then author. Display and print a record.
15. Exit Access.

DB

APPLICATION 2: SCHOOL—POLITICAL CLUBS

1. Create a table named CLUBS with the following structure:

Field Name	Field Type	Width
Clubcode	Text	5
Club_Name	Text	25
Address	Text	25
Zip	Text	5

2. Add the following records to CLUBS and adjust column widths as needed:

Clubcode	Club_Name	Address	Zip
YDC	Young Democrats Club	123 Main St	65432
YRC	Young Republicans Club	456 Maple St	65431

3. Create a table named COUNCIL with the following structure:

Field Name	Field Type	Width
Clubcode	Text	5
Officer	Text	25
Office	Text	15

4. Add the following records to COUNCIL:

Classcode	Officer	Office
YDC	Jeff Murphy	President
YDC	Leslie Thompson	Vice-President
YDC	Linda de la Fuente	Treasurer
YDC	Lisa Rogers	Secretary
YRC	Terry Smith	President
YRC	Mary de la Torre	Vice-President
YRC	Jean Johnson	Treasurer
YRC	Jim Fuller	Secretary

5. Create a report named ADDRESS1 that will be an address list for each member of the officers' council. The report will have each officer's name, club name, address, city and state, and zip code. (Because everyone lives in the same city, the city and state will be literal strings. Pick any city you like.) Print the report.
6. Copy ADDRESS1 to ADDRESS2.

7. Modify ADDRESS2 so that the club name is printed in bold style. Save your changes.
8. Print the modified report.
9. Copy ADDRESS2 to ADDRESS3. Modify ADDRESS3 so that the officer's name is printed in large type.
10. Print a set of labels using ADDRESS3.
11. Design a data entry form named OFFLIST1 that will display the clubcode, club name, address, city, state, zip code, and a list of all officers for that club. Display and print a record.
12. Copy OFFLIST1 to OFFLIST2. Modify OFFLIST2 so that the office held is printed, too.
13. Print the screen.
14. Copy OFFLIST2 to OFFLIST3. Modify OFFLIST3 so that the office held is displayed first, followed by the name. Display and print a record.
15. Exit Access.

APPLICATION 3: READING CLASSIC FICTION

1. Create a table named STYLE with the following structure:

Field Name	Field Type	Width
Code	Text	5
Style	Text	25

2. Add the following records to STYLE:

Code	Style
17th	Seventeenth-Century Classical
Rom	Romantic Poetry and Fiction
GR	Classical Greek/Roman
LG	Lost Generation

3. Create a table named READING with the following structure:

Field Name	Field Type	Width
Style	Text	5
Title	Text	35
Author	Text	15

4. Add the following records to READING:

Code	Title	Author
17th	Gulliver's Travels	Swift
17th	Absalom and Achitophel	Dryden
Rom	Don Juan	Byron
Rom	Frankenstein	Shelley
LG	Sun Also Rises	Hemingway
LG	Wasteland	Eliot
17th	Battle of the Books	Swift
GR	On Duties	Cicero

5. Create a report named BKLIST1 that will be a list of each book on your reading list. The report will have each book's name, author, and style. Print the report.
6. Copy BKLIST1 to BKLIST2.
7. Modify BKLIST2 so that the author's name is printed in bold style and change the report's title to BKLIST2. Save your changes.
8. Print the modified report.
9. Copy BKLIST2 to BKLIST3. Modify BKLIST3 so that the title is printed in large type and change the report's title to BKLIST3.
10. Print a report using BKLIST3.
11. Design a data entry form named STYLE1 that will display the style code, style name, and a list of all titles in that style. Display and print a record.
12. Modify the subform so that the author's name is printed, too.
13. Print the screen.
14. Modify the subform so that the author's name is displayed first, then the title. Display and print a record.
15. Exit Access.

APPLICATION 4: VIDEO COLLECTION

Using the VIDEO table you created in Chapter 2, do the following:

1. Copy those records in the VIDEO table whose TYPE field starts with C to a new table named VIDEO2.
2. Add the records from the VIDEO table to VIDEO2 whose VOLUME field is 102.
3. List all the tables in the database.
4. Using the VIDEO table, create a label report that lists the VOLUME and START fields on the first label line and the SUBJECT on the second line. Print labels for items whose time exceeds 100. (Use Avery 5160 labels.)
5. Modify the label report created in Exercise 4 to include the TYPE and TIME fields on the third line of the label. Print the labels for items whose TYPE field begins with I.

6. Create a customized data entry form that shows "Video Listing" as a centered title and includes all fields in an appropriate arrangement designed by you. You may use borders for emphasis. Display and then print one record.
7. Create a basic column graph for the VIDEO2 table. Print the graph.
8. Modify the graph in Exercise 7 to a bar graph. Print the graph.
9. Create a table called VIDEO TYPE with these fields:

Field Name	Field Type	Width
Type	Text	2
Listing	Text	20

Enter these records into the table:

Type	Listing
C	Children
M	Magic
SF	Science Fiction
A	Action
I	Instruction
O	Old Classic

10. Create a many-to-one form linking the VIDEO table to the VIDEO TYPE table on the TYPE common field. Include the VOLUME, START, SUBJECT, TYPE, and TIME fields for all records. View and print one form.
11. Create a one-to-many form linking VIDEO TYPE to VIDEO using the common TYPE field as a link. Show all fields except TYPE from VIDEO TYPE. Display and print one record.
12. Export the VIDEO table to an Excel spreadsheet.
13. Export the VIDEO TYPE table to a delimited text file.
14. Import the data you exported to the Excel spreadsheet.
15. Import the data you exported to the delimited text file. Rename the fields and adjust the lengths to be identical with the original VIDEO TYPE table.

APPLICATION 5: ADVANCED INVENTORY

Using the MAGIC and MAGVEND tables you have copied onto your disk, do the following:

1. Copy those records in the MAGIC table whose ID field starts with E to a new table named TRICKS. Then copy the entire MAGVEND table to a new table called TRIVEND.
2. Add the records from the MAGIC table to TRICKS whose ID field starts with C.
3. List all the tables in the database.

4. Using the TRICKS table, create a label report that lists the ID and ITEM fields on the first label line and the VENDOR code on the second line. Print the labels for items whose stock exceeds 20. (Use Avery 5160 labels.)
5. Modify the label report created in Exercise 4 to include the COST field on the third line of the label. Print the labels for items whose ID field begins with C.
6. Create a customized data entry form that shows TRICK INVENTORY as a centered title and includes all the fields in an appropriate arrangement designed by you. You may use borders for emphasis. Open the form, display a record, and print it.
7. Create a column graph for the TRICKS table. Print the graph.
8. Modify the graph from Exercise 7 to a bar graph. Print the graph.
9. Create a one-to-many form linking the TRICKS table to the TRIVEND table on the VENDOR common field. Include VENDOR, ID, PRICE, ITEM, and STOCK fields for all records. View and print one record.
10. Using autoform, create a form for TRIVEND and TRICKS. Save the forms under names you select.
11. Create a many-to-one form linking the TRIVEND table to the TRICKS table on the VENDOR common field. Include VENDOR, ID, PRICE, COMPANY, and STOCK fields for all records. View and print one record.
12. Export TRICKS to an Excel spreadsheet named Tricks1.
13. Export the TRIVEND table to a delimited table named Vend1.
14. Import the VEND1 delimited file into a table named VEND2. Change the field names and sizes to match the original values in TRIVEND.
15. Import the TRICKS1 spreadsheet into a table named TRICKS1.
16. Exit Access.

APPLICATION 6: ADVANCED SALES

Using the SALES table you created in Chapter 2, do the following:

1. Copy those records in the SALES table whose CUSTOMER field starts with M to a new table named SALES2.
2. Add records from the SALES table into SALES2 whose CUSTOMER field starts with P.
3. List all the tables in the database.
4. Using the SALES table, create a label report that lists the ITEM field on the first label line and the CUSTOMER code on the second line. Print the labels for items whose price exceeds $100. (Use Avery 5163 labels.)
5. Modify the label form created in Exercise 4 to include the QUANTITY, PRICE, and TOTAL ([QUANTITY]*[PRICE]) fields on the third line of the label. Print the labels for items whose CUSTOMER field begins with M. (Add captions as needed.)
6. Create a customized data entry form that shows "Orders" as a centered title and includes all the fields in an appropriate arrangement designed by you. You may use borders for emphasis. Print one record.
7. Create a column graph for the SALES2 table. Print the graph.
8. Modify the graph in Exercise 7 to a bar graph. Print the graph.

9. Create a table called SALCUST with these fields:

Field Name	Field Type	Width
Customer	Text	6
Name	Text	20
Phone	Text	12

Enter these records into the table:

Customer	Name	Phone
MAR-75	Edward Martin	212-555-1234
PAR-15	Charles Parker	505-555-9876
BON-01	Richard Bonacci	800-555-2468

10. Create a many-to-one form linking SALES to SALCUST on the common CUSTOMER field. Include the CUSTOMER, ITEM, QUANTITY, and PRICE fields for all records. View one record and print the form.
11. Create a one-to-many form that links SALCUST to SALES. Show all fields except CUSTOMER from SALCUST. Print one record.
12. Export the SALES table to an Excel spreadsheet.
13. Export the SALES table to a delimited text file.
14. Import the data you exported to the Excel spreadsheet.
15. Import the data you exported to the delimited text file. Rename the fields and adjust the lengths to be identical with the original SALES table.
16. Exit Access.

APPLICATION 7: LINKING DATA WITH ANOTHER PROGRAM

1. Launch Access and display the READING table created in Application 3.
2. Create a query that displays only LG (Lost Generation) titles.
3. Close the query, saving it under the name of LOST GENERATION.
4. Launch Microsoft Word.
5. Type a reply letter to a friend who has written you asking what titles you might loan her to use for her paper on fiction of the Lost Generation.
6. Link the query results to the letter so that the list of titles will be displayed.
7. Print the letter.
8. Save the letter under the title LOST REPLY, then close the document.
9. Return to Access.
10. Display the READING table.

11. Add two more LG titles:

LG	The Great Gatsby	Fitzgerald
LG	The Old Man and the Sea	Hemingway

12. Switch back to Word.
13. Retrieve the document LOST REPLY.
14. Verify that the new titles are displayed.
15. Print the document.
16. Close all files and return to an empty desktop.

MASTERY CASES

The following Mastery Cases allow you to demonstrate how much you have learned about this software. Each case extends a fictitious problem from Chapter 1 and can be solved using some of the skills you may have learned in this chapter. If you do not have the referenced file, you will have to create it by following the instructions in Chapters 1 and 2. Design your response in ways that display your mastery of the software.

These Mastery Cases allow you to display your ability to:

- Create labels
- Design a customized screen
- Use multiple tables

CASE 1. DESIGNING A CUSTOMIZED ENTRY SCREEN

Using the file and data you modified in Chapter 2's course record, design a screen that will display the title "GRADUATION PROGRESS" centered at the top and effectively display each record's data for review or editing. When completed, print a screen copy of one record using the new design.

CASE 2. USING MULTIPLE TABLES

Using the file and data you modified in Chapter 2's music catalog, create a new file that includes data for album title, year of release, and record company. Then, design master and detail forms to create a one-to-many link that will display the selection titles and play lengths for all records that match each album name in the new file. Print a sample screen from one album.

CASE 3. CREATING LABELS

Using the file you modified in Chapter 2, design a label that can be used to mail a special sale announcement to each client in the database. Include in the label the date of next appointment. When done, print the labels for those clients whose birthday will be coming up next month.

Access 7.0 for Windows 95 Feature and Operation Reference

Note: Access keys include both keystrokes that are common to most Windows applications and those that are unique to Access.

COMMON WINDOWS KEYS

ALT

Pressed alone, the Alt key activates the section highlight on Microsoft Access 7.0's (or any active application window's) menu bar. The highlight may then be moved to a menu bar item using the arrow keys. If you used in combination with other keys, the Alt key is held down when striking another key. The other key is usually a function key (F1 through F12), the underlined letter of a menu item, a button, or another option that has an underlined letter.

- **Alt + F4** exits Microsoft Access 7.0 (or any Microsoft Windows application) or any dialog box.
- **Alt + Backspace** or **Ctrl + Z** undoes the last action.
- **Alt + Spacebar** opens Microsoft Access 7.0 window's (or any application window's) control menu.
- **Alt + – (Minus)** opens the control menu of a document window.
- **Alt + Tab** switches to the last application used when operating multiple applications. Pressing and holding the key while tapping the key scrolls through running applications.
- **Alt + Esc** switches to the next running application when operating multiple applications. An application can be running as a window or a toolbar button.
- **Alt + Enter** switches a non-Windows application that was started in Windows between running in full screen and a window.
- **Alt + Print Screen** will copy an image of the active application window (or dialog box) to the clipboard for future pasting.

ARROW KEYS

- Moves an insertion point one space, or line, at a time in the direction of the arrow when editing data within a text or drop-down box.
- Move the selection highlight in the direction of the arrow, to each item on a menu or list (in a list box or drop-down box).

The arrow keys can also be used in conjunction with other keys to perform such tasks as resizing a window, moving a selection (data, chart, table or object), or moving a drawing or editing tool.

BACKSPACE

Erases single characters to the left of the insertion point.

CAPS LOCK

Keeps the Shift key active so that all characters are typed in uppercase.

CTRL

The Control key is used with another key to invoke a command.

- **Crtl + Alt + Delete** exits the current application if it stops responding to the system.
- **Ctrl + B** turns on/off the bold feature.
- **Ctrl + C** or **Ctrl + Insert** copies a selection (data, chart, table or object) to the Windows Clipboard for future pasting.
- **Ctrl + Esc** opens the *Task List* dialog box.
- **Ctrl + F4** closes the active document window.
- **Ctrl + F6** or **Ctrl + Tab** moves the highlight to another document window or icon.
- **Ctrl + I** turns on/off the italics feature.
- **Ctrl + N** turns off the bold, italics or underline feature.
- **Ctrl + O** opens a file.
- **Ctrl + P** prints the current document or range selection.
- **Ctrl + S** saves the current document to a file.
- **Ctrl + U** turns on/off the underline feature.
- **Ctrl + V** or **Shift + Insert** pastes contents of the Windows Clipboard to a desired location.
- **Ctrl + X** or **Shift + Delete** cuts (moves) a selection to the Windows Clipboard for future pasting.
- **Ctrl + Z** or **Alt + Backspace** undoes the last action.

DELETE

The Delete key erases the following:

- Single characters to the right of the insertion point when editing data in a cell, text box, or drop-down box.
- A selection.

END

- Moves the insertion point to the end of a line when editing data.
- Moves the selection highlight to the last item in a menu, list box, or drop-down box.

ENTER

- Enters typed data into a cell or inserts a hard return.
- Invokes a command from a menu selection or dialog box.

ESC

- Cancels a menu or dialog box before a command is invoked.
- Returns a cell to its previous content before completing a new entry.

HOME

- Moves the insertion point to the beginning of a line of data in a cell, text box, or drop-down box.
- Moves the selection highlight to the beginning of a list in a menu, list box, or drop-down box.

NUMLOCK

Activates the numeric keypad that is on the right side of most keyboards. NumLock works as a toggle key; pressing it once activates the keypad, while pressing it again deactivates the keypad.

PG UP AND PG DN (PAGE UP AND PAGE DOWN)

Moves one screen page up or one page down.

PRINT SCREEN (PRTSC)

Captures an image of a screen to the Clipboard.

SHIFT

Works like the Shift key on a typewriter; when it is held down and a letter or number is pressed, the uppercase letter or the symbol assigned to the number key is produced. Other commands invoked when pressing the Shift key and another key include the following:

- **Shift** + → expands the selection highlight to the right.
- **Shift** + ← expands the selection highlight to the left.
- **Shift + Delete** or **Ctrl + X** cuts (moves) a selection to the Windows Clipboard for future pasting.
- **Shift + Insert** or **Ctrl + V** pastes contents of the Windows Clipboard to a desired location.
- **Shift + Tab** moves the dotted selection rectangle to the previous option in a dialog box.

TAB

Moves the dotted selection rectangle to the next option in a dialog box.

ACCESS KEYS

Special keys used by Access in addition to those used in Windows 95 are described below. For the specific location of these keys, check your particular keyboard.

CTRL+N

Opens a new database.

CTRL+O

Opens an existing database.

CTRL+F6

Cycles between open Access windows.

F11 OR ALT+F1

Brings the database window to the front.

CTRL+F

Opens the *Find* dialog box.

CTRL+H

Opens the *Replace* dialog box.

CTRL+Z

Undoes typing

F12 OR ALT+F2

Opens the *Save as* dialog box

SHIFT+F12 OR ALT+SHIFT+F2

Saves a database object in Design view.

F2

While entering or editing data in Form view or Datasheet view, the F2 function key toggles the edit mode. When edit mode is on, a text insertion point is placed in the field and individual characters can be deleted, inserted, or overtyped.

F7

While entering or editing data in Form view or Datasheet view, the F7 function key initiates a spelling check.

ACCESS MOUSE OPERATIONS

A mouse is an input device that allows you to control a mouse pointer (graphical image) on your screen. As you move your mouse, the mouse pointer moves in a similar fashion.

Your mouse can be used to select Windows 95 and Access features. Some Access special features accessible by mouse are summarized below. Refer to Figure DBA-2 for the location of some of these features. (Detailed applications of these features are incorporated within the "Summary of Common Access Operations" section of this appendix.)

CLOSING AN OBJECT WINDOW

Clicking the *Close* button is a quick way to close that window.

DRAG AND DROP

The Access Drag and Drop feature is a quick way to move a selection of text, a column boundary, or a selected object to another location. This is done by "dragging" the selected item to its new location and then "dropping" it (releasing the mouse button). (Remember, text and objects must be selected first.)

EXITING ACCESS BY MOUSE

Clicking the Access *Close* button is a quick way to exit the program.

MOVING THE INSERTION POINT BY MOUSE

Pointing to a new location and clicking your mouse is an easy way to move the insertion point (or focus) when editing data in a table or when designing a form, report, query, or other object.

RESIZING AND *CLOSE* BUTTONS

Clicking a resizing button is a quick way to change the size of a window. These mouse actions can be used to resize the Access window, the database window, or a window containing an Access object like a table or report. When at maximum size, two of the three Access resizing buttons are displayed to the right of the title bar. To the right of the resizing buttons you will always find the *Close* button. These buttons will also appear in the upper right corner of any window you open within Access, such as a database window or a window containing an Access object.

	Button Name	**Effect When Clicked**
	Minimize	Reduces the window to an icon
	Restore	Restores the window to its previous size
	Maximize	Enlarges the window to full screen
	Close	Exits from the program, closes the database file, or closes the object's window

FIGURE DBA-1 ■ THE BASIC TOOLBARS

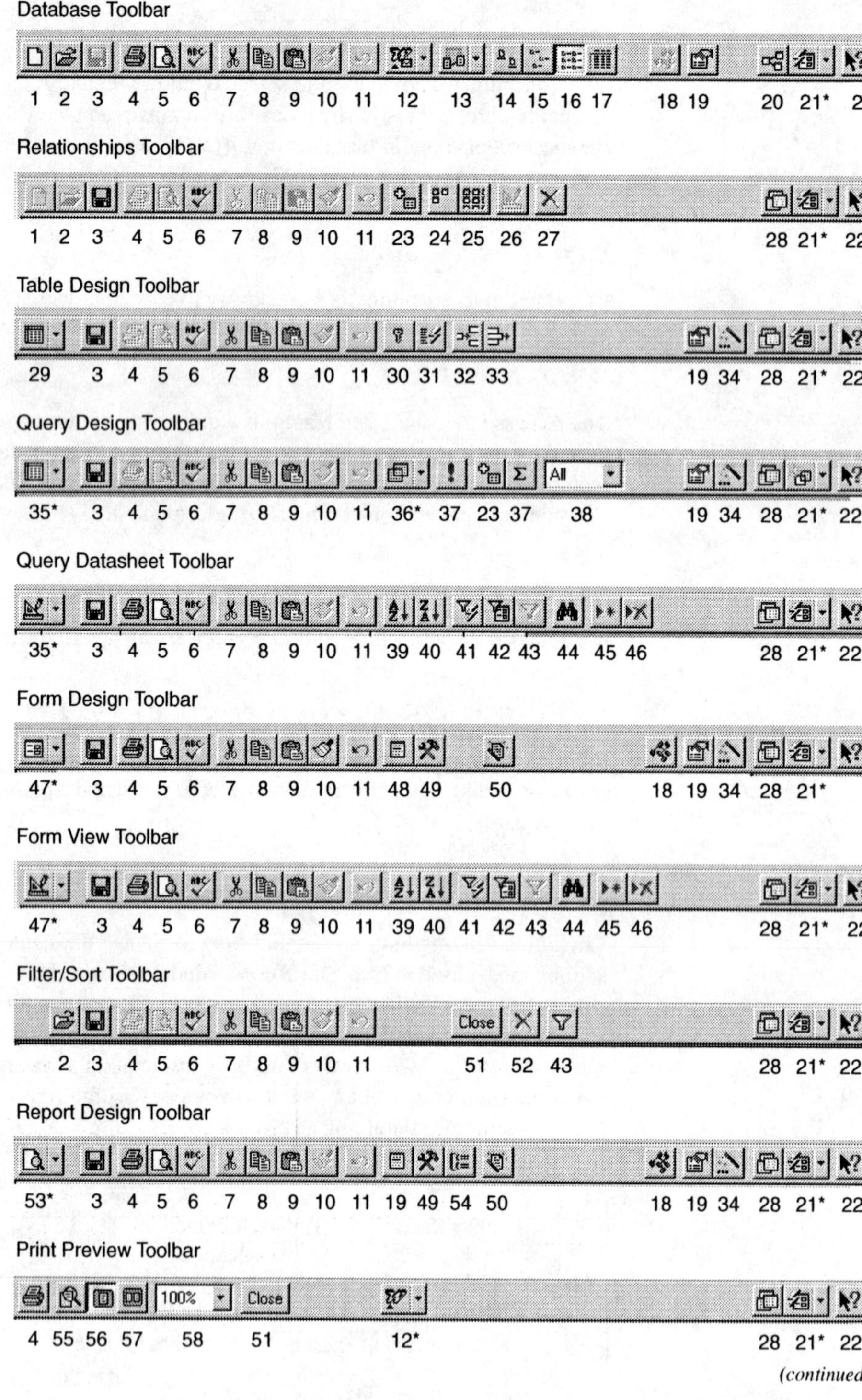

(continued)

FIGURE DBA-1 ■ *(continued)*

Toolbox Toolbar

59 60 61 62 63 64 65 66 67 68 69 70 71 72 73 74 75 76 77*

Formatting (Form/Report Design)

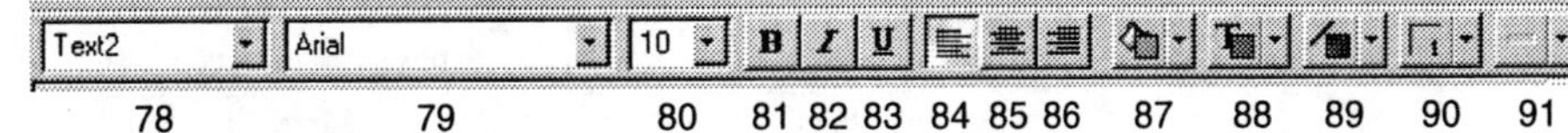

Formatting (Datasheet)

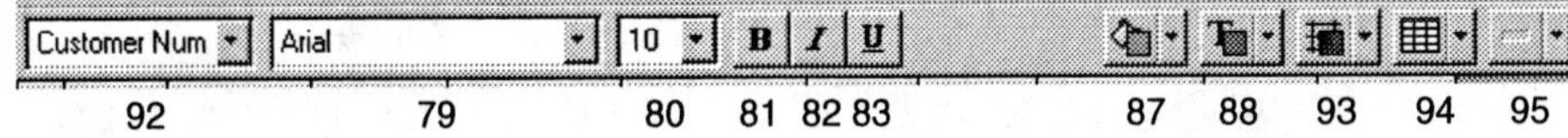

Macro Toolbar

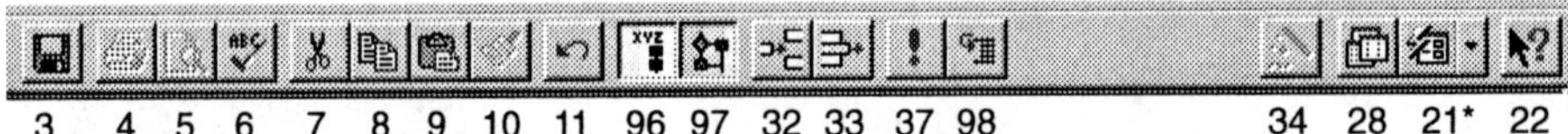

Visual Basic Toolbar

99 100 3 4 11 101 102 103 104 105 106 107 108 109 110 111 112 113 114 34 28 21* 22

Microsoft Applications Toolbar

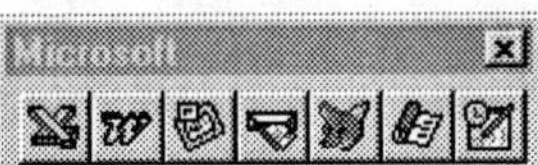

115 116 117 118 119 120 121

#	Button Name	Function
1	New Database	Creates a new empty database file
2	Open Database	Opens an existing database file
3	Save Current Object	Saves changes made to any object in design mode or saves format changes made to a table in datasheet view
4	Print	Prints the current object
5	Print Preview	Displays on screen the print job that would result from clicking the *Print* button
6	Check Spelling	Checks and corrects spelling in your data files
7	Cut	Removes the selected object and copies it to the Clipboard
8	Copy	Copies the selected object to the Clipboard

(continued)

FIGURE DBA-1 ■ *(continued)*

#	Button Name	Function
9	Paste	Copies the data in the Clipboard to the selected object or location of the text insertion point
10	Format Painter	Copies formatting from one object to another object of the same or similar type
11	Undo Last Action	Reverses the most recent action
12*	Office Links	Choices: Merge it with Word, Publish it with Word, and Analyze it with Excel
13*	Analyze	Choices: Analyze Table, Analyze Performance, and Documentor
14	Large Icons	Displays objects in the database window as large icons
15	Small Icons	Displays objects in the database window as small icons
16	List	Displays objects in the database window as an alphabetized list of small icons
17	Show File Details	Displays objects in the database window as a list of small icons with name, description, date modified, date created, and type
18	Code	Displays a Visual Basic module
19	Properties	Displays a list of properties associated with the selected object
20	Relationships	Displays the Relationship window so the relationships among tables and queries can be modified
21*	New Object	Choices: Autoform, Autoreport, New Table, New Query, New Form, New Report, New Macro, New Module
22	Help	Click this button, then click the object on the screen with which you need help
23	Show Table	Displays a list of tables so relationships can be altered
24	Show Direct Relationships	Displays a map of current relationships for the selected table
25	Show All Relationships	Displays a map of all relationships for this database
26	Design View	Displays the selected object in Design view
27	Clear Layout	Clears the contents of the Relationships window
28	Database Window	Displays the Database window
29*	View	Choices: Design view, Datasheet view
30	Primary Key	Selects a field to be the primary key for the table
31	Indexes	Selects fields for indexing
32	Insert Field or Row	Inserts a blank row at the selected location
33	Delete Field or Row	Removes the selected row
34	Build	Displays a builder for the selected item, allowing you to choose among predesigned options

(continued)

FIGURE DBA-1 ■ *(continued)*

#	Button Name	Function
35*	View	Choices: Datasheet view, SQL view, Design view
36*	Query Type	Choices: Select, Crosstab, Make Table, Update, Append, and Delete
37	Run	Runs the query, macro, or module
38	Top Values	Selects the records with the top n% values
39	Sort Ascending	Sorts records in ascending order by selected field(s)
40	Sort Descending	Sorts records in descending order by selected field(s)
41	Filter by Selection	Filters records using the selected field value as a criterion
42	Filter by Form	Opens a form in which the user can enter criteria values for filtering
43	Apply/Remove Filter	Toggles the filter on and off using the criteria
44	Find	Opens the *Find* dialog box
45	New Record	Advances to the blank record at the bottom of the table or dynaset
46	Delete Record	Deletes the current record
47*	View	Choices: Design view, Form view, and Datasheet view
48	Field List	Displays a list of fields that can be placed on the form or report
49	Toolbox	Displays the toolbox buttons
50	Autoformat	Applies predesigned format to the form or report
51	Close	Closes the Filter, Print Preview, or Query window
52	Clear	Clears all values from the query or filter grid
53*	View	Choices: Design view, Print Preview, Layout Preview
54	Sorting and Grouping	Adds or removes group levels to the report
55	Zoom	Zooms in (magnifies) or zooms out (minimizes)
56	One Page	Previews just the current page
57	Two Pages	Previews the current and following pages
58	Zoom Control	Controls the magnification level of the zoom feature
59	Selection Arrow	Changes the mouse pointer to an arrow shape that can be used to select objects
60	Control Wizard	Toggles Control wizards on and off
61	Label	Inserts labels on reports and forms
62	Text Box	Creates text boxes on reports and forms that can display field data from tables and queries
63	Option Group	Creates a frame that can hold option buttons, toggle buttons, and check boxes on a form
64	Toggle Button	Inserts a button on a form that indicates a TRUE value when selected by the user

(continued)

FIGURE DBA-1 ■ *(continued)*

#	Button Name	Function
65	Option Button	Creates one button in a set of single-choice buttons on a form
66	Check Box	Creates a box on a form that indicates a TRUE value when checked by the user
67	Combo Box	Creates a combined list box and text box on a form
68	List Box	Creates a list box on a form
69	Command	Creates a button on a form that can be used to run a macro or a Visual Basic module
70	Image	Creates a frame that holds a static image
71	Unbound Object	Creates a frame to hold an OLE object
72	Bound Object	Creates a frame to hold an OLE object that is a field value in an Access table
73	Page Break	Marks the beginning of a new screen in a form or a new page in report
74	Subform/Subreport	Creates a frame to hold a subform or subreport
75	Line	Draws a line on a form or report
76	Rectangle	Draws a rectangle on a form or report
77*	Custom Control	Adds a custom control to a form or report
78	Object	Selects an object from the drop down list
79	Font Name	Selects a font name from the list of available fonts
80	Font Size	Selects a font size from the list of available sizes
81	Bold	Bolds the selected text
82	Italics	Italicizes the selected text
83	Underline	Underlines the selected text
84	Left	Left justifes the selected text within its frame
85	Center	Centers the selected text within its frame
86	Right	Right justifies the selected text within its frame
87	Back Color	Selects a background color from the palette
88	Fore Color	Selects a foreground color from the palette
89	Border	Selects a border color from the palette
90	Border Width	Selects the width of the frame around the selected object
91	Special Effects	Applies a variety of special effects to the object such as shadowing
92	Select Field	Selects from the list of fields
93	Gridline Color	Selects from a palette the desired color for the lines separating field values in Datasheet view
94	Gridlines Shown	Determines which gridlines will be displayed in Datasheet view

(continued)

FIGURE DBA-1 ■ *(continued)*

#	Button Name	Function
95	Cell Effect	Selects a special effect, such as shadowing.
96	Macro Name	Displays the macro name column in the Macro Design screen
97	Conditions	Displays the conditions column in the Macro Design screen
98	Single Step	Executes the macro one step at a time
99	Insert Module	Inserts a new module
100	Insert Procedure	Inserts a new procedure in the current module
101	Redo	Repeats the last action
102	Debug Window	Displays the Debug window
103	Object Browser	Displays Object Browser to display or insert code templates to the selected object
104	Continue	Continues execution of module
105	End	Halts execution of module
106	Reset	Halts execution of module and clears all variables
107	Breakpoint	Sets or removes breakpoint at the current line
108	Instant Watch	Displays the value of a selected expression (such as a variable) during execution
109	Calls	Displays a list of executed calls
110	Step Into	Executes one statement at a time in a module
111	Step Over	Executes one statement at a time, treating the selected module as one step
112	Compile	Compiles all procedures
113	Indent	Shifts the selected line(s) to the right
114	Outdent	Shifts the selected line(s) to the left
115	Microsoft Excel	Switches to or Launches Microsoft Excel
116	Microsoft Word	Switches to or Launches Microsoft Word
117	Microsoft PowerPoint	Switches to or Launches Microsoft PowerPoint
118	Microsoft Mail	Switches to or Launches Microsoft Mail
119	Microsoft FoxPro	Switches to or Launches Microsoft FoxPro
120	Microsoft Project	Switches to or Launches Microsoft Project
121	Microsoft Schedule+	Switches to or Launches Microsoft Schedule+

*Indicates toolbar buttons that appear in a "stack" of buttons. The last button used remains on top of the stack. To select another button in the stack, click the pull-down arrow.

SELECTING RECORDS, TEXT, AND OBJECTS BY MOUSE

Selection is the process of marking text, records, field values, columns, rows, or objects for application of other Access features. Click the desired item with the mouse to select it. When an item has been selected,

- It can be cut or copied to the Clipboard by clicking the *Cut* or *Copy* button.
- It can be deleted by pressing the Delete key.
- It marks the destination for a paste operation.
- It marks the location where data will appear if you make a keyboard entry.

Multiple objects can be selected using the ruler bars.

RULER BARS. Using the Access rulers when designing a form or report provides a quick way to select objects and makes it easier for you to position objects visually. To activate the rulers while designing a report or form, click *View* and then *Ruler*.

To use the ruler bars to select objects, drag the mouse along either of the rulers. Objects located between the beginning and ending points will be selected.

To Select While Entering or Editing Data in a Table	
For Selection of a	**Use This Mouse Action**
Field Value	Point to the left side of the value and click
Several Field Values	Drag mouse over values
Column	Click the column selector
Row	Click the row selector

To Select While Designing a Report or a Form	
For Selection of a	**Use This Mouse Action**
Object	Click the object
Multiple Objects	Shift-click each object

SHORTCUT MENUS

Shortcut menus provide quick access to a variety of features. To select a *Shortcut* menu by mouse, simply click it (left mouse button). Also, pointing to and clicking the right mouse button in the following locations will open a *Shortcut* menu.

- Title bar
- Toolbar
- Table
- Form
- Report design screen
- Form design screen
- Print preview screen
- Database window
- Object name in the database window

THE TOOLBARS

The toolbars, shown in Figure DBA-1a, provide a quick method of executing frequently used procedures using the mouse. There are sixteen standard toolbars that appear at various times in Access: Database, Relationships, Table Design, Query Design, Query Datasheet, Form Design, Form View, Filter/Sort, Report Design, Print Preview, Toolbox, Formatting (Form/Report Design), Formatting (Datasheet), Macro, Visual Basic, and Microsoft Applications.

Access toolbars are totally customizable, so your system might be arranged differently than shown in the figure. Buttons can be added, deleted, and rearranged on any toolbar. Also, toolbars can be created or deleted. You may activate the toolbar customization capability by clicking *View, Toolbars*, then clicking the *Customize* button on the following dialog box.

Access toolbars are shown in their default arrangement in Figure DBA-1. The number below each button is keyed to the table showing the button name and function. Some buttons are grouped in stacks. One button is always on the top. Clicking this button executes the procedure associated with the button. Clicking the pull-down arrow next to the button causes the entire list of buttons to be displayed. Clicking one of the buttons on the list executes the procedure associated with the button *and* it places the button on top of the stack. These grouped buttons are designated with an asterisk (*) following the reference number. See Figure DBA-1b for a list of all the buttons contained in the stack.

DISPLAYING AND HIDING A TOOLBAR. To display or hide a toolbar:

1. **Click *View*, and then click *Toolbars***
2. **Click the check box to select or clear the desired toolbar**
3. **Click *Close***

MOVING THE TOOLBAR. The toolbar can be moved (and reshaped) from its current location to a new location anywhere within the Access window.

1. **Click within the toolbar and hold the mouse button**
2. **Drag the toolbar to your desired new location and drop it there**

CREATING A CUSTOMIZED TOOLBAR. You can create your own customized toolbar by doing the following:

1. **Click *View*, then click *Toolbars***
2. **Click the check box to display the desired toolbar**
3. **Click the *Customize* button**
4. **Click *New***

5 **Type a name for the new toolbar, then click *OK***

EDITING A TOOLBAR. You may add, move, or delete buttons to or from any toolbar.

To add a button to a toolbar

1 **Click *View*, then click *Toolbars***

2 **Click the check box to display the desired toolbar**

3 **Click the *Customize* button**

4 **Select the category of buttons you want displayed**

5 **Drag the desired button to the appropriate toolbar**

6 **Click *Close***

To move a button

1 **Click *View*, then click *Toolbars***

2 **Click the check box to display the desired toolbar**

3 **Click the *Customize* button**

4 **Drag the button to its new location and drop it there**

5 **Click the *Close* button**

To delete a button

1 **Click *View*, then click *Toolbars***

2 **Click the check box to display the desired toolbar**

3 **Click the *Customize* button**

4 **Drag the button off the toolbar**

5 **Click the *Close* button**

INSERTION POINT MOVEMENT

The text insertion point can be located where you desire while entering or editing data in a table or form, typing text in a label box, or entering values in a dialog box. You can place the insertion point in a location by double-clicking the location or by pressing F2 while the location is selected. The insertion point can be moved within the location as desired.

The Insertion Point Moves	When You Press
One Character Right	→
One Character Left	←
One Word Right	Ctrl + →
One Word Left	Ctrl + ←
To the beginning of the current line	Home
To the end of the current line	End

SUMMARY OF COMMON ACCESS OPERATIONS

Following is a brief, step-by-step summary showing how to perform several common Access tasks.

ARRANGING DOCUMENT WINDOWS

It is possible to have several windows open within Access at the same time. For example, you might have the database window, a table, and a Report Design screen open at once. Often these windows overlap or completely obscure each other. When this is not convenient, the windows can be arranged in vertical tiles, horizontal tiles, or cascaded. To arrange windows,

1. **Click *Windows***
2. **Then click *Tile Horizontally*, *Tile Vertically*, or *Cascade***

CANCELING A COMMAND

If you have begun an operation or procedure that you wish to halt, you can cause Access to return to its previous state by one of the following methods, depending on the action initiated:

If you have pulled down a menu that you want to remove from the screen,

1 **Click a portion of the screen that is not on the menu**

If you have opened a document that you wish to close,

1 **Click the *Close* button**

If you have opened a dialog box that you do not want,

1 **Click the *Cancel* command button**

If you have sorted or filtered records in a way that you do not desire,

1 **Click *Records*, then click *Remove Filter/Sort***

If you have begun a print job that you want to stop,

1 **Click the *Cancel* command button on the *Printing* dialog box**

If Access has changed the shape of the mouse pointer to that of an hourglass, the procedure has begun. It cannot be canceled until the mouse pointer changes to another shape. Remember that the best protection against damage done to your data by human error is to keep current backup copies of all your data.

CLOSING A WINDOW

All Access objects, documents, and files appear in a window. Closing the window causes the object, document, or file to disappear from the screen. If any data has not been saved to the disk, it will be saved when the window is closed or a dialog box will ask you if you want to save changes to your data. Never turn off the computer without closing all windows that may contain unsaved data. To close a window,

1 **Click the *Close* button**

COPYING DATA

Records in a table can be copied to the Clipboard. Once on the Clipboard, they can then be pasted (inserted) to another Access table or to other Windows applications. To copy records,

1 **Display the table containing the records**

2 **Select the records**

3 **Click *Edit*, *Copy*** Ctrl + C

COPYING OBJECTS

An object can be a table, query, report, form, macro, or module. To copy one of these objects so that its entire contents can be inserted in the same database file or another database file,

1. **Display the database window**
2. **Click the tab corresponding to the object's type**
3. **Select the object's name**

4. **Click *Edit, Copy*** **Ctrl + C**

Tables and queries can be copied to the Clipboard and then pasted into other applications. Reports, forms, macros, and modules can only be pasted into Access database files.

CREATING A NEW DATABASE

To create a new database file,

1. **Click the *New Database* button or click *File, New Database***

Access will open a dialog box where you can choose to create a *blank* database file (one which contains no objects) or select from among many predesigned files that contain objects like tables, reports, and screen forms.

2. **Select the icon representing the type of database file you wish to create, then click *OK***

If you have selected *Blank Database*, Access will create an empty file in which you must design and save the objects you intend to use. If you have selected one of the other choices, Access will activate a wizard which will guide you through a series of customization steps so that you can make decisions like adding or removing fields from tables, altering the style and format of reports, and so on.

The pre-designed formats are as follows:

Asset Tracking	Friends	Order Processing	Students and Classes
Book Collection	Household Inventory	Picture Library	Time and Billing
Contact Management	Inventory Control	Recipes	Video
Donations	Ledger	Resource Scheduling	Wine List
Event Management	Membership	Service Call Management	Workout
Expenses	Music Collection		

When you have completed the *Wizard* dialog boxes, Access fills the database file with the objects that are necessary for you to manage that type of data. Of course, any of the objects can be redesigned later.

DELETING DATA

Records in a table can be deleted two ways: using the mouse or using a query.
To delete records using the mouse,

1. **Display the table containing the records**
2. **Select the records**
3. **Press Delete**

You can also delete a group of records by using a Delete Query window. Records that match the specified criteria in the query will be removed from the table.

1. **Open the Query design screen**
2. **Click the drop-down button next to the *Query Type* button, then select *Delete Query***
3. **Select the fields to be used by dragging the field names to the field rows of the columns of the query**
4. **Type the appropriate criteria in the criteria rows beneath the fields**

5. **Click the *Run* button**

Access opens a dialog box to warn you that a specified number of rows are about to be deleted. To affirm the deletion of the selected records,

6. **Click *OK***

DELETING OBJECTS

Objects (tables, queries, reports, forms, macros, or modules) and their entire contents can be deleted from the database file.

1. **Display the database window**
2. **Click the tab corresponding to the object's type**
3. **Select the object's name**
4. **Press Delete**

A dialog box opens to ask you to confirm the deletion of the object.

5. **Click *Yes***

If you have inadvertently deleted an object that you shouldn't have, you can restore it by clicking *Undo Delete* on the *Edit* menu.

DRAG AND DROP FEATURE

Selected objects can be moved across the screen using the drag and drop feature. The variety of objects that can be manipulated using drag and drop include the following:

- Object icons displayed in the database window
- Objects placed on reports and forms (in Design view) such as a *text box* or an *unbound object frame*.

To move one of these objects

1. **Open the window in which the object is to be found**

2. **Select the object**

3. **Point to the object with the mouse**

In the case of design objects placed on forms and reports, it will be necessary to point to the selected object's move handle.

4. **Click and hold the left mouse button**

5. **Drag the object to the desired location**

6. **Drop the object by releasing the mouse button**

EXITING ACCESS

To exit Access the easiest way,

1. **Click the *Close* button**

Be sure, if multiple windows are displayed, that you select the *Close* button on the Microsoft Access title bar. If any data or changes to designed objects have not been saved, Access will open a dialog box asking you if you want to save or abandon changes. Never turn the computer off with Microsoft Access running. Always shut down cleanly and safely by exiting Access. Then follow the standard Windows 95 shut down procedures.

EXPORTING DATA

Access can export data (save data in a format readable by other applications) by using the *File, Save As/Export* command. The only kind of Access object that is exportable is the table. Other objects (reports, forms, queries, etc.) can be copied to other Access database files, but they cannot be exported to other applications.

To export table data,

1. **Display the database window and select the *Tables* tab, if necessary**

2. **Select the table to be exported**

3. **Click *File, Save As/Export***

On the resulting dialog box,

4. **Select *To an External File or Database*, then click *OK***

Access will open the *Save Table ... In* dialog box.

5 Use the pull-down arrow to designate the file type, then click *Export*

Depending on the export file type, Access will either export the data immediately or initiate a wizard to step you through certain choices about your data.

FINDING A RECORD CONTAINING A PARTICULAR VALUE

Access has a sophisticated ability to search through the records of a table to locate a record or those records containing a particular field value. There are basically three methods you can use:

THE *FIND* BUTTON. To locate records containing fields with a specified value,

1 Place the text insertion point in the significant field

2 Click the *Find* button

Access will display the *Find* dialog box. Because the text insertion point was in the field selected in Step 1, Access presumes that you are hunting for a value in that field.

3 Type the criterion value in the *Find What* text box

Wildcard characters may be included in the criterion value. (See "Wildcard Characters in Searches, Filters, and Queries" presented later in this appendix.)

4 Indicate the direction in the *Search* box

5 Indicate which part of the field must correspond to the criterion value in the *Match* box

6 Click *Find First*

Access searches in the *Search* direction for the first record containing the criterion value. If such a record is encountered, Access selects the field value. To continue searching,

7 Click *Next*

This process can be repeated until the last matching record is encountered.

FILTERING. Filtering is another way to identify those records which match a certain value. When a filter has been established, Access suppresses the display or printing of those records that do not match the filter's criteria. To limit the display of records to a specific value,

1 Display the table

Next, indicate any cell containing the value that you want to filter by.

2 Click (or tab to) the column containing the field value you wish to filter by (in any record)

For example, if you wanted to see only the records of inventory items manufactured by Acme Corp, you would place the focus or text insertion point in a field containing that value, thus pointing this value out to Access.

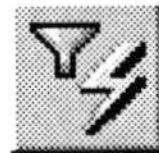

3 Click *Records, Filter, Filter by Selection*

Access displays only those records whose manufacturer value is identical to the value that was selected when the filter command was executed. Records can be edited, deleted, or printed. The filter remains in effect until you cancel it by clicking the *Apply Filter* button to deselect it.

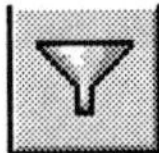

4 Click *Records, Remove Filter/Sort*

All records are again displayed. Access remembers the last filter that you used, and it can be applied again at any time. To re-impose the same filter condition as before,

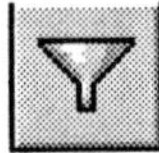

5 Click *Records, Apply Filter/Sort*

Then, remove the filter:

6 Click the *Apply Filter* button

Remember, the *Apply Filter* button acts as a toggle. If a filter is active, clicking this button again will deactivate the filter.

If you wanted to use wildcard characters (see "*Wildcard Characters* in Searches, Filters, and Queries") in the filter process or if you wished to filter by more than one field value, you would use the *Filter by Form* process.

1 Display the table

2 Click the *Filter by Form* button

Access displays an empty table. In the appropriate field columns,

3 Enter the values (including wildcard characters if desired)

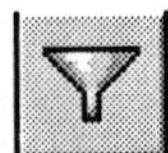

4 Click *Records, Apply Filter/Sort*

Then, remove the filter:

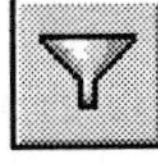

5 Click the *Apply Filter* button

THE SELECT QUERY. The third method that you can use to locate records containing certain field values is to design and run a Select query, which allows you to find records that:

- Match criteria exactly
- Fall within an acceptable range of values

- Fit a pattern
- "Come close" to search values
- Do <u>not</u> match criteria

You can also combine criteria.

To design and run a Select query, display the table and do the following:

1 Click the *New Object* button, then select the *New Query* button

A dialog box will ask you to choose between *Query Wizard* and *New Query*.

2 Select *New Query*, then click *OK*

You now see the empty Select Query design screen. Select the fields that you want to display in the answer.

3 Click and drag the desired field names from the list of fields to the field row of the query

This identifies the field columns that will appear in the answer. To restrict the records that will appear by specifying the search criteria:

4 Type the desired values in the criteria row (include wildcard characters as logical connectors if desired)

5 Click the *Run* button

The answer to the query appears on your screen. The answer table (dynaset) is dynamically connected to the underlying table, so edits made to the dynaset are passed on to the table itself.

HELP FEATURE

The Access Help feature is always available with context-sensitive help. There are several methods by which you can ask for help.

To display the Access Help screens,

1 Click *Help*, then click *Microsoft Help Topics*

THE *HELP TOPICS* DIALOG BOX. Access opens the *Help Topics* dialog box. Note that this dialog box has four tabs representing four ways of searching through the Help text. Select the tab that offers the kind of help you think you need.

When You Click This Tab...	You Get This Kind of Help...
Contents	Select a topic from a list of logically arranged topics.
Index	Type a word or phrase which Access will try to find in its Help index.
Find	Type a word or phrase. Access will search through its Help screens for that word or phrase.
Answer Wizard	Type a simple question or statement describing the task you are trying to perform. Access will try to reply by displaying the appropriate Help wizard.

THE *HELP* BUTTON ON THE TOOLBAR. The toolbar contains a *Help* button. Its function is to help you identify the features you see on the screen.

1. **Click the *Help* button**
2. **Point to a feature on the screen and click**

Access displays a brief description of that feature.

THE *HELP* BUTTON ON DIALOG BOXES. Every Access dialog box also contains a *Help* button. It provides help with the features of that dialog box.

1. **Display any dialog box**
2. **Click the *Help* button in the upper right corner of that dialog box**
3. **Point to a feature on the dialog box and click**

Access displays a brief description of that feature.

THE F1 FUNCTION KEY. Pressing F1 causes Access to display a Help screen associated with the task then underway or the *Help Topics* dialog box.

IMPORTING DATA

Access can import data (read data in a format created by other applications) by using the *File, Get External Data, Import* command.

To import table data,

1. **Display the database window**
2. **Click *File, Get External Data, Import***

On the resulting dialog box,

3. **Select the type, location, and name of the data file to be imported**

Depending on the type of file that is being imported, Access will start an Import wizard that will step you through the import process.

LINKING A TABLE FROM ANOTHER DATABASE FILE

Normally, Access displays only the names of objects contained within a database file in the database window. However, at times, data from a table or query contained in another file is needed. A table from another file can be linked to a particular database file. The name of this table will be displayed in the database window as if it were an object within that file. To link an external table to a database file, perform the following steps:

1. **Display the database window**

2 **Click *File, Get External Data, Link Tables***

On the *Link* dialog box,

3 **Indicate the name of the Access database file containing the table you wish to link, then click the *Link* button**

On the *Link Tables* dialog box, Access will display a list of tables in the file you selected.

4 **Select the table name or names you desire, then click *OK***

The names of the linked tables will be displayed in the database window and the data in those tables can be used just as if the tables were objects in the database file. To remove the link,

5 **Select the name of a linked table and press Delete**

The link will be removed and the table name will no longer display in the database window. However, the table's data in its parent file will not be deleted. Only the linking information will be deleted.

LOGICAL CONNECTORS

The following logical connectors can be used to identify a group of values in a query.

Operator	Example	Explanation
<	<500	Less than
>	>500	Greater than
=	=500	Equal to
<=	<=500	Less than or equal to
>=	>=500	Greater than or equal to
AND	>5 AND <10	Logical AND connector; both conditions must be true
OR	>5 OR < 10	Logical OR connector; either condition must be true
NOT	NOT 500	Logical NOT expression; all values except 500

MACROS

A *macro* is an Access object. Like Access, macros provide a way to automate repetitive procedures. The steps involved in creating and running a macro are simple, but mastering the process well enough to automate a sophisticated application is challenging. The steps in creating a macro are as follows:

1 **Display the database window and click the *Macro* tab if necessary**

2 **Click *New***

Access will display the Macro Design screen, which consists of two columns. In the left column,

3 Enter the commands that the macro is to execute

When the text insertion point is in a row in the left column, a pull-down arrow appears. Clicking the pull-down arrow causes a list of available commands to be displayed. When you select a command, Access asks for any arguments that must accompany that command. In the right column,

4 Enter an optional comment explaining the command to the left

The macro is saved as any other object would be. To run the macro,

5 Click *Tools-Macro*

On the resulting dialog box,

6 Select the macro name and click *OK*

The actions will be executed from top to bottom.

OBJECT LINKING AND EMBEDDING (OLE)

Objects come in a variety of forms and the term is widely applied. However, anything referred to as an object is a collection of data assembled into a meaningful form that has a discrete identity. An object could be a graphic image like a Windows bitmap, a sound file, a video clip, a file produced by a word processor or spreadsheet, an Access object like a form or a report, the contents of the Clipboard, and so forth. In Access, an object (like a graphic image containing a company logo) can be placed on a form or report during the design process. An object can also be a field value in a table. For example, a digitized photograph of each employee could be stored in the employee's record.

Objects can be *embedded* or *linked.* When an object is *embedded,* it is placed in the Access file and becomes part of the file. When an object is *linked,* Access retrieves a copy of the file each time the object is viewed, printed, or otherwise referred to by Access.

INSERTING AN EMBEDDED OBJECT ON A FORM OR REPORT. To insert an object on an Access report or form,

1 Open the form or report in design mode and display the toolbox

2 Click the *Unbound Object Frame* button and draw a rectangle to contain the object

On the *Insert Object* dialog box,

3 Click *Create from File,* then type the name of the file in the text box

4 Click *OK*

The object will be placed in the *Unbound Object* rectangle and has become a part of your report or form.

INSERTING A LINKED OBJECT ON A FORM OR REPORT. To insert a linked object on an Access report or form, follow the same steps given above for an embedded object. On the *Insert Object* dialog box, be sure that a check mark is placed next to *Linked.*

INSERTING AN EMBEDDED OBJECT INTO AN ACCESS TABLE. First, the table must be designed to accept the object. To do this, designate the field that will contain the object as the *OLE Object* data type. When entering data in the table (whether in Datasheet view or Form view), use the following steps to insert the object in the desired record:

1. **Select the field in which the object is to be inserted**

2. **Click *Insert*, then click *Object***

You will see the *Insert Object* dialog box. The process for filling out this dialog box is exactly the same as that given earlier. When you have completed the dialog box, the object is inserted into the Access table and has become a part of its data.

INSERTING A LINKED OBJECT INTO AN ACCESS TABLE. The process for inserting a *linked* object into an Access table differs from that of inserting an embedded object only in that the *Linked* option must be checked on the *Insert Object* dialog box. Access will look up the file containing the object and will insert it in the table. However, you may control when and how often Access looks at the original file to get an up-to-date image. You may choose to have the link

- *Automatically* updated. Access will update the image every time the record is printed, displayed, copied, or otherwise referred to in an Access process
- *Manually* updated. Access will update the image when the user desires

To choose which of the update methods is used in a particular case,

1. **Open the table for editing**

2. **Select the field containing the object**

3. **Click *Edit*, then click *OLE/DDE Links***

Access displays the *Links* dialog box, where you can indicate your preferences about the update method, among others. To change the update method,

4. **Select the object name in the *Links* text box**

5. **Select either *Automatic* or *Manual*, then click *OK***

To update a manual link,

6 **Display the *Links* dialog box using the steps shown above, click the *Update* button, then click *OK***

OBJECT TYPES

Access database files can contain six types of objects:

- Table—The primary container of data. Access tables are made up of records containing fields of various types. Each record contains a single observation about the class of things that the table is designed to contain, like a single invoice or a single employee.
- Query—A question asked of the data. Access queries examine a table or tables searching for the answer to the question. Queries can select certain records, perform summary statistics on tables, delete records, append records, and create new tables.
- Report—A display of Access data designed for the printer. Access reports are made up of design objects placed on the report by the user. Reports are banded, consisting of the page header, report header, detail band, report footer, and page footer. Also, additional group bands can be added to group the data on the report meaningfully.
- Form—A display of Access data designed for the screen. Access forms are made up of design objects placed on the report by the user.
- Macro—A list of menu commands that can be executed automatically. An Access macro contains any number of commands. The list can be created or edited by the user for the purpose of automating frequently repeated procedures.
- Module—A procedure associated with an object. The procedure is written in Visual Basic for Applications, which is the object-oriented programming language that is associated with Access. The procedures can be created and edited by the user. Procedures can be activated by an event, such as a mouse click, a change in the data, or the opening of a file.

A list of objects of each type in a database file can be displayed by clicking the appropriate tab on the database window.

OBJECT WINDOWS

When an object is open for viewing or design, Access displays the object's data in an object window. This window is contained within the database window. Like all other windows in Windows 95, it can be resized using the size buttons, closed using the *Close* button, moved using click and drag, and its boundaries can be adjusted using the mouse. If the object contained in the window has been changed and not saved, you will be prompted to save changes. An open object window can be brought to the front by clicking *Window,* then clicking the window's name.

PASTING OBJECTS OR DATA FROM THE CLIPBOARD

To paste objects or data that have been cut or copied to the Clipboard,

1 **Select the area where the object or data is to be pasted**

When inserting data in a table, select the field where the data is to be inserted. When designing a form, draw a rectangle to contain the object or data by clicking the appropriate button on the toolbox.

2 **Click the *Paste* button**

Note: If you are pasting one or more entire records that have been cut or copied from another Access table, click *Edit*, then click *Paste Append*

PRINTING A REPORT

To print a report,

1 **Display the database window**

2 **Click the *Reports* tab, then select the report name**

3 **Click *Preview***

An image of the report as it will appear on the printer is displayed on the screen. If the report looks satisfactory,

4 **Click the *Print* button**

PRINTING A TABLE

To print a quick copy of the data contained in a table,

1 **Display the database window**

2 **Click the *Tables* tab, then select the table name**

3 **Click the *File, Print, OK*** [Ctrl + P , ↵]

RELATIONSHIPS

Data among several tables can be linked together in a relationship. The relationship is typically defined by a common field—called a *key* field—which is contained in the two tables to be related. The key field must be of the same data type and width in both tables. For example, a table containing a list of customers could be linked to a table containing a list of invoices. The key field would likely be a customer number that would be contained in both tables. Then, when invoices were printed, Access could draw customer name and address information from the customer table by looking up the customer number found on the invoice record.

When two or more tables are related, one table is the *master* table. It is the table that contains the observations of primary interest to the user. Other tables in the relationship are called *detail* tables. When the user scrolls to a record in the master table, Access scrolls the detail tables until a record with a matching key field is found.

Relationships can take various forms:

- One-to-Many—One record in the master table can match any number of records in the detail table(s).
- Many-to-One—Any number of records in the master table can match a single record in the detail table.
- Many-to-Many—Any number of records in the master table can match any number of records in the detail table(s).

Tables can be linked in three ways in Access.

DESIGNING A FORM OR A REPORT USING DATA FROM LINKED TABLES WHEN THE SUBFORM/SUBREPORT ALREADY EXISTS. In the process of designing a form or report, data can be drawn from more than one table. The data from the detail table will be displayed on a *subform* or *subreport.* If you intend to use a form or report that has already been designed as the subform or subreport, it can be inserted directly into the report or form. With the form or report displayed in Design mode, perform the following steps to insert the subform or subreport:

1. **Click the *Subform/Subreport* button, then draw a rectangle to contain the subform/subreport**

2. **Open the *Properties* dialog box**

3. **Click the drop-down button next to data source, then select the name of the object to be used as a subform/subreport**

4. **Click the ellipsis button next to *Link Child Fields***

On the *Subform Field Linker* dialog box that follows,

5. **Select the key fields on which the two tables will be linked, then click *OK***

6. **Save the form or report in the normal way**

USING A WIZARD TO DESIGN A FORM OR REPORT DISPLAYING DATA FROM TWO OR MORE TABLES. The Access wizards will design both the form and subform for you.

1. **Open the database window, click the *Forms* (or *Reports*) tab, then click *New***

On the *New Form* dialog box,

2. **Select the name of the master table, select *Form Wizard,* then click *OK***

On the *Form Wizard* dialog box,

3. **Select the fields from the master table you want on the report**

4. **Click the drop-down button next to *Tables/Queries,* then select the detail table**

5 **Select the fields from the detail table you want on the report**

6 **Complete the remaining *Form Wizard* dialog boxes in the normal way**

LINKING TABLES. Tables can be linked directly without using the design screens or wizards. To link two tables:

1 **Display the database window and click the *Tables* tab if necessary**

2 **Click *Tools*, then click *Relationships***

Access opens the *Relationships* dialog box. The next step is to display the tables you want to link. If they are not displayed,

3 **Click *Relationships*, then click *Show Table***

Access displays the *Show Table* dialog box.

4 **Select the tables you want to link, then click *Show***

5 **Using click and drag, draw a line connecting the key fields on the two tables**

Access should graphically display the link between the two tables by displaying a line connecting the two fields.

SELECTING TEXT AND OBJECTS

Access data is contained in objects. If you want to work with the data in an object, you must first select the object. The rules for selecting objects vary with the nature of the object.

To Select This	Do This
One object name in the database window	Click the object name
Several object names in the database window	Shift-click each object name
An object in a Report or Form design screen	Click the object
Several objects in a Report or Form design screen	Shift-click each object, or drag the mouse along a ruler
One or more text characters in a text box	Double-click the text box to place the text insertion point, then use the shift key in combination with the arrow keys to select text
One or more characters in a field in a table	Select the field, press F2 to place the text insertion point, then use the shift key in combination with the arrow keys to select text

SORTING A TABLE

To sort the data in a table,

1. **Display the table or form**

2. **Tab to a value in the field you wish to sort by**

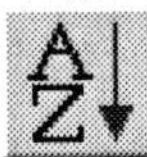

3. **Click the *Sort Ascending* button**

The table displays records sorted by that field. Clicking the *Sort Descending* button places the data in reverse order. To return the table to natural order,

4. **Select *Records*, then select *Remove Filter/Sort***

SPELLING AUTOCORRECT

Access will check the spelling of the words in a table. To perform a spelling check,

1. **Display the table**

2. **Press F7 or click *Tools*, *Spelling***

VIEW

Access displays objects in one of three possible views:

View	Purpose
Design	The object's components are displayed as design objects that can be created, deleted, and edited by the user.
Datasheet	The table or query is displayed in columns and rows. Each row is a record. Each column is a field.
Form	The table is displayed as a screen form, usually one record per screen

WILDCARD CHARACTERS IN SEARCHES, FILTERS, AND QUERIES

The following wildcard characters can be used in searches, filters, and queries to specify a group of values (all customers with zip codes beginning with 799) as opposed to a single, specific value (only those customers in zip code 79968).

Allowable wildcard characters include the following:

Character	Substitutes for	Example
*	Any group of characters.	Sm* matches any group of characters beginning with "Sm" like "Smith," "Smell," and "Small arms fire"
?	Any single character	Sm??? matches "Smith" and "Smell" but not "Small arms fire"
#	Matches any single numeral	1#3 matches 123 and 183 but not 1R3
[ ]	Matches any of several characters within the brackets	N[JY] matches "NJ" and "NY" but not "NC"
[-]	Matches a range of characters	799[01-05] matches zip codes "79901," "79902," "79903," "79904," and "79905" but not "79906"

THE ACCESS MENU SYSTEM

The Access menu bar provides a menu system that allows you to access its features by mouse or keyboard. Figure DBA-2 provides an overview of each menu bar item's submenu.

FIGURE DBA-2 ■ THE ACCESS' MENU SYSTEM

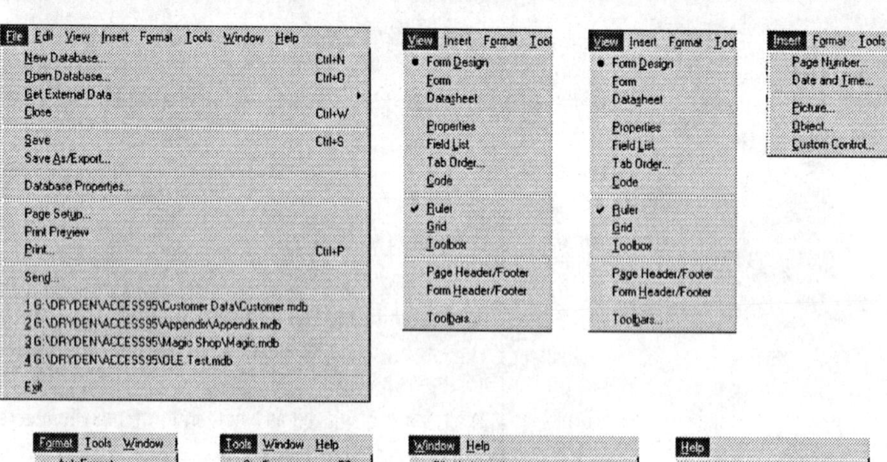

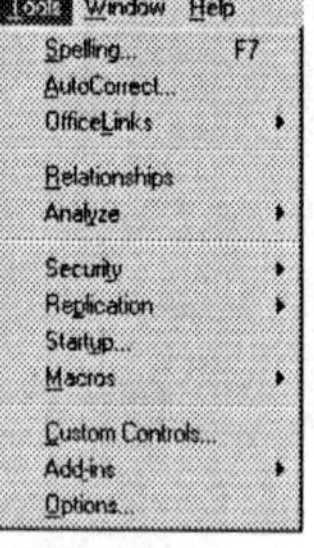

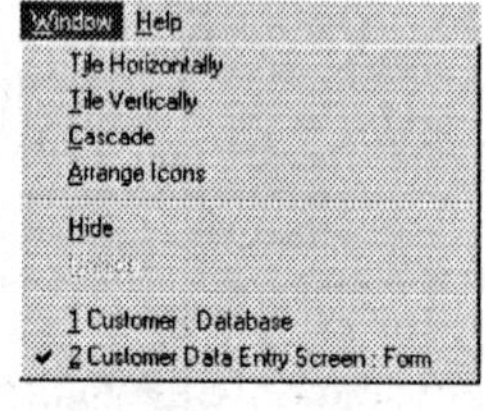

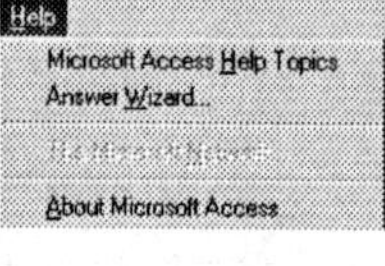

GLOSSARY

Allow zero length. A property indicating whether a zero-length string (" ") will be permitted as a field value. (DB28)

ASCII. A standard format adopted by the computer industry for representing typed characters. ASCII (pronounced "ask-key") is an acronym for American Standard Code for Information Interchange. (DB212)

Average. This command computes the arithmetic mean (average) of all numeric fields or expressions. (DB141)

Band. In a banded report, a section. All objects in a section will print at the same time. (DB95)

Banded report. A type of report design consisting of several sections, called bands, that organize the report into areas. The areas will print together, such as Page header, page footer, etc. (DB95)

Border. The frame or boundary around a window or other object. (DB182)

Button. A graphic representation on the screen of a process that will be initiated when the button is clicked. (DB3)

Calculated field. A value based on data from other table fields that have been combined or calculated. A calculated field displays results that are not normally contained within the table. (DB184)

Caption. A property containing the text that will be displayed on the status bar when the field contains the text-insertion point. (DB27)

Clicking. Pressing the left mouse button. (DB5)

Conditional expression. An expression that Access evaluates to determine whether or not an action will be performed. The expression is compared to data in the table and either matches the data or doesn't. (DB51)

Context sensitive. A response from the program that is appropriate for the task being performed by the user. (DB12)

Count. An Access function that returns the total number of records or the total number of records meeting the specified condition. (DB142)

Database. A collection of data or objects related to a particular topic or purpose. A database file can contain tables, forms, reports, and queries. (DB2)

Database file. An Access file that contains any combination of the table, query, report, form, macro, or module objects. (DB19)

Database window. The standard display of object names in a database file. (DB19)

Datasheet view. A column-and-row tabular display of the table. (DB30)

Data type. The attribute of a field or variable that determines what kind of data it can hold. (DB25)

Decimal places. The number of places to the right of the decimal to be displayed. (DB28)

Default value. The value provided by the program that will be used (as in a dialog box) if the user does not change it. (DB27)

Delete. A button or command that removes a file or record. (DB167)

Delimited file. An ASCII text file in which filed values are separated by commas, trailing blanks are removed, and text is enclosed within quotation marks. This format is particularly useful for merging with form letters in word-processing programs. (DB214)

Design view. A window that shows the design of a query, form, report, or table. From Design view, you can create new database objects or modify existing ones. (DB30)

Detail band. The band in a report that prints one time for every record. (DB95)

Detail form. A subform contained within a master form. The Detail form displays data from the detail table. (DB189)

Dialog box. A window in which options are selected to configure program commands. (DB3)

Double-clicking. Pressing the left mouse button twice quickly. (DB5)

Drag and Drop. The process by which an object can be moved using the mouse. Point to the object, click, and—as you move the mouse—the object will move on the screen.

Dynaset. A table-like data set produced by a query. Edits done to the dynaset are passed on to the underlying table. (DB49)

Edit. To change one or more field values in a record. (DB130)

Embedding. The process of inserting an OLE object into another file. (DB217)

Exporting. An output technique that saves data in a format readable by other programs. (DB211)

Field. An individual element of data that contains one or more typewritten character of image. (DB3)

Field name. A unique name, up to 64 characters, assigned to identify a field. (DB24)

Field selector. A small rectangle above a field column in a table display. When the field selector is clicked, the entire column will be selected. (DB45)

Field size. The maximum width in characters that a field can contain. (DB26)

Field value. The data contained in a given field. (DB25)

Find. The process of locating records that contain specified values. (DB42)

Format. The property that specifies the appearance of a field value, such as currency, date, etc. (DB25)

Forms. An Access object that defines the way a record will be displayed on the screen. (DB36)

Graph. A pictorial representation of data. (DB202)

Group band. A band that prints every time the value in a specified field changes. (DB95)

Handles. Small rectangles on the border of a selected object that indicate where the mouse pointer must be placed to move that border. (DB99)

Importing. An input technique that retrieves data, which has been saved in another format. (DB211)

Index. A feature that speeds searches and sorting in a table. Indexes are created in the Indexes Window or by setting a field's Indexed Property to YES. (DB28)

Input mask. A user-specified format that assists data entry in a field or control. It indicates where data is to be entered, the kind of data allowed, and/or the number of characters that may be entered. (DB27)

Key field. A field common to two tables by which the tables are linked. (DB202)

Linking. The process of connecting two or more tables by a common field. (DB217)

Literal. Text in a report that is reproduced exactly as it is entered without being replaced with table data. (DB27)

Many-to-one link. A technique for linking tables in which a group of master records are linked to one detail record. (DB199)

Master form. The portion of a form that displays data from the master table of a set of linked tables. (DB189)

Mouse. A pointing device used with Windows programs. (DB5)

Mouse pointer. A graphical image (arrow, hand, etc.) that moves across the screen as the mouse is rolled across the desk. (DB5)

Move handle. The solid square in the upper-left corner of a selected control that is dragged to move the control to a new position without altering the control's dimensions. (DB181)

Natural order. Record number order. (DB187)

Object. Any collection of text, graphics, sound, or video that can be shared, via linking or embedding with OLE; in Microsoft Access 7.0, an object may be a table, form, report, or query. (DB19)

One-to-many link. A technique for linking tables in which each master record is linked to a group of detail records. (DB190)

Page footer. The band in a report that will print at the bottom of every page. (DB95)

Page header. The band in a report that will print at the top of every page. (DB95)

Pointing. Moving the mouse pointer to an area of the screen. (DB5)

Portrait. A printing orientation in which the printed figure is upright when the shorter edge of the page is "down," a vertical orientation. (DB91)

Properties. A feature that determines how an object will behave in the Access environment. (DB26)

Query. A question that is asked of a table to select specific records or restrict field displays. (DB48)

Record. The portion of a table that contains information about an individual entity—a person, place, or thing. One record is represented in each horizontal row or table. (DB3)

Report footer. The band in a report that will print on the last page of the report. (DB95)

Report form. A display of data designed to be printed. (DB87)

Report header. The band in a report that prints on the first page of the report. (DB95)

Required. A property specifying whether or not a value must be placed in a field for the record to be saved. (DB28)

Scroll. Moving forward or backward in the table, from record to record. (DB42)

Scroll buttons. Buttons displayed at the bottom of the screen which, when selected, advance to the first, previous, next, or last record. (DB42)

Select. The action of choosing an object to be edited, moved, etc. by clicking it with the mouse. A selected object becomes highlighted or surrounded by borders and handles. (DB96)

Shortcut keys. Key presses, usually involving Ctrl, Alt , or Shift keys, in combination with another key to perform a menu action. (DB7)

Sorting. Rearranging table records in a particular order, alphabetically or by other criteria. (DB83)

Sort direction. A positive or ascending sort direction arranges records in order from smallest to largest (0–999, A–Z, Jan 1–Dec 31) by the key field(s). A negative or descending sort direction arranges records in the opposite order. (DB122)

Status bar. The horizontal bar at the bottom of the Microsoft Access 7.0 screen that displays information on commands, tool bars, and other options. (DB11)

Structured Query Language (SQL). A common database language that is used to query, update, or manage a database. In Microsoft Access 7.0, SQL queries can be viewed or written by using the *View, SQL* command.

Sum. An Access function that returns the numeric total of the selected numeric fields of all records or the numeric total of the selected numeric fields of records meeting the specified condition. (DB138)

Table. A two-dimensional representation of data in which rows represent records and columns represent fields. Also, a database document that stores data. (DB3)

Tabular report. A report organized in the form of a column and row table. (DB91)

Toolbar. A set of buttons that carry out common menu commands, usually found near the top of the Microsoft Access 7.0 screen. (DB11)

Validation rule. A property specifying a test that must be passed by data, which is entered into a field. (DB27)

Validation text. Text that describes the validation rule and that is displayed when the text-insertion point is in the field associated with the rule. (DB27)

Windows. Microsoft Windows is a product of the Microsoft Corporation. (DB3)

INDEX